KOREA, CHINA
and the WORLD

IGSC Institute for Global Strategy and Cooperation

The Korea Herald

KOREA, CHINA and the WORLD

Edited by Hwang Jaeho

HU:iNE

Going Global, Staying Together

With the emergence of Donald Trump in 2017 and the outbreak of COVID-19 in 2020, the international community has been fully experiencing the surrealistic international order of self-reliance and the law of jungle. As Joe Biden took over the power in 2021 and as we got used to COVID-19 in 2022, we are now trying not to slip the tail of the liberal international order. This comes from the fear that we have no idea of what the new international order will be like once we lose it.

Whenever domestic and foreign issues broke out, the media strived to faithfully report the views and voices from various fields in Korean society, including the Korean government, bureaucrats, scholars and expert groups, businesses and entrepreneurs, and NGOs and civic groups. The key messages and main contents were generally well reported, however, personally, it seemed things were largely determined by the media's choice. Then I was thinking how nice would it be if the full, broad, and in-depth conversations made by the people who are cited by media and people could be delivered to others. Also, how nice would it be if the voices of related experts abroad as well as experts in the field at home were directly delivered?

In autumn of 2021, the Korea Herald timely sympathized with my thirst for contributing to policy and public goods, and in the end we could run a series of joint interviews for more than a year. This collaboration was a great fortune, joy, and reward for me. Since early December 2021, nearly 80 domestic and foreign experts have participated in 43 interviews, starting with interviews with Kim Jonghwi, the former Senior Secretary for Foreign Affairs and Security, who planned and directed diplomatic ties between Korea and China behind the scenes on August 24, 1992.

The total nationality of those who participated in the interview are from 12 countries. I sought to analyze the issues and see alternatives, focusing on various questions that were pending at the time when the respective interviews were hold. Originally, the title of this interview series was 『China and the World』, however, the title of this book is decided as 『Korea, China and the World』 considering that there were many issues about Korean diplomacy as well. As the title of this book, it goes with three parts of Korea, China, and the World, and one more part related to Korea-China relations and regional order is added as the fourth part.

The first part is Korea's foreign policy with five chapters. It deals with the diplomatic environment surrounding Korea, Korea's traditional and public diplomacy, what is Japan and NATO to Korea, and other major relations including the one with North Korea. The second part is about China's foreign policy, which is divided into four chapters. It covers China's respective foreign policies and mutual competition, China's relations with other major countries including Russia and Japan, and China's growing intangible competitiveness. The third part is issues from the world and regional level and is divided into four chapters. In addition to issues in the Indo-Pacific region, Europe and North America, and Eurasia, this chapter contains the Taiwan issue also. With two chapters, the last and fourth part discuss Korea-China relations and cooperation at the East Asian level. It reviewed and analyzed how Korea-China relations have developed over the past 30 years since diplomatic relations were established, followed by various areas of cooperation in East Asia.

In fact, I cannot tell how time has passed. The overall path to the publication was a series of tension every time. I had to search the timely topic and invite the expert about a week or two weeks ago, and the recording and organizing interviews was quite a tough process. But as always, the past year or so has been with my veteran warriors (researchers Ko Sunghwah and Shin Euichan) from our Institute for Global Strategy and Cooperation. My team was able to learn a lot from the professional consciousness and sense of duty from the journalist fields by discussing timely topics and meeting the deadlines for articles. I would like to take this opportunity to express my sincere gratitude to managing editor Lee Joohee, desk editor Choi Heeseok, and reporter Shin Jihye of The Korea Herald, who planned and contributed together for this publication. They have always been open to the topics and approaches we have proposed and have not put any strain on editing and direction at all. The Korea Herald, as an excellent platform for domestic and foreign intellectual interactions and public opinion-building, was a great partner in this cooperation.

Now, according to the Korean calendar we are standing at the end of January 2023, the black rabbit Gyemyo year, the year of wisdom and prolificacy. Going through interviews, I could accumulate wisdom and experience from a number of experts at home and abroad. Although we have differences in conservatives and liberals, and countries and races, we were united in wishing for peace, stability, cooperation and prosperity for Korea and the international community. I am very pleased to publish this book on the spring day of this Gyemyo Year. Hopefully the results of the past year can provide abundance and prosperity of knowledge in perceiving the fields, just like the black rabbit of 2023 stands for prolificacy.

January 31, 2023

Hwang Jaeho
Professor, Hankuk University of Foreign Studies
& Director, Institute for Global Strategy and Cooperation

Foreword

When insight is desperately needed

Throughout the year 2022, The Korea Herald had the valuable opportunity of collaborating with Professor Hwang Jaeho by publishing his interviews with distinguished experts across the globe discussing current events and their implications for foreign relations.

The convoluted rivalries among the major powers, together with the pandemic and the war in Ukraine, have led to the rise of detrimental protectionism as the norm, with smaller states struggling to subsist strategically and economically.

The long-standing ideological confrontation has developed into a technological duel, with its consequences being felt across the world and by important economic players.

Whether security precedes economy or vice versa, the two go hand in hand with a leader's decisions playing a pivotal role.

For South Korea, which has always lived in a haunting geopolitical shadow and the remnants of invasions and war, the latest developments are of great importance.

All affairs around the world are intertwined, more so for South Korea, as its geopolitical and economic stances often put it in a dilemma, as eloquently described by Professor Hwang.

As Asia's fourth-largest economy with unprecedented global presence in terms of technology and culture, South Korea's bearing may, and should be different from the past.

Roadblocks to such efforts to avoid repeating the past come from within the country as well, with public apathy and sociopolitical division often clouding what is really important.

Rather than just looking at world affairs from the local point of view, it would be equally important to look from the outside, to hear what the other stakeholders and onlookers have to say, and how other states are coping with tricky situations and, or turning them into opportunities.

Professor Hwang's China and the World provides just that, by bringing together experts from Korea, China, the US, Japan and other countries of Europe and Asia.

Questions posed by professor Hwang do not aim to impart South Korea's perspective, but rather give the experts and readers an opportunity to see the same issues from different angles.

Professor Hwang's commentaries at the end of each interview remind the readers why we should care and how to decipher each interviewee's viewpoint.

The yearlong project of Hwang's China and the World was by no means an easy task, but was definitely an undertaking that we desperately needed and will continue to need.

We are living in the time of quick headlines that bombard us, or jolt us, leading us to often choose to bypass them altogether the next day.

Fragments of news shape the main stream of history and Hwang's project reminds us that the more we hear, the more we are aware.

The Korea Herald expresses its sincerest thanks to Professor Hwang and his team for sharing this valued opportunity of learning various insights.

February 2, 2023

Lee Joohee
Managing Editor, The Korea Herald

Contents

II. China's Diplomacy and Security

China and US's Diplomacy

China-US Relations

China's Foreign Relations with Others

III. Global Issues and Views

Issues and Views in Eurasia

Taiwan Problem

IV. Korea-China Relations and East Asia Cooperation

Korea-China Relations

East Asia Cooperation

I

Korea's Diplomacy and Security

Looking on New Northern Policy, from the origin

Dec 13, 2021

Kim Chongwhi

Former Senior Presidential Secretary for Foreign and Security Affairs under Roh Taewoo government

The death of Roh Taewoo, who was president from 1988 to 1993, in October put a spotlight on his historical achievements. His foreign policies, such as hosting the Seoul Olympics, joining the UN, and promoting the Northern Policy, are seen as major diplomatic moments in modern Korean history. Behind the scenes of it all was the Presidential Secretary Kim Chongwhi. Kim served as the senior presidential secretary for foreign and security affairs in the Blue House at the time and has since served as a professor at National Defense University, the president of the Korean Association of International Studies, deputy representative at the Inter-Korean High-Level Talks, and a distinguished visiting fellow at the Heritage Foundation in the US. At the end of November, I met Kim, who now works as a "diplomatic strategist" at a cafe in downtown Seoul.

Hwang You stood by President Roh for five years as his foreign affairs and security adviser. I would like to start with how you evaluate the Roh administration's achievements in diplomacy and security.

Kim First of all, the operating system in the Roh administration was very comprehensive and properly integrated. At that time, Korea already had a National Security Council similar to what the US has, but it was more likely to function as a separate organization. It was the 6th Republic when the current form of Blue House presidential secretary for foreign and security affairs was established.

Secondly, our position was quite firm: To take the lead when it comes to the inter-Korean or unification issues. I believe this stance eventually led us to achieve the Basic Agreement and regain peacetime operational control, which was another achievement we made at that time.

Third, our stance was to implement the preemptive foreign and security policies. In that sense, the Roh administration could initiate the inter-Korea talks, Northern Policies, and Yongsan Garrison. Last but not least, the president himself led the diplomacy and security aspects from a long-term perspective with a larger flow, since the frequent changes and short term of office at minister level certainly had limitations.

Hwang I personally have this impression that Korean diplomacy had its great takeoff, heyday, golden age, or whatever we name it, when you served.

Kim Korea certainly is a small country, but at the same time, we know that it is a country that can play a significant role as a catalyst. Since the end of the Cold War, Europe and the Western world have gone through numerous events both in terms of international or historical significance. Let's say the unification of Germany, for example. On the other hand, there have not been many changes in Asia. Meanwhile, Korea attempted to bring about changes by establishing diplomatic ties with Russia, China, and Vietnam. I would dare to say, but am confident, that Korea was the catalyst that created a crack in the existing order, but also reformed the order.

Hwang In the late 80s, the Roh administration presented a forward-looking policy toward China and former Soviet countries, though they were longtime enemies of Korea since the Korean War. Where did this title "Northern Policy" come from?

Kim Actually, Foreign Minister Lee Beomseok from the 5th Republic used the term in his lecture at the National Defense University, and we adopted it later. The Roh administration was stepping toward a new diplomacy with China and other former Soviet countries, then we started using the terms "Northern Diplomacy" and "Northern Policy" afterward. At the very beginning, Northern Policy was not the most representative slogan.

Hwang What was the blueprint of the Northern Policy? And what was its ultimate goal?

Kim Above all, we aimed to expand our foreign network through the Northern Policy. The primary goal was to build a Korea with influence greater than its actual national power. To do so, we had to stretch over to Russia, China, Vietnam, and others, beyond the Western countries that we were already had diplomatic ties with. Also, joining the United Nations was part of the plan. That was the diplomacy we were thinking of.

Secondly, we tried to extend the fields that the Korean economy could enter. We thought of the necessity of increasing the export volume by targeting Russia, which has a massive amount of natural resources, and China, which has a massive population.

The third goal of the Northern Policy was to strengthen the security system. The interactions with China and Russia through the Northern Policy actually played a huge role in reducing the arms supply chains to North Korea, which streamed down from China and Russia. As a consequence, we could cut down the spending that we were pouring into national defense, and instead focus the national budget on other areas, such as economy or social welfare. Additionally, the consideration of unification is reflected in the Northern Policy as well. Not only simply building embassies in China or Russia, but also lowering their antagonism toward Korean unification was part of the plan. In the end, the Northern Policy was quite an important step in building a peaceful and cooperative atmosphere.

Hwang When it came to the Northern Policy's implementation, establishing diplomatic ties with the Soviet Union came before China. Was there any particular reason for this approach?

Kim Back then, hostility toward the Soviet Union was pretty harsh. President Reagan even called the Soviet Union the "Evil Empire." The majority of people were in fact anticipating diplomatic relations with China to happen sooner. Korea and China were already having exchanges and several talks regarding trade and commerce took place. Therefore, establishing diplomatic ties with China seemed bright and feasible. However, even under these circumstances, I thought ties with Russia would be a bit smoother. Considering the geographical aspect, Russia is basically a European country and was facing a deterioration in the sense of international politics. I guess the Soviet Union presumed that opening a new trade and commerce route and seeking an economic revival by holding Korea's hand would be a better choice, because North Korea's relations with China was more concrete than that with the Soviet Union, even in economic aspects. With all these realistic conditions interlocking together, Korea's diplomatic ties with the Soviet Union could move on constructively.

Hwang Some say that the Roh administration brought up the Six Party Talks.

Kim Well, that is not exactly fact. It is true that President Roh mentioned the Six Party Talks in his first speech at the UN, but it was the US who had suggested the idea of Six Party Talks. Fortunately, it was actualized, but fundamentally holding Six Party Talks meant dragging the complicated Korean Peninsula issue into a deeper swamp. Because that meant inviting six guests to the table when the negotiation between only two Koreas is already difficult enough. Historically, China and Japan had hard feelings and the conflict between the US and Russia did not seem to be helpful to inter-Korean relations. On this basis, we were rather reluctant about the Six Party Talks.

Hwang In reality, the Six Party Talks is quite nominal under today's circumstances. Some members are currently discussing the possibility of opening the Four Party Talks. How do you observe the overall situation? Do you think that resuming the Four Party Talks would help resolve North Korea's nuclear issue?

Kim Basically, what we have to keep in mind is to set the conditions where North Korea would be willing to talk. In other words, North Korea would come to the table when it is cornered and face the difficulty. The Roh administration was working on the conversations with North Korea, but China was implicitly and repeatedly supporting North Korea, then eventually there was not much progress in talking with North Korea at the end of President Roh's administration. Later, during President Kim Daejung's administration, North Korea could receive considerable economic support and this led North Korea to only be willing to talk directly to either the US or Russia. North Korea put the least effort into talking to Korea. Continuing, even when today's Moon Jaein administration opened the window and set the talking channel between North Korea and the US, Pyongyang was only interested in facing Trump one on one. Its attitude was relatively reluctant to have South Korea on the same table and seemed to be trying to exclude South Korea from the board. I also feel terrible to say this, but the best way to have North Korea seated with us for a talk is to create a desperate condition. Moreover, when we finally have North Korea seated, the talks must be flexible but very firm at the same time.

Hwang When you look back at that time, do you also have anything in mind that you think could have gone better?

Kim I personally wonder how inter-Korean relations would have gone if we had one or two more years at the very end of the administration. I assume we could have made some progress. Back then, we could complete signing the Inter-Korean Basic Agreement, but could not make practical output. The fact that we could not develop the steps further always remains in my mind. To add one more, I would like to cautiously say that today's society is way too immersed in liquidating the past or purging evils. Every administration or every government certainly has its merits and demerits. Merits must continue and be advanced, while demerits must be corrected and moved on from. However, we tend to completely erase the past and reset the board as every new administration comes into power. This is one thing that could have gone better I guess.

Hwang The Moon administration has presented the New Northern Policy as one of its major foreign policies. I wonder how it comes across to you.

Kim I personally cannot tell the major difference between Moon administration's New Northern Policy and the original one. But in short, I see it is a meaningful trial in the sense that it succeeds the Northern Policy from Roh Taewoo's administration.

Hwang When you were serving, Korea did not have the dilemma, for example, caused by standing in between the US and China as it does today. I wonder if you expected or predicted today's US-China competition or Korea's current dilemma.

Kim China's diplomacy and negotiating attitude used to be to keep a low profile. China evaluated itself as an under-developed country while praising Korea as a developed one. They used to mention that they were looking forward to learning a lot from Korea. On the other hand, I knew China would grow at some point, but could not expect it to become such a "big power" that it is today.

Hwang How can we overcome Korea's dilemma, standing in between the US and China?

Kim Geopolitically, Korea is surrounded by China, Japan, and Russia, and it seems like standing in a very uneasy position in terms of making strategies. However, if we just simply flip our perspective, Korea could be seen as a strategically priceless location. In my opinion, Korea should strategically make its stance more undaunted and dignified when it is stuck between the US and China. There is no reason to be obsequious to one side or to be too offensive to the other one.

The term we commonly use to describe Korea's foreign policies toward China and the US is "Security to the US and economy to China," but this in fact is impossible in practice. That is the reason why Korea has to react flexibly in facing the US and China relations. For instance, it is not necessary for Korea to join QUAD at all, because Korea is directly and geographically bumping shoulders with China, unlike any other QUAD country.

Hwang China is soon hosting the Beijing Winter Olympics in February. Biden, on the other hand, is already making moves to prepare a diplomatic boycott, and some US allies seem to be on board with his plan.

Kim For this instance, I guess we need to stay still and see how things flow. But at least, the president of Korea should avoid paying a visit to Beijing in person.

Hwang As Korea will be welcoming a new administration next year, I believe it is time for Korea to make a new leap in diplomacy. What could be the direction for Korea's future?

Kim Continuity is what Korean diplomacy is most in need of. The policies are severed every time there is a new administration coming in. This should be highly discouraged. In particular, what we have to do is to distinguish the merits and demerits of past foreign policies, and to put efforts into succeeding and developing the merits. Being way too buried under the frame of liquidating the past might be unhealthy, because it leads to policy severance.

Hwang In that sense, the current administration has made efforts to succeed and promote the past administrations' outcomes, such as the Park Geunhye government's Trust-Building Process on the Korean Peninsula or the Northern Policy from Roh Taewoo's era. If there could be any policies that you consider should be continued for the sake of Korea's national interest, what would you choose?

Kim Personally, I suggest the next government work on practical preparations for unification in earnest. No one can tell when Korean unification will come true, and it will be a change in our daily lives. We can only work to minimize errors and ultimately reduce the unnecessary costs when we are ready to face and adopt sudden unification. Whenever there is sustained peace on the peninsula is the right time to prepare for welcoming any unexpected unification.

Hwang The Korean government has been more focused on peace rather than unification for the last few years.

Kim In order for Korea to play a more significant role in international society, first of all, it has to grow the national scale. Korea's national scale by today's standards is still very tiny compared to neighboring countries such as China, Russia or Japan. Once Korea unifies and the two Koreas can finally combine after a peace and co-existence era, Korea will have a population of about 70 to 80 million. This is a larger number than even the populations of the UK and France. Korea will be able to make the final leap to becoming a developed country that can influence international society, only when it promotes the country based on national scale. This energy of unification will become the background for national development and growth and will lead Korea to stand as a leading country on the international stage. This stage will be beyond the East Asia region. In short, Korea's unification is the destiny of this country, and we must be ready with full effort.

Hwang Would you share one scene that made an impression on you that you will never forget?

Kim I guess that would be the moment when we could successively make the Korea-Russia Summit happen in San Francisco. As I recall, all the talks and decisions were intimately made at such a tense speed. The Russian side had offered me a meeting for a talk, then we were able to sit and discuss holding the summit. Back then we were anxious over whether this summit would really happen, but in the end, President Roh Taewoo and Mikhail Gorbachev met in person. The successful moment of arranging the summit must be the most unforgettable moment in my life.

Hwang If there is a single word that represents yourself, what would that be?

Kim I define myself as President Roh Taewoo's "adviser." I first met Secretary Kim Chongwhi in person at the 20th anniversary celebration of the establishment of Korea-China diplomatic relations in 2012. His temperate attitude and language left an impression both back then and today. The conversation we shared today was based on his accurate memories and logic. Just as President Nixon and Henry Kissinger's teamwork transformed the global diplomatic topography, Roh and his adviser Kim preemptively and unprecedentedly led the changes of circumstances that surround the Korean Peninsula.

Above all, the Northern Policy is remarkably brilliant. If Korea was taking a defensive stance, building diplomatic ties with 45 countries including China and the Soviet Union, in such a short term would have been impossible. The Roh government's successful Northern Policy is splendidly meaningful in the sense of completing Korea's diplomacy, by adding the "left half" to the "half" that was only focused on the Western world. Northern Policy was "an ambitious blueprint and practice that flipped the existing inter-Korean frame" with one finger snap. It was a strategy that contained mid- and long-term strategic mind and insight, and considered the future unified Korean Peninsula's position and policy within Northeast Asia that would go way beyond North Korea.

Back then was the era when Korea could clearly show off its dynamic continental disposition. This has unknowingly become some kind of a diplomatic exemplar to the following administrations. Every administration endeavored to come up with new foreign policies, pursued making actual output, and worked on including and promoting the attention to the areas that are still not on the list.

In this way, today's Moon administration is focusing again on the Northern areas by reviving the original Northern Policy, three decades later. The New Northern Policy emphasizes former Soviet Union countries rather than China. Additionally, the New Southern Policy could be specified as a strategic balancing approach, which embraces ASEAN and India.

The Northern Policy was the one that stimulated the creativeness of Korean diplomacy and moved on. We are looking forward to seeing another Northern Policy from the upcoming administration, continuing the Moon administration's New Northern Policy.

Korea's future diplomacy — 'pragmatic' or 'strenuous'?

Jan 3, 2022

Sohn Yul

Professor, Graduate School of International Studies at Yonsei University

Chun Chaesung

Professor, Department of International Relations at Seoul National University

Seo Jungkun

Professor, Department of Political Science at Kyung Hee University

The tension of the upcoming presidential election is not as heated as usual, as COVID-19 keeps people from gathering. Although the surface seems relatively calm, the candidates are somehow preparing their own policies.

The diplomatic security policy might attract less attention than the domestic circumstance, however, it might be more urgent, requiring prompt action. While domestic politics is about dividing and distributing the interest pie among the inside powers, international politics is under the law of the jungle. It is the world where states are distinguished according to their power, the weak fall prey to stronger predators in a blink, and all these processes go on in different languages. Therefore, beyond words, the new leader's diplomatic philosophy, strategy and policy matter.

There are two candidates from the ruling and opposition party running in the presidential election next March. Lee Jaemyung from the ruling party put pragmatic diplomacy at the very front while candidate Yoon Seokyoul from the opposition is imploring strenuous effort diplomacy.

Observing the situation in an ideological lens, both sides of the progressives and conservatives are insisting on different external approaches. However, they in fact share a common core, which is pragmatism. Both candidates are ultimately chasing after the national interest as the top priority, but from different directions. This interview has invited three prominent scholars from international politics to theoretically look into how the progressives and conservatives have performed pragmatic diplomacy since the founding of South Korea, and to seek out what foreign policies the new government would present after the presidential election next year.

The below interview introduces professor Sohn Yul from the Graduate School of International Studies in Yonsei University, who also serves as the president of East Asia Institute, professor Chun Chaesung from the department of international relations in Seoul National University, who is now the president of the Korean Association of International Studies, and professor Seo Jungkun from the department of political science at Kyung Hee University.

Hwang The trend of pragmatism is known to root in the US. I would like to ask your thoughts and views on pragmatic diplomacy.

Chun When we discuss the term "pragmatism," what must come first is clearly classifying pragmatism and pragmatic diplomacy. Pragmatism basically comes from philosophy.

William James, John Dewy and other distinguished philosophers founded pragmatism after the US Civil War (1861-65) and it is usually said to be the only philosophy that developed in the US. However, when we move on to pragmatic diplomacy, it rarely has the pragmatism that I just introduced as its philosophical frame. Pragmatic diplomacy, which Korea has sustainably asserted and practiced, also can be said that it is more likely to come from a pragmatic background, not a diplomatic pragmatism. Additionally, pragmatic diplomacy has its significance in the actual practice and implementation rather than the theoretical or speculative approach. Therefore, building consensus in society is the critical matter.

Sohn Observing from the view of diplomatic policy, pragmatic diplomacy can be understood with the practical outcome from diplomatic policy, rather than its purpose, principle or the legitimacy of process. Based on this condition, pragmatic diplomacy can be defined as diplomacy that selects issues among massively various international problems and particularly focuses on the ones that are directly related and influence our daily life. In the same context, pragmatic diplomacy has some aspects that can be compared from diplomacies that are based on ideology, norms, ideals or values.

Seo First of all, if we broadly define this pragmatic diplomacy, most of the diplomatic measures which are not biased in ideological perspective can fall into this category. On the other hand, in the active definition, pragmatic diplomacy can be called competence diplomacy or performance diplomacy, which pins down the problem and ambitiously makes outputs by solving that problem.

Hwang Do you have any country in mind that performs or has performed successful pragmatic diplomacy around the world?

Sohn I guess Deng Xiaoping's concentration on China's economic policy in the late 1970s can be an example, since it put great weight on solving the problem. In a more comprehensive perspective in pragmatic diplomacy, pragmatic diplomacy itself must be one pillar of the weak state's diplomacy. The primary goal of a weak state in international politics is survival. Under this condition, it is quite difficult for weak states to go after any form of ideology or value. In other words, the weak must seek ways to survive today and continue tomorrow, therefore, the moves made must be pragmatic diplomacy. On the other hand, strong states present and suggest the international order they have established. As they are the ones who have suggested the large outline, their national interest and universal ideology must be pursued within the frame that they have made. Because of how this framework works, strong states usually tend to combine their national interest and value, rather than emphasizing unconditional pragmatic actions.

Chun In my view, I would like to point to France under President Charles de Gaulle and the current Taiwan government as the most successful cases. First of all, President Charles de Gaulle successfully avoided ideological diplomacy and could claim national interest, even amid the Cold War. It was the time after the Second World War ended and the US and Soviet Union were making acute ideological confrontations. President Charles de Gaulle demonstrated considerable influence over international society by asserting autonomous diplomacy from the US through implementing distancing tactics, promoting relations with the Soviet Union and East Germany, proceeding in nuclear developments, withdrawing from NATO and so on. Moving on to the current Taiwan government, it has clearly set a national goal, beyond ideological aspects. It is flexibly operating the semiconductor industry, prevention of the pandemic, military areas and its relations with China for its own sake. As a result, it is obtaining the largest reflective interest even in the middle of US-China competition.

Seo Thinking about your question, I was wondering why we could not find such a successful story of pragmatic diplomacy from the US in the other way around. After the Cold War, the ideological war ended and the US definitely must have had space to settle its pragmatic diplomacy. However, unlike how we generally expect, there were no specific discussions on the US' pragmatic diplomacy. The first and the largest reason that pragmatic diplomacy could not be institutionalized in the US is in its domestic political system, where the diplomacy of checks and balances goes back and forth. The US is a country that basically has elections every two years, which means the president's policies are evaluated through elections every other year. Under such a domestic political system, the success or failure of foreign policies are regularly and publicly judged and the direction of diplomacy can be revised. Based on the conditions explained above, the election naturally forms checks and balances regarding foreign policies. Therefore, there is no extra space for the US to make pragmatic diplomacy from the national level, and in fact there was less necessity of it.

Hwang What can be the main characteristics of Korea's diplomacy since the establishment of this country?

Seo Basically, when we combine Korea's diplomacy or the history of Korea's diplomacy with the term pragmatism, we must deeply think about how far we can understand and set the boundary of Korea's diplomacy under the concept of pragmatism. In Korea's case, it could achieve a democratic society, industrialism and economic development through the US-Republic of Korea alliance, which is the military one. On the other hand, it has also limited and decreased the stretch of Korea's pragmatic diplomacy. In a realistic perspective, the pragmatic diplomacy that Korea has implemented is dispatching troops to Iraq and signing the US-ROK free trade agreement under President Roh Moohyun's government and President Park Geunhye's "Unification Bonanza" slogan. However, on top of that, what must be considered first is whether this pragmatic diplomacy has made actual and practical outcomes.

Sohn Nevertheless, if we define pragmatic diplomacy in the empirical traditional sense, which is comparable with ideology and value, President Park Chunghee's ROK-

Japan normalization of diplomatic relations and South-North Korea Dialogue can be the representative examples. Although the era had severe conflicts from history, Korea's establishment of diplomatic relations with Japan and taking advantage of the financial system in economic cooperation was a very pragmatic approach, because it eventually led us to industrialization. Additionally, the effort to accomplish the South-North Dialogue and improvement of the two Koreas' relations back in 1972 can be evaluated as active and pragmatic moves Korea made amid the big changes in international society, known as the Nixon Doctrine.

Chun Korea's status and influence in international society is growing, and under the circumstances, one of the toughest challenges that Korea's diplomacy is facing remains seeking the space where Korea can practice pragmatic diplomacy, with the US-ROK alliance at the center. The next significant figure of Korea's diplomacy is the problem in defining the relationship with North Korea. Lastly, the essential characteristic of pragmatic diplomacy depends on how perceptively we are analyzing and predicting the trends of international politics. Once we are not able to read the flow accurately and make the right decision, the possibility of implementing pragmatic diplomacy drops in the end.

Hwang Then what can be the differences between the pragmatism of progressives and conservatives? Also, can pragmatic diplomacy be both sides' common diplomacy?

Sohn I see domestic politics as the most critical obstacle in performing pragmatic diplomacy. The logic of the bloc is based on Korea's diplomacy and the confrontation is applied to most of the diplomatic issues. This is the variable that limits Korea from stepping forward to a pragmatic approach. How the progressives and conservatives look at North Korea, the US, Japan and China are totally different depending on which bloc they belong to, and the gap can hardly be overcome. After all, it will be the great challenge for the Korean government, including the upcoming one, to overcome the domestic political conditions, which are bisected when it comes to the diplomatic area, to pursue the national interest and to convince the people in order to establish and implement pragmatic diplomacy.

Chun Pragmatic diplomacy can be the common tenet and principle for both progressives and conservatives. However, Korea's diplomacy from both sides is hard to be said as pursuing pragmatic diplomacy, since it still has space to develop in responsibility. The current progressives and conservatives are carrying pragmatic diplomacy to raise the national interest as their banners. However, as mentioned above, these approaches must also consider the potential possibility that pragmatic diplomacy can fall off the rails.

Seo Regardless of the blocs, they must define national interest and concentrate their full political efforts in actively persuading the opposing side. Paving the way to positively persuade those opposed is the essential part of pragmatic diplomacy in the future. Understanding pragmatic diplomacy as the process of persuasion and building domestic consensus can be the right direction for our diplomacy to develop further.

Hwang What could be your suggestions on either the vision or the spirit of the era, and the directions for Korea's pragmatic diplomacy?

Seo I personally believe the first thing we have to do for Korea's further pragmatic diplomacy in this era of US-China competition is shifting our discussion from which side we must choose to what we shall do for ourselves. The discourse of choice between the US and China must move on to what Korea's diplomacy can proactively do within our capacity. Only then, Korea's diplomacy can set its vision and meet the future. In these aspects, from now on, what matters most is clearly defining the national interest and working on the persuading process, and during the process the leader -- I mean the president -- should break from the obsession to cover all areas. Honest discussions will lead to honest policy.

Sohn According to research from the East Asia Institute last October, there were several international issues that Koreans are perceiving as external threats. From the prior ones, it goes from the COVID-19 situation, climate change issues including fine dust, technology competition and conflicts, then the North Korea issue followed. This research shows that the North Korea issue is now quite far from what people are perceiving as the threat, however, the current government is still pouring its full diplomatic effort and capacity into pulling out the declaration of the end of the war. From now on, I would like to say Korea must focus on the international affairs that the people are actually feeling by their skin and rearrange the priority list accordingly for Korea's diplomacy to develop in a pragmatic term.

Chun I contemplate that the policy measures to practice as the most important component in Korea's pragmatic diplomacy, rather than a vision or a goal. We must precisely narrow down what the policy measures we have in our hands are, what we can do, and what we cannot. Especially, fully understanding the neighbor countries' relative national powers and recognizing the things that we cannot handle is critical. In addition, based on what I have mentioned before, we also need to analyze the losses and risks that can happen in case we perform a particular diplomatic policy, then prepare the preventive and responding capacity.

Hwang Do you think we can put the value of diplomacy or norms beyond pragmatic diplomacy as the motto for foreign policy? If not, what if Korea puts the norms and values at the very front of foreign justification and melds the pragmatic approach in the context?

Chun As Korea's influence is growing larger, we need to enter into the procedure of defining new international problems and raising it into the discourse by ourselves. Furthermore, Korea's value diplomacy has a great foundation to grow once Korea can integrate its domestic political capacity.

Seo Entering the 20th century, Korea is the only country that has achieved democratic society and industrialization at the same time, therefore, a number of developing countries are trying to emulate Korea's successful case and requesting cooperation. This can be Korea's identity and value for the future pragmatic foreign policy that we can actively utilize and promote.

Sohn In the case of the middle powers like Korea, putting too much emphasis on pragmatism itself will lead to the risk of the middle power's trap of reading and checking the flows, particularly trying to read the strong powers' thoughts. Therefore, to make a certain voice in international society as a middle power and to perform one's own influence, we must parallel value diplomacy based on national identity and see beyond the national interest.

Hwang Lastly, what should be the next government's priority in management among diplomatic issues?

Sohn It must be the follow-up actions of the 5.21 US-ROK summit. All the issues that were discussed in the US-ROK summit are comprehensively interrelated to the Korean Peninsula, Northeast Asia and also to the stability and order of the Indo-Pacific region.

Chun I also agree. There must be some specific actions that can contribute to the stability and peace of the Korean Peninsula and Northeast Asia, based on the discussed results in the US-ROK summit.

Seo Only when we can solve North Korea's nuclear issue, the Korean Peninsula's peace and Northeast Asia's regional order can be stably maintained.

All the experts in the conversation agreed on at least one point, which is the necessity of all-party supported pragmatic diplomacy. Looking back at Korea's history, there was ideological separation and confrontation between anti-communism and pro-unification during the Cold War, then that continued to the group supporting the US-ROK alliance against those supporting South Korea and North Korea's reconciliation and cooperation after the Cold War. Today, both the progressives and conservatives attempt to formally use or utilize pragmatism in a policy context, as a breakthrough to overcome the ideological diplomatic approach, which are for instance the alliance first and unification first.

It stands out that both are considering pragmatic diplomacy as an important matter. Nevertheless, the thing is that both sides are thinking on the premise that the opposition would yield, therefore, realizing the diplomacy that pursues national interest and gets all parties' support is never easy. Adding more, if Korea fails in making successful and flexible but principles-based diplomatic moves toward neighboring strong states, pragmatic diplomacy must face the great challenge of abandonment and entrapment. Concluding today's discourse, pragmatic diplomacy can only be achieved when we have the substance, competence and practice.

Tough diplomatic security environment waiting to greet the next administration

Dec 27, 2021

Kim Kijung
President, Institute for National Security Strategy

Korea's national security can be mainly divided into the policy toward North Korea and toward the others. Since last week's interview with the president of KINU (Korea Institute of National Unification) covered Korea's policies toward North Korea, the interview this week is about Korea's overall national security. Kim Kijung, the president of the Institute for National Security Strategy (INSS), has shared his views on the Moon Jaein administration's national security strategy over the past five years and the diplomatic security that will be greeting the next administration.

Before joining the INSS, President Kim was a professor of the department of political science and diplomacy at Yonsei University and has served as the second deputy at the Office of National Security at the very beginning of the Moon administration. He is also the so-called designer of the 'Peace Process on the Korean Peninsula' which is the core of the Moon administration's North Korea and diplomatic policies. At the same time, he is also a poet and has published multiple pieces.

Hwang To begin with, I would like to ask how you evaluate Moon Jaein administration's past five years from the aspect of diplomatic security policies and the outcomes.

Kim It is quite a misfortune that the two Koreas lost the momentum to move forward since the No-deal in 2019 Hanoi, however still, I also agree that the Moon Jaein administration's most noticeable achievement is building the foundation for the momentum in the Inter-Korean relations and peace. In the long-term perspective, I assume the Moon administration's five years have contributed a significant role in leading Korea to reach the ideal nation that we have dreamt about, which is a Korea that shows its competence to the international community with a concrete economic capability. Under the acceleration of the US-China competition, Korea has just stood on tiptoe to be a greatly significant nation to both the US and China in strategical terms. During the Moon Jaein administration, Korea was invited to attend the G-7 summit twice, and also performed successful and noteworthy management of the coronavirus pandemic. Korea could strengthen its national brand within the international society by showing its national capacity to the world.

Hwang How do you view the circumstances surrounding diplomatic security that the next administration will bump into?

Kim For Korean diplomacy, the main and core challenges that we used to confront against would be still there no matter which administration comes into power. When we narrow down the prospects to the Northeast Asia region, the diplomatic security circumstances that Korea will face has more unstable and vulnerable factors that would stand out more than the stable ones. Particularly, Northeast Asia is where the vulnerable variables were sustainably reproduced over and over. Such issues of North Korea, territorial disputes, or ethnic conflicts are escalating and maintaining the vulnerability. Since World War II, these regional problems in Northeast Asia seem to expand and raise conflicts. In addition, in recent days the Northeast Asian countries are escalating the arms race. This arms competition is simmering year by year. Lastly, when it comes to the Korean Peninsula problem, the peace and coexistence could not be settled till today, and the solution to institutionalize the peace and coexistence is still not there yet.

Hwang Considering that the US has set two pillars in its foreign policy, which must be the Atlantic and Pacific, seemingly there are some signs of changes in the Pacific side. During the reorganizing era after the world wars, China has been partially dragged into the center of the world by the US. However, it seems to take up the center of the world by its own capacity. Also, watching Japan's moves, it seems to be immersed in the competition with China within the Northeast Asia region to make its last jump since its "Two Lost Decades."

Kim In Korea's perspective, the main reason for all these issues actually start from the point after World War II. How Japan has readjusted during the postwar period and how the situations were managed after the Korean War can be the representative points. What the current Korean Peninsula is struggling with is also partially related to all these post-war readjustment errors. We can conclude that the Northeast Asia region was rather a history of segmentation and distrust than a history of cooperation and harmony. What we are carrying on our backs have their roots in history.

Hwang I guess we can understand that the decline of the US and Japan and the rise of China and Korea eventually have built up the current unstable Northeast Asia's political circumstances. In the end, it could be thought that it is time to rearrange the power distribution as one side is declining. Taking these historical flows into consideration, what capability and qualification should the leader of the next administration have?

Kim Historically, Korea used to have one extraordinary leader who is responsible for the national operations and the country was anticipating him/her to play the right role in the regional; or international stage. Therefore, people's expectation level toward the leader is usually extremely high. We are desiring a leader who has great insight into the further direction that Korea should walk toward, as well as the one who can be the leader of Korea but also the one who can present the future and historical direction of the regional diplomacy in Northeast Asia. To sum it up, I think the insight and the capability to read the era is the most significant and essential qualification that the next administration's leader must possess.

Hwang What would be the spirit of the times for today's international society?

Kim For the thousand years of the history of civilization, human beings have pursued the values of freedom, equality, justice, and life and peace. Therefore, what the present and future spirit of the times require would not be far away from this frame of values. In my personal opinion, I would like to emphasize more on the value of justice and fairness, both on the domestic and international stages. Furthermore, from the perspective that we desire Korea's leader to be the leader of the time in Northeast Asia, settling down with the peace problem might be the most exigent matter. The core of the political situations surrounding the Korean Peninsula and the core of the characteristics of Northeast Asia's regional order meet each other. In this sense, the most ideal flow would be the one if the stable and peaceful existence of the Korean Peninsula that we pursue, successfully turns into the peaceful order of Northeast Asia.

Hwang Every time the new administration comes in, their main emphasis on diplomacy tends to change accordingly. What would be the next administration's diplomatic emphasis?

Kim The Korean Peninsula is divided into half while Korea is geopolitically located at the center of Northeast Asia and is surrounded by strong states regardless of our own wills. Looking at Korea from the world map, Korea relatively belongs to a remoted area far from the world and confronted various challenges. Nevertheless, it has overcome the obstacles and has reached today's status. As we have dreamt for so long, Korea is actually heading toward the center of the world. Under this environment, up to how far are we going to draw the line of diplomatic strategy would be the matter of political decisions.

Hwang Since we are looking forward to the upcoming presidential election, what strong points would Korea's diplomacy have if either the conservative or progressive comes to power?

Kim I guess the conservative administration has its strength in the perspective of the US-ROK alliance, because it would be able to utilize the US in practical measures. On the other hand, if we think about the strategic decisions and peaceful resolution of the North Korea issue, progressives seem to have relative advantages. Above all, I value strategical flexibility as the most important factor that both the conservative and progressive must keep in mind. In specific, Korea should make a step away from the discourse of obsession in selecting one when it comes to US-China relations.

Hwang There are quite a number of voices that understand the current US-China relationship as the New Cold War, both domestically and abroad.

Kim Unlike how it was back in the US-Soviet Cold War, the current US and China are under a relationship of extremely high mutual dependency. In addition, back in the US-Soviet Cold War, there was a political and ideological confrontation which later was expanded to worldwide military conflicts. However, today's US and China are sharing massive economic benefits under mutual dependency. Therefore, the core of the conflict between the US and China is rooted in who takes the larger pie. To sum it up, their relations is rather a political competition or a power game for the sake of having a larger piece of the pie.

Hwang Probably the core of the US-China relations might be new technology. What would be Korea's countermeasure to this flow?

Kim One of the most essential parts of the core of US-China competition is the technology hegemony. Science and technology will steadily play a larger role in a broader area, which will eventually have a greater influence over international politics. For Korea to successfully adjust to the future science and technology competition, we might need a strategy at the national level, which goes beyond the interests only of the enterprises. In other words, there must be support or assistance in building the cooperative structure between the nation and enterprises in the national strategic aspect.

Hwang The end-of-war declaration is the last but the main diplomatic agenda for the Moon administration. I wonder what discussions there was between the US and Korea and what different viewpoints they had in their opinions.

Kim As far as I know, the US Department of State and the Korean Ministry of Foreign Affairs at least have made some successful agreements at the working level. Korea has consistently reminded the fact that Korea is the one that is most engaged in solving the Korean Peninsula issue in a peaceful way, and that Korea can be the only one that is able to sustainably raise this issue. However, the truth is that the Korean Peninsula issue is very low in the US' priority since the US itself is facing difficulties in domestic politics.

Hwang Recently, the US is trying to encourage the diplomatic boycott of the Beijing Olympics along with the sanctions on North Korea. Adding all these circumstances into the calculation, the possibility of the declaration of the end of the war seems to fade away.

Kim The expectations that the Beijing Olympics would be the turning point seemed to come from the PyeongChang Olympics. As the PyeongChang Olympics could fully perform its strategic and periodic value, the Beijing Olympics also might have looked forward to a similar effect. But the thing is that while PyeongChang Olympics was successfully hosted, the following Tokyo Olympics lost its sincere meaning due to the coronavirus crisis, and Beijing Olympics is at the forefront of concern. Under the conditions, the possibility to accelerate the declaration of the end of the war with the momentum from the Beijing Olympics is barely there. I do not take this as the failure of Korea's diplomacy and therefore there is no need to be too much disappointed. In fact, the declaration of the end of the war also is a political and symbolic action, and the best place to declare it would be Panmunjeom, not Beijing. To conclude, what must be considered most important is understanding the meaning of the declaration in terms of the periodical turning point. Utilizing this symbol as the diplomatic measure is unlikely to be the right approach.

Hwang How should the next administration set up Korea's relations with China?

Kim I agree that Korea and China are tied under competitive relations due to the industrial and investment areas. However, in the longer term, both countries must maintain mutually friendly relations. From Korea's perspective, we are standing on the point of maintaining the strategic relations with China but at the same time required for the De-Sinicization. In the end, we need to continue the relations with China with a flexible approach, but to use the pivoting strategy to strengthen the partnership with China amid US' emphasis on the alliance. Only by expanding the space of diplomatic decision, Korea will be able to develop its status within the US-China relations.

Hwang Please share your thoughts on Korea's relations with Japan in the next administration.

Kim The Moon administration has come up with a two-track strategy for its diplomacy toward Japan. It was basically to separate the historical issue from further cooperation. Although the Moon administration's two-track strategy did not make a noticeable outcome, I still think we need to maintain this two-track approach. Also, if possible, a multitrack that covers multiple aspects on multiple levels seems like an idea. Two countries were tied with knots of anticommunism and the liquidation of colonialism since the Year 1965 System, and today might be the right timing to come up with a new strategy. We must continuously bring up the suggestions and discourses to break from the post-Year 1965 System and make a new move.

Hwang In order to strengthen Korean diplomacy's competitiveness, what would be the necessary reformation, for instance, organizational restructuring or reformation of human resources?

Kim Korea has several other diplomacy departments besides the Ministry of Foreign Affairs. For instance, the Ministry of Economy and Finance, Ministry of Trade, Industry and Energy, Ministry of Education, or Culture, Sports, and Tourism are actually implementing diplomatic roles. Along with the government departments, what really matters is the role of Blue House. Considering the relations between the Blue House and the Ministry of Foreign Affairs, the messages from Blue House must be clearly delivered to the Ministry of Foreign Affairs, so that the ministry can develop and practice the diplomatic strategies based on the streams from the Blue House. Additionally, the Ministry of Foreign Affairs should increase its discussions and talks with the external think tanks and go deeper in mapping out the strategies.

Hwang Should the new administration establish an additional government organization like Japan's Ministry for Economic Security or do you have any suggestions on reforming the overall formation?

Kim I agree that Korea also needs a new department that is in charge of economic security. The reason that Japan founded the Ministry of Economic Security is not only to create great benefits from the economic field, but also to respond to the crisis of the international supply chain. Therefore, the economic flow could be interpreted within the security terms. I anticipate an organizational restructuring that could connect science technology with international politics, and eventually can contribute to diplomatic strategies.

The past administrations' foreign policies had different diplomatic strengths and emphases. Regardless of whether all those foreign policies and diplomacies were actually implemented or not, the highlights were all distinguished. Geographically, they were all different starting from the Korean Peninsula, moving on to Northeast Asia, East Asia, Asia, and finally to the global level. Ideologically, there were voices from one side that actively support the US-ROK alliance under the US' alliance policy to the other side that would reflect the realities by putting more weight on the relationships with China. However, even though the past governments attempted to expand the diplomacy with new agendas, the discourse could not overcome the Korean Peninsula due to the risk of North Korea. Though Korea desires to make a new voice in between the US and China, the alliance with the US and China's support on the North Korea issue were always what Korea was tied up with. In the end, Korea was trapped in a dilemma, stuck in between the US and China.

However, since the outbreak of the coronavirus pandemic, Korea's diplomatic security environment and status met a great change. Korea could stand up as an advanced country in the international society with a new pride, that Korea is no longer in the position to focus only on passive diplomacy or the unrequited diplomacy toward North Korea. Now, the people have perceptions of being the citizens of an advanced country. They have the ambitions of being global citizens. All these changes will give attention to the new administration's foreign policies, and its influence would never be small. Therefore, the new administration is under considerable pressure to perform a new diplomacy that fulfills the expectations both from the inside and outside. Now is the era that requires leadership with fresh and dynamic diplomatic capacity, which goes beyond ideology, party, or interest conflict, than any other time. The presidential election on March 9 is coming right in front of us. The time to present the new diplomacy is ticking.

Korea's foreign policy, time to keep eyes on new economy and new security

Feb 16, 2022

Cho Kyunghwan
Member, The Presidential Commission on Policy and Planning

Kim Younkyu
Professor, Division of International Studies at Hanyang University

Kim Sangbae
Professor, Department of Political Science and International Relations at Seoul National University

There are some fields that previous forms of Korean diplomacy could not fully cover, but had to be dealt with. Those must be the new security and new economic issues. We are facing newly emerging security issues with roots in technological innovation -- for instance, the "fourth industrial revolution." From 5G, quantum computers, semiconductors, and other areas, existing hegemonies face a variety of new technological challenges. Technical standards are another significant confrontation. New security issues besides technology are rising to the surface, such as climate change, environment, health, quarantine, cyber terror, and so on. In the end, these areas will be as important as North Korea's nuclear programs and the four great powers, the US, China, Japan, and Russia, that surround the Korean Peninsula. This week's discussion invited Cho Kyunghwan, who is a member of the presidential commission on policy Planning, professor Kim Younkyu from the division of international studies at Hanyang University, and professor Kim Sangbae from Seoul National University, who is also the current president of the Korean Association of International Studies, to take a precise look into these emerging security issues.

Hwang Regarding the security issues that do not belong to traditional ways and types, we use several terms including human security, non-traditional security, or new security.

Cho I would say we can distinguish this concept so-called emerging security or the new security by periods and sectors. Firstly, in periodical flow, national security or traditional security was the major priority in terms of security concepts since the end of the Cold War after World War II. From the 1990s, new security areas emerged and were established. For instance, the UN Development Program came up with stories of human security and led the changes. Secondly, we can distinguish security depending on areas and sectors. Now our daily lives are facing new and various threats that we have never experienced before. Under these circumstances, states have obligations to protect their people from the new security threats by getting involved in their lives.

Kim Y. When we define the term emerging security or new security, it can change according to whether we will embrace the economic security issue or not. Personally speaking, the practical emerging security issues and economic security issues may be included in the definition of non-traditional security.

Kim S. The thing is that, regardless of the terminology, emerging security or new security, the paradigm of security is changing. Currently, the spectrum and the contents of security are continuously transitioning and the actors or their roles in resolving the issues are also changing accordingly. In this context, classifying some areas into the traditional security and some as the new is practically difficult. We may have to change the way we recognize "security" from the root.

Hwang It seems the proportion of new security in the general concept of security will expand further. How far do you expect it to stretch?

Cho From now on, the importance of this concept "new security" will grow larger and larger. Also, since the security paradigm itself has changed, respective states must respond with a comprehensive and deep understanding of the wide spectrum of newly emerging security threats. Moreover, states need a clear counterstrategy against new security and emerging security from the state-leading presidential level. These fields must be essentially included in the president's tasks.

Kim Y. The very surprising change in terms of the newly emerging security issues is that such trade, industrial, or enterprise issues were transferred into the sector of national security. When we see the US today, the State Department is intervening in battery and semiconductor issues, while

President Biden is directly mentioning a "battery arms race" in person. Compared to the past, when the US and the Soviet Union competed through the number nuclear weapons they possessed during the Cold War, the US and China are now confronting each other with the number of semiconductor and battery factories they have today.

Kim S. The weight of emerging security will rise for sure. However, I personally consider we have to slightly change the question in order to read the current security paradigm more precisely. What is more concerning than whether the proportion of new security will grow or not is the fact that the security threats we will face from now on will be under the mechanism which works with the logic of emerging security. What we have to do is figure out how to counteract this process.

Hwang Looking at the Huawei case, the competition for technological hegemony between the US and China is quite intense.

Kim S. The history of such conflicts, for instance, the ones that emerged from US's sanctions on China's telecommunication companies like Huawei, is already more than 10 years old. It just reached its peak in 2019. Since then, there is no particular report that says significant national information or data were extracted from Huawei equipment and caused any crisis in national security. Perhaps what happened surrounding Huawei can be examined as the preparation for the threat in the future, rather than the actual threat that exists today. In other words, we can see this in the context of the US' subjective process of securing itself from the potential threat that might break out under crisis, which does not happen during peacetime. Furthermore, the US has imposed sanctions on the industries that were in charge of supplying semiconductors or components to Huawei. This eventually shook the fundamental structure of the global supply chain that both the US and China built together under globalization for the last 30-40 years. Decoupling or reshoring between the US and China followed and bilateral competition and confrontation got more severe in succession.

Kim Y. Continuing the discussion on the reorganization of the supply chain, the US is relatively weak when it comes to the newly emerging semi-conductor and battery field. Because the US is usually in charge of designing and planning, and got used to the structure of gaining benefits from technology, 70 percent of semiconductor production and 90 percent of battery production gathered in East Asia. Under such a situation, one of the great goals the US is aiming for today is to move the semiconductor and battery supply chain that is already constructed in East Asia to US territory, and to build its own independent structure.

Hwang The geopolitical concept that we knew is changing.

Kim S. We are heading toward the network-oriented competition, going beyond the resource-oriented power race. Additionally, the weaponization of interdependence is ongoing to utilize this network mechanism. Again, this means the dominant power follows depending on how you use the network and interdependency, regardless of how many resources you have. In particular, as the US and China form their own networks, Korea is standing on a critically important edge of the selection. We might consider the fight between the US and China surrounding the supply chain of semiconductor and battery production creates an unfavorable atmosphere for Korea, but it can provide Korea with a point of strength in terms of establishing a network depending on our further choices.

Hwang Do you consider the new security feasible as the soft security agenda when it comes to the Northeast Asian security cooperation regime?

Cho Under the current situation, the pandemic can be the trigger for future connection that links South and North Korea, the US, China, and probably Mongolia to establish a cooperation mechanism for soft power issues. Now the border between new security and old security has collapsed, and therefore we can come up with OSCE in the East Asian version. Of course, whether it is able to happen in parallel with the US-South Korea alliance or not is the problem. However, I assume both the US and Korea can find a point of nexus where both states' benefits meet and the new security sector would be that critical meeting point of cooperation.

Hwang As the US-ROK alliance was as advanced as the global alliance, Korea will probably see more space to contribute to international society in the new security sector. What would it be if the US requires Korea to join the QUAD?

Cho The QUAD has organized working groups on new technology, climate change, and vaccines. These are fields where Korea also has great capability and can cooperate from case to case even though we do not necessarily join the QUAD. Also, cyber cooperation that was mentioned in the US-Korea summit is another field we can consider. Within that context, actively stepping in with a practical approach seems reasonable, regardless of the hegemonic frame between the US and China.

Hwang The new security issues are more closely connected to daily life than the traditional security issues and the government can get involved in them at any time. Do you have any suggestions that should be reflected on the mechanisms to respond to this?

Kim Y. Recently Korea is going through discussions on the reorganization of the supply chain and it mainly focuses on what position Korea should maintain. As we are all aware, the US in the past did not put its weight on manufacturing, therefore, most of the manufacturing industry is concentrated in China. Korea also has very close relations with China when it comes to export, import, raw materials, and intermediary goods. Under the condition, the US has declared the reorganization of the supply chain as well as the revival of manufacturing market, and Korea is in the position of disputing whether this can be the opportunity or the risk for Korea's sake accordingly. Currently, Korea is attempting several diversifications in resources through resource cooperation with Australia and others, following China's weaponization of resources. Korea is seeking to find ways to minimize the risk that comes from China. It must be the next administration's task to comprehend and consider deeper and respond in making decisions at the middle of the US and China as well as the reorganization of the supply chain.

Hwang Do you think it is necessary for Korea's next government to newly establish a department or maybe a control tower in Blue House that manages new security issues including the economy, cyber, infectious diseases, and others?

Kim Y. The prime minister's office is not quite appropriate in dealing with emerging security issues. In order to accurately counteract the emerging security issues and to lead the related policies from the front, the Office of National Security at the Blue House should cover the emerging security with the president standing at the core. Furthermore, if in need, an additional security office should be established along to handle the new security in dramatic situations.

Kim S. As far as I know, adding one more security office has its limits, since it would cause hypertrophy of the Blue House. However, in a similar sense, we could think of having the 3rd deputy director who is in charge of the emerging security sector in the current Office of National Security, following the 1st (national defense) and the 2nd (foreign affairs), instead of founding an additional security office as an alternative. National Intelligence Service is already running its organization in this way, for instance, its 3rd deputy director is covering a particular area such as space or AI weapons. It might differ indeed depending on the political positions, however, it seems more reasonable to gather all the scattered emerging security issues in one organization and let it manage them.

Cho The current 1st and 2nd deputy directors in the Office of National Security are way too focused on inter-Korean relations. In this sense, we may have to reduce and rearrange the tendency and found or expand the function of new security related departments.

Hwang Do you have any additional words to add?

Kim Y. Climate change is not just a simple environmental issue, but is closely related to electric motor vehicles, semiconductors, and batteries. Considering the facts, we must put more emphasis on the connections between the emerging security issues.

Kim S. From the perspective of the emerging security issues, it is necessary to reestablish our view toward the two Koreas' relations. Whenever inter-Korean relations and emerging security issues come up together, cooperation on quarantine, health, human rights, climate change and others are always mainstream topics. However, new security basically emerges from the conflicting and threatening factors. Considering these, the representative new security issue between the two Koreas is cybersecurity. In addition, several other new security issues are still rising in between two Koreas and will only emerge more. So far, the North Korean nuclear problem is the most critical issue, which tends to crowd out other areas. Nevertheless, we all have to be settled on how to respond in case we face new security problems that go beyond the nuclear problem, and therefore a new perspective in reading inter-Korean relations must be established.

Cho I would say the logic of ideology should not be applied to new security issues. Personally, I anticipate the next president to be the one who makes a clear position regarding the emerging security, as the leader of the country.

Standing at the current position, where the uncertainty of the international order and instability of the Korean Peninsula is expanding, setting the further direction and counteractions in Korea's diplomacy is more urgent than any other time. An in-depth discussion on Korean diplomacy's vision, dignity, direction and positioning amid the heated US-China competition, as well as the arrangement and rearrangement of the overall organizational framework is required in order to maximize Korea's diplomatic competitiveness. It follows that the discussion on what kind of function should be added, where, and from which sector, could be referential advice for the new government's implementation of foreign policy from May.

What concerns me the most is the need for an operating system that can comprehensively deal with both traditional and newly emerging security issues. Japan has recently established a new position of economic security minister, which is specified into only the economic security issues. For Korea to blend traditional and new security issues effectively, it also has to develop either a department or a mechanism that it can implement at the national leadership level. Sufficient responses to coping with the new economy and new security are essential for national prosperity and the welfare of the people.

Toward the Korea-Japan relations of vision and coexistence

Apr 20, 2022

Lee Wondeog

Professor, Department of Japanese Studies at Kookmin University

Jo Yanghyeon

Professor, Korea National Diplomatic Academy

Nam Kijeong

Professor, Institute for Japanese Studies at Seoul National University

Historically, Korea and Japan have long been in conflict and contradiction. Since Japan's colonization of Korea, it has deepened what some observe to be Japan's sense of superiority over Korea and Korea's sense of inferiority toward Japan. Japan's "Lost Decades" – a period of economic stagnation caused by an asset price bubble collapsing in the 1990s -- and Korea's rise in national power in the international community brought some tension to bilateral relations. During the Moon Jaein administration, historically latent anger and debt relief measures were interspersed with legal and social policy responses and confrontations on old historical issues. The new government, which will be inaugurated in May, is emphasizing the improvement of Korea-Japan relations, unlike the existing progressive government. Nevertheless, we see a number of constraints still in place. This week's panel discussion will attempt to conduct a diagnosis and evaluation of the Moon Jaein administration's Korea-Japan relations. It will also examine the goals and constraints that the Yoon Sukyeol administration will face in trying to establish a new relationship with Japan. It will also present specific solutions and road maps for the process of normalizing Korea-Japan relations. The panel includes distinguished researchers on Japanese international affairs: professor Lee Wondeog from Kookmin University, professor Jo Yanghyeon from the Korea National Diplomatic Academy, and professor Nam Kijeong from the Institute for Japanese Studies at Seoul National University.

Hwang This is commonly referred to as the worst period for Korea-Japan relations since the two countries established diplomatic relations in 1965. Observers are also saying that relations have worsened under the Moon administration.

Lee I do not completely agree with such statements. In fact, relations between Korea and Japan have worsened structurally since 2012 (before the Moon administration took office). We can say the conflict has intensified and deepened because problems were not resolved. Beyond the governmental dimension, anti-Japanese or anti-Korean sentiments are reaching a climax in both countries. On top of that, communication between national leaders has been cut off, which has continued this situation under an absence of trust. I would add that the interruption in human resource and private exchanges due to COVID-19 are additional obstacles in improving Korea-Japan relations.

Hwang How do you evaluate the Moon administration's handling of Korea-Japan relations?

Lee I would largely divide it into two parts. The first half of the Moon administration's term (2017-2019) can be assessed as an omnidirectional conflict with Japan. This conflict arose from issues related to politics, history, security, and approaches toward North Korea. Most of all, wartime sexual slavery and forced labor issues were the largest factors of conflict. They triggered an economic hit from Japan's export regulations, which excluded South Korea from its "whitelist" of countries with preferential trade status. This later escalated into Korea's "No Japan" movement boycotting Japanese products. In terms of security, there was also mutual distrust that resulted in disputes, such as the 2018 radar lock-on dispute or announcement on the temporary termination of the General Security of Military Information Agreement (GSOMIA). When it came to policies toward North Korea, the Moon administration considered Japan as an obstacle in reaching peace on the Korean Peninsula. Japan regarded the Moon administration as anti-Japan and pro-North Korea as a result. In the latter half of Moon's term, there were efforts to improve relations with Japan through a two-track approach following US President Biden's inauguration. However, not much came of this approach. There was no clear consensus on the sexual slavery issue, nor on compensation for forced labor. On the other hand, Japan was likely watching Korea like a teacher "waiting for the homework to be done with his arms crossed," rather than positively responding to the Moon administration's efforts.

Nam I guess it is hard to tell if we can blame worsened Korea-Japan relations on the Moon administration. I can see factors that limited the Moon administration's diplomacy with Japan. The Moon administration conceptualized national identity as based on constitutional principles, and valued judicial judgement based on the separation of legal, administrative, and judicial powers. It also valued an international norm which focuses on victims. Under the given reality and conditions, at times the Moon administration decided to take a very realistic approach toward Japan, which even disappointed and confused the Moon administration's supporters. Also, due to the politicization of history, the government paradoxically happened to take the burden of resolving historical issues. This eventually resulted in civil society organizations' excessive politicization of certain historical issues meeting resistance. The Moon administration's diplomacy with Japan is within the realm of pragmatic diplomacy to a certain level. As such, if the new administration excludes these strategies it would actually narrow down the spectrum of pragmatic diplomacy. Moreover, if it chooses to accept Japan's one-track approach, it will face considerable domestic opposition. Moving forward, if the politicization of history gets toned down, the new government must remember the possibility that it might have to deal with massive resistance from civil society organizations.

Hwang I would like to hear your outlook on further changes in relations with Japan after Yoon Sukyeol's inauguration.

Jo I personally think we should avoid overly positive expectations of Korea-Japan relations under the Yoon administration. Of course, the new administration seems to be concerned with Korea-Japan relations. Cooperation between the US, Korea and Japan has become more significant due to the war in Ukraine and heightened animosity against China and North Korea. The Kishida administration's leadership is maintaining stability with 50 to 60 percent support domestically. The Japanese public seems to have very low expectations regarding Korea-Japan relations. The Biden administration also is continuously stressing US-Korea-Japan relations. All these factors point to better relations between Korea and Japan. However, Korea's pro- or anti-Japanese framing and the majority opposition and minority ruling party structure in parliament has a high possibility of constraining the implementation of specific policies toward Japan. Conservatives in Japan with former Prime Minister Abe have created a "historical war" framing which is now acting as a constraining factor on Prime Minister Kishida and Foreign Minister Hayashi in regard to bilateral relations. Since the two countries still have domestic political obstacles, both Korea and Japan should utilize well the momentum of Korea's new government.

Lee When we look into President-elect Yoon's overall pledges and remarks made during his campaign, he mainly emphasizes setting a future oriented and cooperative relationship with Japan – not one buried under historical issues. He has consistently called for negotiating a comprehensive deal that covers all the current major issues of conflict between Korea and Japan. This includes compensation for forced labor, export regulations, interruption of GSOMIA, and so on. He also mentioned his intent to upgrade the Japan–South Korea Joint Declaration of 1998 between Japanese Prime Minister Keizo Obuchi and South Korean President Kim Daejung. Moving forward, the Yoon administration's diplomatic strategies are generally in pursuit of a comprehensive US-Republic of Korea (ROK) alliance; strengthened US-Korea-Japan security cooperation; gradual participation in the Quadrilateral Security Dialogue (Quad); and cooperation on the US' Indo-Pacific Strategy. In this sense, I see a high possibility for Korea-Japan relations to naturally turn into a cooperative one.

Hwang Despite all these optimistic prospects, I guess we can still see restrictive factors from home and abroad.

Lee Yes. First of all, we can think of Korea-Japan relations within the context of Northeast Asian geopolitics, where strategic competition between the US and China is intensifying. Transitions are taking place with the flow and balance of power. Additionally, as Korea-Japan relations have gone from vertical to horizontal, there is disharmony and maladjustment. Under structural limitations, this new dynamic cannot be easily and naturally overcome even with a new government in Korea. Furthermore, domestically Korea's opposition party holds the majority of seats in parliament. In addition, civil rights and historical victims' organizations continue to take a resolute stance against Japan. Thus, if the new administration takes a passive stance to Japan regarding historical issues, these organizations will denounce the new administration's policies as a humiliation. This will give rise to anti-Japan public sentiment, and the new administration will have to undertake the task of persuading the public otherwise.

Hwang What would be a specific roadmap for improving and normalizing Korea-Japan relations?

Lee We need to reopen communication between leaders on both sides through a summit. So far, Korea and Japan have maintained abnormal relations for 11 years without a single summit. Since a meeting is crucial in recovering Korea-Japan relations, we must consider the possibilities of holding a summit close to the time of Yoon's inauguration. I see either Prime Minister Kishida's visit to Yoon's inauguration ceremony or President-elect Yoon's participation in the Quad summit scheduled in Tokyo at the end of May as likely to happen. The period after Korea's local elections in June or Japan's House of Councilors elections in July is also a feasible time. This shuttle diplomacy based on leaders' restoration of trust and communication is critical. In case a summit of the two leaders is unavailable for some reason, they could start thinking of holding a trilateral summit. The summit can be one of either US- Korea-Japan, or Korea-China-Japan.

Jo The Yoon administration's policies toward Japan seem to deal with issues in a comprehensive way. However, negotiations and talks between Korea and Japan can reach a more effective outcome by using multiple gradual approaches, not a package deal. In particular, Korea and Japan must recognize that they must cover both areas of diplomacy and domestic politics at the same time. Accordingly, this approach would take some time. I also agree with the significance of Japan taking cautious moves regarding Korea-Japan relations until the House of councilors election, though the inauguration of Korea's new government will be a worthy opportunity. From the Kishida administration's view, President Biden's visit to Japan will be a necessary opportunity for the election. In this context, I would like to recommend that Japan seek a similar method in improving its relations with Korea. Lastly, I am a bit worried about Japanese politicians who are insisting on very firm hardline policies toward historical and territorial issues.

Nam The new government is planning on a "Joint Declaration 2.0" through an inclusive approach. However, the declaration back then was achieved through sharing a common goal, which was to build an East Asian community. Both Korea and Japan came to a consensus on planning a vision for peace, as well as solving and moving on from historical problems. That is why former President Kim Daejung assessed Japan as having contributed to the development of international society as a peaceful country after World War II when mentioning Japan's postwar constitution. If the new administration strives to upgrade the Joint Declaration, how it does so will be its critical challenge. If these problems are not seriously dealt with, a final and irreversible crisis may once again strike Korea-Japan relations.

Hwang It seems that the forced labor issue, the biggest area of conflict between Korea and Japan, must be resolved.

Jo When it comes to the resolution of the forced labor issue, subrogation in a broad sense stands on extending the Declaration of Waiver of Compensation against Colony, also called the "YS Formula." When we interpret subrogation within a wide spectrum, it is to require an apology and show of regret from Japan. Also, it is to have the Korean government provide material compensation to victims and the bereaved. Then it has a certain point of intersection with the YS Formula. If the Yoon administration can come up with a measure combining these two alternatives and present them to the people, I think it will be a more persuasive approach.

Lee I think it is necessary to resolve the issue after the measures to withhold cashing through consultation with victims' groups are taken. The scope of the conscription issue is quite wide, and I personally believe the cases won in the Supreme Court should be given priority for resolution. This means 50 billion to 300 billion won ($40 million-$242 million) should be paid to approximately 34 to 200 people. The ways to solve this conscription problem are through fundraising and subrogation through legislation. Also, they can be resolved through the International Court of Justice, the Arbitration Commission and the YS Formula. Considering the current situation, subrogation through legislation and the YS Formula might be possible.

Hwang How about the sexual slavery issue?

Lee I actually do not think it is the biggest issue at hand in terms of Korea-Japan relations. The essence of resolving the sexual slavery issue is restoring the dignity and honor of the victims through an apology from the Japanese government. To that end, we must solve it with a sexual slavery agreement fully involving both parties. Currently, the Research Institute on Japanese Military Sexual Slavery under the Ministry of Gender Equality and Family provides unpaid compensation to survivors and bereaved families. This compensation comes from a fund which includes 5.4 billion won from the Japanese government and 10.4 billion won from the Korean government's gender equality funds. This fund also allows the implementation of symbolic projects for historical research, memorials, and future education about the issue. An example would be building and maintaining a historical museum for the victims.

Hwang What other efforts can be made for better Korea-Japan relations?

Nam The tenuous disputes today between Korea and Japan trace their roots to the system in 1965. In fact, the principle of compensation was transformed into a form of economic cooperation under the Park Chunghee regime, which resulted in Korea losing its right to make further compensation claims. Within this context, the Yoon administration is trying to normalize Korea-Japan relations. Following the Moon administration's oppositional approach, the system back in 1965 lingers as a reminder of conflicts between Korea and Japan. Moreover, as Korea has recently shifted to a "middle power" mentality, progressive cooperation and development in Korea-Japan relations may meet some difficulties. In this respect, I think that the Japanese government should consider these issues cautiously and make active efforts to solve these problems.

Lee Korea needs to utilize a private-public mix. Those standing between Korea and Japan should be considered from the "1.5 track" perspective. In particular, it is important to take into account the experiences of public-private joint commissions or studies on a new era for Korea-Japan relations. A Korea-Japan public-private institute can find an efficient resolution for further improvement of bilateral relations. Additionally, we may be able to develop the Joint Declaration 2.0 while preparing for the 60th anniversary of normalized diplomatic relations between Korea-Japan in 2025.

Yoon displayed bold, decisive diplomacy at NATO summit

Jul 7, 2022

Song Whasup

Senior Research Fellow, Korea Institute for Defense Analysis

Hiroyasu Akutsu

Professor, International Politics and Security Studies at Heisei International University

After the previous summit with US President Joe Biden in May, President Yoon Sukyeol's attendance at the NATO summit was a straight one-two punch that proved a change in the new Korean government's foreign policy. Contrasting with the Moon Jaein government's friendly stance toward China, Yoon instead moved boldly without hesitation. He chose to prioritize the alliance with the US. Under the framework of a Korea-US-Japan cooperation, this could be understood as a signal of a narrowing of the sentimental distance between Korea and Japan, which was suffering from a deep emotional cleavage stemming from historical issues. It does not necessarily mean that Yoon's government will turn the previous foreign policies totally upside-down, however, it will be distinguished from the last five years for sure, posing a dilemma for China. Both leaders from Korea and Japan have attended the NATO summit this time. In contrast to how Japan was being criticized for harboring wicked intentions to pressure China by bringing NATO into the game, Beijing, which still holds some expectations for Seoul, has displayed a much milder response toward Korea. This week's discussion invites Senior Research Fellow

Song Whasup from the Korea Institute for Defense Analysis and Hiroyasu Akutsu, professor of International Politics and Security Studies at Heisei International University, who has served at the National Institute for Defense Studies, to discuss Korea and Japan's foreign policies starting from the NATO summit.

Hwang How do you evaluate President Yoon Sukyeol and Prime Minister Kishida's visits to the NATO summit?

Song President Yoon Sukyeol's participation at the NATO summit can be a huge diplomatic asset, as it presented an opportunity to communicate with numerous leaders from various countries. Furthermore, it can be evaluated that his participation has established a meaningful diplomatic foundation for his term of office, as he played the diplomatic sales card in terms of nuclear power plants and the defense industry, as well as promoting Korea's bid to host the 2030 World Expo in Busan. In the case of Prime Minister Fumio Kishida, he highly evaluated that the US, Korea, and Japan have agreed on trilateral cooperation for North Korea's denuclearization at the US-Korea-Japan Summit. Considering the security situation surrounding the Korean Peninsula, holding a US-Korea-Japan summit must have contributed to strengthening the deterrence against North Korea.

Akutsu Although both Japan and Korea are nonmembers of NATO, the participation of both President Yoon and Prime Minister Kishida was a clear message that both countries stand on the side of democracy in its fight against authoritarianism.

It may be too early to evaluate their participation in detail, but at this early stage, I can raise a few points at least. First, Yoon, the first-ever Korean president to attend the summit, reminded the world that North Korea's nuclear and missile threat is growing and continues to be a global issue while NATO members have tended to pay more attention to Russia and China. Second, Kishida, the first-ever Japanese prime minister to attend the summit as well, was able to realize his proposal in the meeting with Korea, Australia and New Zealand on the sidelines of the summit. Third, both countries, in close coordination with the US, effectively utilized this opportunity to resume the Japan-US-Korea trilateral security cooperation meeting for the first time in four years and nine months.

In addition to the above second point, to my understanding, Korea had a few specific purposes beforehand. It includes strengthening the "value alliance" based on a liberal democracy with the 30 NATO member states and partner nations; building the foundation for a comprehensive security network with NATO states and exploring ways to effectively respond to emerging security threats, such as cyber and aerospace threats and climate change; and establishing a NATO mission in Brussels to increase information-sharing and strengthen our networks with NATO members and partner nations. Obviously, Korea was well-accepted as a key partner that shares common values with NATO and the past cooperative achievements were appreciated at the summit. As for economic, cyber and aerospace security, climate change and so on, Korea is expected to play a meaningful role in the future.

Hwang What are the prospects for the Yoon and Kishida governments' development of relations with NATO?

Akutsu Prime Minister Kishida already stated that in order to open up horizons for Japan-NATO cooperation, Japan will accelerate the work to substantially upgrade the Japan-NATO Individual Partnership and Cooperation Program, the cooperation document that exists between Japan and NATO, and develop Japan's cooperation in the cyber, emerging technologies and maritime security fields. As for defense cooperation, Japan will dispatch Self-Defense Forces officials to the NATO headquarters and expand mutual participation by Japan and NATO as observers in the other's exercises.

As for Korea, Korea and NATO have also been committed to strengthening relations to address shared security challenges, including cyber defense, nonproliferation and counterterrorism. NATO and Korea have been engaged in dialogue and cooperation since 2005. Like Japan, Korea is also one of NATO's "partners across the globe." Since 2012, work has been taken forward through an Individual Partnership and Cooperation Program and was renewed in 2019. Political dialogue and practical cooperation are being developed across priority areas, including nonproliferation, cyber defense, counterterrorism, security-related civil science projects, interoperability, chemical, biological, radiological and nuclear defense, as well as civil preparedness, resilience and disaster relief. Yoon's participation in this year's summit will accelerate further cooperation between Korean and NATO in both general and specific terms.

Song Korea formally joined the NATO Cooperative Cyber Defense Center of Excellence in May, and is preparing for the establishment of the NATO mission. It seems Korea's further cooperation with NATO in nontraditional security areas will grow stronger, and military exchanges might be expanded, including mutual visits of vessels and so on. However, when we look into NATO's characteristics, the possibility of fully holding military cooperation with Korea is quite low. Instead, I assume Korea would rather share a strategic consensus with NATO and the response to the international security threats.

Japan established its NATO mission in July 2018, and has conducted a joint exercise with vessels. As Prime Minister Kishida mentioned in the recent summit, security in the Indo-Pacific region and NATO are at an inseparable point. In this sense, cooperation to solidify the connection between the Indo-Pacific region and NATO is expected in the upcoming future.

Hwang What is the background of Prime Minister Kishida's proposal for the Korea-Japan-Australia-New Zealand Summit?

Song The Japanese government has been opposing the change of status quo by force. It seems Prime Minister Kishida has determined that sharing the principle of opposing the change of status quo by force with its partner countries is significant, as he witnessed Russia's invasion of Ukraine.

Moreover, Japan might have wanted to show off its leadership in promoting the cooperation between NATO and Indo-Pacific partner countries.

Akutsu In April, China signed a security pact with the Solomon Islands in the southwest Pacific Ocean. In response, Australia stepped up efforts to prevent the Solomon Islands from officially signing the agreement and accelerated diplomatic efforts to oppose the security pact. Regarding the US, which already announced in February a plan to open an embassy on the Islands to deepen cooperation with Pacific Island partners, immediately accelerated its diplomatic engagement with the Islands. Naturally, the concern was shared with New Zealand and Japan as well.

Both the US and its allies in the Asia-Pacific have realized that security issues cannot be resolved by one single superpower and that the US allies have to strengthen their capabilities to "help themselves" as well as to "help the others between and among themselves." As a policy simulation and wargame designer, I would ask: What if US security resources became so sparse in multiple contingencies occurring almost simultaneously in the region that the US allies and partners have to get together to compensate? Japan, South Korea, Australia and New Zealand are not members of NATO, but they have been invited as partners to the NATO summit this time, so I assume that Japan decided to seize this opportunity to meet with the other US allies to forge positive chemistry among them at least to alleviate the above concern.

Hwang What could be the meaning of Korea's establishment of the NATO mission?

Song Once the NATO mission is established, communication with NATO will be systemized and access to information on the agenda that are discussed in NATO will be easier. In other words, we will be able to get the information about NATO's projects, which basically will extend the range of opportunities to cooperate with NATO in the defense industry along with emerging security areas including cybersecurity. Additionally, starting with NATO itself, opportunities to cooperate with respective NATO member countries in the defense industry, nuclear power plants and emerging security will also be enlarged.

Akutsu In light of Japan's experience, Korea's establishment of the NATO mission means the possibility of deepening and widening cooperation between Korea and the alliance. Korea is expected to increase information-sharing and strengthen its networks with NATO members and partner nations. In Japan's case, the mission of Japan to NATO was established on July 1, 2018. The North Atlantic Council agreed in May 2018 to accept Japan's request to designate its embassy to Belgium as its mission to NATO. Then, the ambassador of Japan to Belgium became the head of the mission of Japan to NATO.

Hwang What direction should Korea-US-Japan cooperation take in the Indo-Pacific Strategy Framework?

Song The most critical threat in the Indo-Pacific region is North Korea's nuclear program. The US-Korea-Japan Summit has agreed and emphasized the fact that North Korea's nuclear issue is what the three countries must emergently respond to. Moreover, as the summit has concentrated on bringing highly intensified economic sanctions to resist North Korea's further development of nuclear and missiles, the efficiency of sanctions on North Korea will increase. Also, it has not been particularly mentioned in this summit, but the US-Korea-Japan cooperation is expected to play an essential role in establishing the rules of the Indo-Pacific Economic Framework.

Akutsu The existing trilateral cooperation is mainly focused on North Korea's nuclear and missile threats, so its function should be expanded to be able to deal with those issues, mainly concerning China, that the other partners in the Indo-Pacific Strategy Community are expected to deal with. Given that three partners have already highlighted the importance of peace and stability in the Taiwan Strait and expressed strong opposition to unilateral actions in the South China Sea and increasing tensions in the Indo-Pacific, the further direction for the framework should take those issues into consideration.

Hwang What are the prospects for security and military cooperation between Korea and Japan, including GSOMIA?

Akutsu Both Korea and Japan have emphasized the importance of resuming stronger security cooperation within trilateral, not bilateral, security cooperation. So the bilateral cooperation would be improved, including the General Security of Military Information Agreement, within Korea-US-Japan trilateral security cooperation. Given that fact that the issue of history has still been lingering around the bilateral relations, this should be taken as relatively a good start, if not perfect.

Song Though the GSOMIA between Korea and Japan still exists, practical intelligence sharing is pretty limited. Given that Korea and Japan has announced totally different results on North Korea's missile test, the intelligence sharing between the two is not going well. First of all, it is necessary to strengthen the intelligence sharing between Korea and Japan on North Korea's nuclear and missiles to strengthen deterrence against North Korea. On the other hand, as the security cooperation between Korea and Japan has confronted limits due to historical issues, we usually expect the cooperation will meet its limit as long as these issues are not settled. However, when it comes to critical security issues, it is necessary to enhance close communication and cooperation.

Hwang What are the possibilities and limitations of mini-multilateral cooperation, for instance, between Korea-Japan-Australia-New Zealand?

Akutsu It has often been pointed out that in Asia or the Asia-Pacific, the NATO type of multilateral cooperation would not work. However, I have some points to raise here. First, multilateral cooperation would be more successful if it were specifically issue-oriented. The newly born four-nation framework among Korea, Australia, New Zealand, and Japan would work better if it was narrowed down to one or two specific areas or issues for cooperation such as maritime security, capacity-building aid, infrastructure construction aid, economic security and supply chains, cybersecurity and technological innovation. If such a grouping were to become comprehensive and cover many areas or issues for cooperation in the first place, it should separate those areas and issues into working groups. Second, however, the major limitation would be the absence of the US especially when deterrence fails and contingencies occur. If the US were not readily available in a contingency in this region, then the other partners have to work together until the US could spend more time and resources to deal with the contingency. Another limitation would be divergence of interests among US allies and partners stemming from different geographical locations. In my experience of imaginary policy simulations and wargames regarding multilateral security cooperation, some allies and partners tend not to take part in specific joint responses and actions in a contingency. This could happen in the real world in the future.

Song Among Korea, Japan, Australia, and New Zealand, Japan and Australia are Quad members, and Korea and New Zealand are not. Therefore, there is a possibility of a new mini-multilateral cooperation, whether it can be realized or not depends on deciding which countries will exercise leadership, or whether they have sufficient mutual trust and common interests to work together. At this point, the strongest obstacle is that there is no leader for this cooperation yet. If Korea-Japan relations improve, there might be a possibility to drive such mini-multilateral cooperation.

Hwang How did you evaluate President Yoon's three-minute speech on North Korea?

Song President Yoon pointed out that North Korea's nuclear and missile threats are a major challenge not only to the Korean Peninsula but also to the international community's peace. He appealed that the international community has to show and prove how much stronger its willingness to denuclearize North Korea is, than North Korea's willingness to develop nuclear programs and missiles. It was a declaration of his North Korea policy to respond in solidarity with the international community against North Korea's nuclear threat, and meant the perception that the international community's willingness to denuclearize North Korea can also be a deterrence to North Korea.

Akutsu As I already pointed out in response to your first question, President Yoon's three-minute speech successfully stressed Korea's commitment to achieving the denuclearization of North Korea. It is natural that NATO's current concern is the ongoing situation in Ukraine, not the Korean Peninsula, so President Yoon's speech was a very timely one. Furthermore, the strong message from the Korean Peninsula was persuasive at the right time at the right place. For this reason, too, President Yoon made the right decision to attend the NATO summit this time.

Hwang Would these flows cause any conflict with China?

Akutsu China has often negatively reacted to US-led or US-centered multilateralism or minilateralism as efforts to "contain China" or to establish "an Asian NATO," and so on. Australia, New Zealand and Japan have already been criticized individually by China over issues concerning the Solomon Islands, Taiwan, and so on. Both Japan and Korea have already expressed concern about Taiwan in the context of the Japan-US alliance and the Korea-US alliance, respectively, so the possibility is not so low in terms of the way China views any grouping that involves Japan and, Korea especially outside the issues concerning North Korea.

Song NATO pointed to China as a systemic challenge in its new strategic concept. However, President Yoon expressed only the basic principles of diplomacy that it is important to follow the universal values and norms, and that violations should be jointly condemned and sanctioned, and did not directly mention China. Prime Minister Kishida also only mentioned that changes in the status quo by force are not acceptable. China has indirectly checked the moves by saying that it will not neglect any situations that go against China's interests. I would rather say that how Korea and China would manage the Korea-China strategic partnership is a more critical issue than interpreting whether these flows would cause conflicts with China.

Hwang What are your suggestions to improve the overall Korea-Japan relations?

Akutsu Since the question is about "overall relations," let me put it in general terms. In my personal view, the bad part of the relations between Japan and Korea has tended to be caused by media emotionalism or sensationalism and political populism. When both media and politics emphasize the negative part of history and relations, both factors often interact to create inconvenient complexities. Once this process starts, things tend to go out of control. At the popular cultural level, the overall relations are positive, but this does not translate into politics. Even when political and diplomatic relations are relatively positive, sensationalism at the popular level often keeps them from moving forward. By now, it seems that only at the time of change of political leadership, to a degree, expectations for better relations rise in both media and politics. Now is such a time. So my suggestion is for both media and political leaders in both countries to maintain discipline, self-restraint and mutual respect. But in terms of Japan-US-Korea trilateral security cooperation, the current early phase is not necessarily negative, so I will keep my fingers crossed.

Song Although the Korea-Japan Summit was not held during the NATO Summit, it could be understood that the two countries are taking a cautious approach to improve Korea-Japan relations. Furthermore, sufficient time is required to improve Korea-Japan relations. Fortunately, the leaders of Korea and Japan have confirmed that they will communicate closely after this opportunity, so I guess the speed of negotiations to resolve pending issues will accelerate. President Yoon insists that pending issues and the future can only be discussed when there is progress in resolving the issues from the past, therefore, both the past and future must be put on the table at the same time. It is necessary to advance the discussion on improving Korea-Japan relations by embodying a future-oriented vision on cooperation between Korea and Japan.

We need public diplomacy that fully contains the scent of Korea

Mar 2, 2022

Han Dongman

Executive Advisor, Pyeongtaek International Exchange Foundation

Kim Daesik

Deputy Secretary General, Governors Association of Korea

Lee Jongkook

Executive Vice-President, The Korea Foundation

Korea's public diplomacy so far has been characterized as a state-centered one that focuses on popularizing itself. However, it is a fact that Korea is now facing needs and expectations to play a role that goes beyond it from home and abroad. Given that Korea's status and capabilities have developed considerably in the international community, its way of lending a hand should also be tailored to what the other desires and needs. Now, giving off the messages that Korea has in its own principles, values, and norms is truly meaningful. The transition of consciousness from the idea of "helping the other" to "helping each other" is paramount. In the future, Korea's public diplomacy should move toward the direction that can draw forth the sharing and understanding of mutual awareness through communication with others. Therefore, the value that Korea should advocate to the international community must first build the internal consensus on what the international community can accept. I guess it would be a Korean version of public diplomacy that fully contains the essence of Korea.

Based on this as the foundation, this week's discourse invited three distinguished experts from public diplomacy. The former Ambassador of Korea to the Philippines Han Dongman, who is currently serving as the Executive Advisor at Pyeongtaek International Exchange Foundation, the former Ambassador of Korea to Kazakhstan Kim Daesik, who is also the Deputy Secretary General of the Governors Association of Korea, and the former Ambassador of Korea to Libya Lee Jongkook, the current Executive Vice-President at The Korea Foundation. The three came together to discuss Korean public diplomacy's process of development, current status, and further directions.

Hwang When is the first time that Korean public diplomacy began? Also, please tell us what development process it went through.

Han Korea's public diplomacy started in earnest since 2010, when the Korean Ministry of Foreign Affairs and Trade officially set public diplomacy as a major diplomatic goal along with governmental affairs and economic diplomacy. For a successful outcome, the Korea Public Diplomacy Forum was launched as a 1.5 track semi-governmental consultative mechanism to enhance mutual understanding and reinforce the foundations of further cooperation with people from other countries. The first Korean Ambassador for Public Diplomacy was nominated in 2011, and the Public Diplomacy Act and Enforcement Decree went into effect in 2016. Later in 2017, Korea's First Basic Plan on

Public Diplomacy (2017-2021) was implemented under a five-year project. Also, since the Moon Jaein administration came in, the concept of "people diplomacy" was added on the original definition of public diplomacy. It was to aim for public diplomacy that the people can run together. As a result, the People Diplomacy Center was established in 2018. For now, a number of Korean universities are hosting lectures that are related to public diplomacy, and people's interest and attention toward public diplomacy is increasing day by day.

Hwang What could be the strong point or competitive edge for Korean public diplomacy?

Lee Since World War II, Korea has had its unique specialty among countries in the world in the sense that it has successfully achieved both economic growth and democracy. Additionally, Korean people have their own national traits. These traits show their diligence as well as their peace-loving attitudes, although they are living in a divided country. These traits are what could be a magnificent asset in Korea's public diplomacy and it is actually contributing to building up Korea's new national brand. Furthermore, Korea's various modern cultural contents, along with its traditional culture, are based on our historical dynamics, creativeness, and universality. These are sweeping all over the world. Ever since the COVID-19 crisis broke out, Korea is now being judged highly as an exemplar country that handled quarantine well from the international community. Korea has proven its remarkable distinction in the aspect of crisis management and stability that goes beyond its quarantine restoration capabilities. Lastly, I would say Korea's proficiency in IT technology development and related infrastructure is already well known worldwide.

Hwang Then what is the challenge that Korean public diplomacy must overcome on the other hand?

Kim First of all, current Korean public diplomacy is very focused on central government-oriented policies. While respective local areas' cultural capabilities are growing sustainably, most public diplomacy-related projects are concentrated in the central government, including the Ministry of Foreign Affairs. Due to this structure, there are certain limits in supporting local governments and furthering their activities.

Han I see six "T"s as critical when we talk about public diplomacy. The first T stands for Theme. The Korean Ministry of Foreign Affairs has set the theme "Connecting Koreans with the World, Charming Korea" and is putting efforts to actualize it. The second T stands for Target. The target of public diplomacy embraces not only foreign citizens and the public, but also extends to foreigners who are currently living in Korea. This also includes the 7.5 million overseas Koreans. The third T is Timing. On top of Korea's existing basic plan for public diplomacy, which was set to a five-year timeline, I see the necessity of making a more detailed approach, as in short-term, mid-term, and long-term. The fourth T is Tailor-made. The target and practice subjects are quite broad, so it must be implemented on a case-by-case basis. For instance, as K-food would be more suitable for African countries rather than K-pop, a customized strategy should be settled for sure. The fifth T is for Together. When it comes to implementing public diplomacy, we are dealing with a variety of actors and targets. In this sense, for example, the US forces in Korea can be the major target for the city of Pyeongtaek's public diplomacy. Lastly, the sixth T stands for Tool. Local governments' role matters significantly. To share one example, Pyeongtaek is hosting World Culture Week, which cooperates well with Embassies in Korea.

Hwang As seen from the controversy surrounding Hanfu at the recent Beijing Winter Olympics, it might be a cause of conflict in Korea's public diplomacy.

Kim Of course, I would say it is a regret that such a controversy arose at an international festival like Olympics, where countries are supposed to represent and symbolize themselves. However, regardless of what happened this time, I think it is unnecessary to confront other countries by emphasizing one country's own creativity and originality in terms of their culture. The flow of the times is that the entire world is being integrated into a global village and cultural differences are united. Culture is the area where inclusivity and understanding must come first. Escalating people's emotions and politicizing them should not be the most pursued attitude.

Hwang How do you draw the direction of public diplomacy in this era of COVID-19 and the Fourth Industrial Revolution?

Han Under the digital era, media is stretching its influence farther and farther. We can actually see the world leaders propagating foreign policies through social media networks like Twitter and Instagram, and not only through traditional press media anymore. Going one step further, in recent days, the virtual metaverse world has appeared throughout the world on a full scale, and its influence is skyrocketing. It's to the point that even Facebook has set itself on a goal to bring the metaverse to our lives as its mission. As it is shown, under a circumstance where the metaverse is stretching its influence to the real world, the traditional digital media world is transforming into a totally new one. Accordingly, we need public diplomacy that can follow this trend. For public diplomacy to effectively discover or make these new types of content, we must move on from a government-oriented and unilateral information providing approach. Sincere and meaningful public diplomacy or digital public diplomacy will only be possible when various actors from local governments, academia, NGOs, markets, the press, and others could come up together.

Lee Under COVID-19, we moved on from face-to-face meetings and now are running seminars through webinars, and the education field is expanding e-learning. In the context of public diplomacy, projects are focusing on spreading Korean culture through YouTube or other social media networks. Also, there are projects promoting Korean language classes through e-learning actively under implementation. For another example, a project named "Learn Korean with BTS" is winning great popularity in educating people about the Korean language overseas. This system combines digital technology with Korean textbooks and adds BTS members' readings. I can tell this is one of the most successful cases of public diplomacy in the new digital era.

Hwang What could be youths' roles in public diplomacy?

Lee Watching today's trend, the utmost consumer of Korean cultural diplomacy and the Korean wave are youth, from both domestic and abroad. The thing is that they are consumers but also spreaders at the same time. In other words, they are superior assets we have in our public diplomacy today. It is quite thought-provoking from the aspect that young peoples' use of social media and their digitalization leads their boundary of activity to become transnational. Additionally, I would like to emphasize that it is the youth who are the consumers and the spreaders once again for the "knowledge public diplomacy," which goes beyond cultural public diplomacy including K-pop and dramas. Government, its agencies, and other institutes such as the Korea Foundation which deal with public diplomacy should work more on attracting potentiality from young people.

Kim Continuing on, once the new government takes over, we might need to provide opportunities to youth by institutionally managing an internship system in which they can spend about six months to a year at official institutes abroad and experience life overseas. Since the youth are critical consumers and spreaders of public diplomacy in the new digital era, it must be an efficient option to let them do public diplomatic duties, rather than others.

Han I also think that the contributions and roles of youth are very important within the flow of grassroots public diplomacy. In this sense, as far as I know, we have a wide spectrum of support. They range from the Public Diplomacy Youth Camp under the Korea Foundation to the Digital Library of Korean Literature, the Digital Diplomacy Ambassador for Dokdo program, and the Honorary Ambassador on Cultural Heritage under the Voluntary Agency Network of Korea. Also, with COVID-19 and the oncoming Fourth Industrial Revolution, some are saying it is time to nurture more than 100,000 digital youth ambassadors for public diplomacy. Today we have 178 diplomatic missions, and we are required to institutionalize public diplomacy-related internships and expand resources. Moreover, it would be best if we can provide them with incentives when they come back and seek jobs.

Hwang I understand that there are several institutions in charge of public diplomacy in Korea. In your view, do you think it would be more efficient if there is a certain control tower within the government or at the Blue House?

Kim When we look into cooperation between the Ministry of Foreign Affairs, the Ministry of Culture, Sport and Tourism, and the Ministry of Education -- the major actors of the Public Diplomacy Committee -- I would say there are some areas that can be improved greatly. Nevertheless, if a control tower is established in the Blue House and managed formulaically, I assume the sincere traits and effect of public diplomacy would decrease

Han It would be better if the Blue House can manage and support the operation of public diplomacy in a more interactive and bottom-up approach. Then its role could be elaborating its public diplomacy message, which is currently scattered all over. It can also concretely build consistency. For the Blue House to begin with its role, the president as the head of the country must clearly be aware of the significance of public diplomacy.

Lee Korean public diplomacy surely has to be improved, considering its segmentation and redundancy. For one instance, the assignments on Korean (language) education both domestic and abroad are dispersed into three institutions. Therefore, problematic issues were continuously raised. Within the process of segmentation, the absence of a certain institution that manages, supervises, and coordinates cooperation as a whole downgrades the efficiency of work. In this regard, there is a need to improve at a governmental level in terms of distributing and arranging resources, tasks, and manpower.

Hwang Would you introduce any countries that Korea could learn from? Also, please share with us what aspects made you think so.

Han I would recommend Germany. It has reached a fruitful outcome in a hybrid structure, where the government level presents guidelines while sub-institutions and private organizations conduct the projects. Particularly, it has achieved successful results in culture and language with the Goethe Institute and Academic Exchange Office at the center. France has also obtained considerable results in public diplomacy through an integrated approach in the cultural public diplomacy field. In addition, Israel is traditionally the most active country in public diplomacy, and has established the world's first public diplomacy ministerial position.

Lee In the case of Japan, what the Japan Foundation is doing gives us significant suggestions that the Korea Foundation can adopt. Sweden is also well-known as a welfare country, along with gender equality and democracy. It is recently putting great capabilities in science and technology.

Kim Watching Denmark, there are aspects that we can look up to in terms of their value-oriented concepts such as peace, gender equality, democracy, and so on. Also, New Zealand is another example that we can learn a lot from, since it is pursuing eco-friendly values and implementing them well.

Hwang What could be the portion that public diplomacy takes in current Korean diplomacy? How much do you expect it to take up? What direction should the new government set for further public diplomacy? What should be stressed in particular?

Lee When it comes to Korea, it is necessary to expand capabilities in the field of values and policies in relation to soft power in a cultural aspect. What I mean by the field of values is that issues such as climate change, human rights, refugees, and peace should be on the agenda and applied to public diplomacy. Furthermore, from the perspective of technology, we must try to enhance the development of new technologies that are suitable for the digital era such as the metaverse, as well as taking advantage of using social media and new media. By doing so, we need to strengthen networking cooperation in the international community. Finally, it seems necessary to supplement institutional infrastructure. For example, expanding offices in major overseas bases to further Korean public diplomacy.

Kim Propagating Korea's traditional values, such as the humanitarianism of "Hongikinkan" (benefiting mankind) or "Innaecheon" (human beings and the heaven are the same) can be one way. Based on these values, we must progressively put our efforts into strengthening Korean public diplomacy's capacity and infrastructure.

Han Firstly, considering Korea's current economic scale and its status in the international community, I would like to stress the necessity to expand public diplomacy budgets, manpower, and infrastructure. Secondly, education on the importance of public diplomacy must be conducted at the national level. Thirdly, the Ministry of Foreign Affairs is currently strengthening its foundation for digital diplomacy based on "DNA" technology. Here, D stands for data, N stands for network, and A for artificial intelligence.

Also, as part of science and technological public diplomacy, it is necessary to continuously increase the capacity of digital public diplomacy.

In the end, what must be involved in the process of implementing public diplomacy is that its goal should not only be the realization of the national interest through enhancing the national image. The goal of public diplomacy is to contribute to the international community through the creation of global norms and values. Once these goals are achieved, the rise of national image and realization of national interests will naturally follow as a result. In carrying out public diplomacy, it should not just fully depend on the government's lead. It should be in a cooperative direction where various actors including local governments, businesses, media, civil society, and youth are involved and communicate with each other. Even if some level of inefficiency takes place, it is still important to develop a wide spectrum of cooperation in complex and multiple ways based on diversification and decentralization.

What comes after BTS?

Sept 1, 2022

Cho Sungeun

Professor, Department of English for International Conferences and Communication at Hankuk University of Foreign Studies

Deepa Prakash

Associate Professor, Political Science at DePauw University in Indiana

Noel Sajid Murad

Assistant Professor, Department of Marketing and Advertising in De La Salle University located in Manila

The prominent idol group BTS is something we cannot be unfamiliar with. They are a different type from a number of previous Korean idols and have become a global sensation. So many people around the world were fascinated by BTS dances and read into the messages of social reform in their lyrics. BTS was understood as the ultimate peak of K-pop and we saw the possibility of the Korean Wave being able to stand proudly in the mainstream of global culture.

BTS is recognized as the spearhead of Korea's public diplomacy, and their "Permission to Dance" performed at the United Nations made us feel the universal values of mankind. Now this BTS phenomenon has stretched far beyond Korea to the entire international community. How influential BTS has been is easily recognized through domestic and foreign media, but the fact that there is an academic conference going on regarding this phenomenon is not very well known.

Moreover, this conference has been internationally held multiple times already. The first BTS Global Interdisciplinary Conference was held at Kingston University in London in January 2020, while the second was held online by California State University, Northridge in Los Angeles at the height of the pandemic.

The third conference just wrapped up this summer at Hankuk University of Foreign Studies in Seoul, held on July 14 and 15. While the first two BTS conferences were very academic, the most recent one covered many interesting and diverse academic sessions, for example, sessions on fandom and politics, new media and technology, business, marketing and so on.

The biggest difference in the third conference is that it tried to make significant social and political changes. In order to figure out what interesting stories were discussed in the conference, this week's interview invites three experts.

First, we have professor Cho Sungeun from the English for International Conferences and Communication department of Hankuk University of Foreign Studies, who was a member of the organizing committee of the third BTS Global Interdisciplinary Conference. From abroad, associate professor of political science Deepa Prakash from DePauw University in Indiana and assistant professor Noel Sajid Murad from the department of marketing and advertising in De La Salle University located in the Philippines capital Manila joined the discussion.

Hwang Recently the BTS conference was held in Seoul, where you contributed as a member of the organizing committee. Would you share with us some of the background and maybe evaluate the performance of the conference?

Cho BTS Global Interdisciplinary Conference wished to show that the BTS fandom is not just about rooting for their favorite band. We wanted to send a message that the Army fandom is doing exciting work, that their emphatic and enthusiastic actions are being appreciated by people all over the world. Moreover, the non-Army academics who are interested in this social phenomenon realized that not only is BTS a cultural phenomenon worth of receiving critical analysis, but the participatory working of their fandom Army is another social phenomenon worth investigating. The conference highlighted the BTS Army fandom as representatives of "the new humanity," who come together to take action in promoting diversity, education and fighting to see a change in the world.

Hwang BTS is being really hot, so much that we are now having these particular conferences. How can we understand these aspects?

Cho Korean culture, or the so-called "Hallyu," has become the focus of unprecedented attention during the last few years. The global accomplishment of a Korean boy band recording several Billboard No. 1 hits and conquering the American music scene has naturally received a lot of scrutiny. This phenomenon is calling for a new framework for investigating the transnational production, distribution and consumption of K-pop and Korean popular culture. BTS's impact is not just limited to their musical success. As mentioned above, the participatory action of the fandom is also the focus of a lot of academic attention. Numerous M.A. and Ph.D. dissertations, books and journal articles are highlighting BTS' musicality and social significance.

Hwang In terms of Korea's public diplomacy, how should we evaluate BTS?

Cho BTS leader RM's speech at the 76th UN General Assembly showed how a country can strategically employ their cultural capital as an attractive tool for South Korean public diplomacy. BTS' "Love Myself" campaign has successfully raised more than $3.6 million globally for UNICEF's work to end violence against children and young people. Unlike traditional diplomacy that is carried out by diplomats, BTS can exert their influence to a younger, wider and a more diverse audience. As the executive office of the president stated, BTS has delivered messages of comfort and hope to the entire world, and their attendance at the UN General Assembly this time is expected to serve as a meaningful opportunity to expand communication with future generations around the world and draw their sympathy on major international issues. Engagement on important issues can be conveniently created by the extensive network of BTS' worldwide fandom. The fans' enthusiasm and especially their empathy is concentrated on social issues, and they raise awareness of social concerns or support the ideals expressed by the group.

Hwang Actually there have been many other idol groups before them, but what could be the particular reason that brought BTS such worldwide success?

Cho Different people cite different reasons for BTS' success. Some of them talk about how BTS effectively used social media platforms like YouTube and Twitter or new media -- platforms like Twitter, Instagram, Facebook -- to communicate with their fans. In my opinion, the keyword to BTS' success is "authenticity." There has been a conventional perception that K-pop idols are inauthentically manufactured. The members of the group (BTS) are very actively involved in creating their own music. They actively participate in the musical production of their songs and often write their own lyrics which talk about themes universal to their generation. I believe the reasons for BTS's success and popularity is the lyrics of their music. They talk about their own lives, their thoughts, their worries, struggles and their failures. Who doesn't have worries or struggles? So, their lyrics touch something in the listeners. The lyrics have a lot of layers and can be interpreted in various ways according to the receivers' state of mind.

Hwang Fans say the lyrics of BTS songs are very touching. How do you interpret their language between the lines and what are the cultural meanings and codes of the times?

Cho The language of BTS songs deal with very relatable messages. I believe the authenticity of their message is the impetus in making the fans passionately appreciate and enjoy their songs. Just as Big Hit Entertainment's CEO, Bang Si-hyuk, said in an interview in Time magazine, "They don't shy away from speaking about the pain felt by today's generation. They respect diversity and justice, the rights of youths and marginalized people. I think all of these factors worked in their favor." For example, the song "Epilogue: Young Forever," which was listed in their very popular "The Most Beautiful Moment in Life: Young Forever" album, talks about the despair felt by young people when their dreams are frustrated. The song tries to send an encouraging message and tells them they can find a way out of their pain.

Hwang BTS consists of all Korean members and was initiated by a Korean company. We cannot deny that there is a language barrier. Despite the given facts, how do you explain the millions of fans around the world?

Prakash I think that the combination of the universality of the music and BTS' message, their extremely charismatic and appealing personalities of the members and Big Hit/Hybe's excellent marketing has to do with this. Also, Army as a force is important in making BTS' music and message intelligible and transmittable -- they do a lot of the work of translation and spreading the BTS message in different countries and contexts, and that work would be difficult for Hybe to manage on its own, even with all its resources. Beyond that, I think the appeal of non-Western artists cannot be underestimated -- it is refreshing and special for fans around the world to follow artists who are not created by the Western system. But beyond that, it is something indefinable and unplannable. You can't engineer the success of a group like BTS -- otherwise other companies and groups would be able to do it. However, you can't capture lightning in a bottle twice as the saying goes, and something about it is sheer magic.

Hwang According to your presentation, you have evaluated that BTS has increased Korea's brand power. Could you talk about this more specifically?

Prakash We know some of the well-known metrics: tourism, BTS' association with well-known Korean brands, etc. I think what is significant is that BTS (and other music groups and cultural products) is one of the main ways that young people in particular come to develop an interest in Korea. It is amazing to see young people all over the world learning Korean (whether formally or informally) with BTS as their original motivation to do so. And this results in official collaborations such as BTS' promotion of Hangeul or being ambassadors of Seoul. At an official level, their campaigns and presentations at the UN (both before and with the Sustainable Development Goals efforts by the previous Moon Jaein administration) have taken this brand into the area of diplomacy.

Hwang Do you think BTS shows and contains Korean "color" – or qualities – a lot, or does it go beyond it?

Prakash Yes, undoubtedly so. Whether it is in symbolism and lyrics (there are some very Korean references and metaphors in their music), in activities and promotions (making kimchi or makgoeli in their show, wearing hanbok), in visual images (such as the video and performances for "Idol") or in their choice of venues for international performances (Gyeongbokgung, Incheon Airport, etc.) -- they seem to be very conscious of their role as ambassadors for Korea. We can see the latest manifestation of this with their role as ambassadors for Busan's World Expo bid. I think their "Korean-ness" is very appealing to most real fans and an integral part of their identity.

Hwang BTS is about to discontinue its activities as a group for a while. How would this affect the spread of the Korean Wave and Korea's soft power?

Prakash Well, as any Army will tell you, it is Chapter 2, not discontinuation! But jokes aside, I think the Korean Wave goes beyond BTS (as they will also agree) -- K beauty, K dramas, K-pop are forces of their own. Some fans may be disappointed and there may be a loss of some specific tourism revenue, but I don't think it will be devastating at all. BTS has cemented their own legacy and neither them, nor the larger Hallyu wave will be affected by their decision. What can affect this spread are other mistakes or an attempt to overly control artists.

Hwang At this conference, you have delivered a presentation on the political mobilization strategies of the Philippine BTS fandom. Could you briefly elaborate what it is about?

Murad In the Philippines, we recently concluded the 2022 national elections and I believe the Filipino BTS fandoms played quite a significant role during the period. An unprecedented number of pop culture fandom-strategized political mobilizations were felt and witnessed in different social media platforms. There were two particular fandom groups and they were mostly active on Facebook and Twitter -- social media platforms teeming with fake news and misinformation. There also were K-pop group fandoms who were delivering political supports. Not long after, online "troll" activities had established the blatant dichotomy between these two opposite representative supporting groups, including K-pop fandoms, and were compelled to counter these tactics.

Hwang What could be the reason that young Filipinos are so enthusiastic about BTS?

Murad Before they had their major breakthroughs in the music scene and established a worldwide presence with millions of fans rooting for their continued success, BTS was always considered the underdogs. The Filipino millennials and Generation Z deeply relate to that aspect because there are so many challenges that might seem to deter us from living our best lives. We feel that we are going up against a lot and that the system is rigged so much so that there are hardly any winners in life. But just like the songs of BTS that carry with them the message of hope, love, healing and growth, we always stick to the possibility of a better world where we can be exactly who we want to be and where we all care for the welfare of one another. Moreover, the Philippines is a "song and dance" country, very much like South Korea, so the music that BTS creates truly inspires us Filipinos to work hard on our goals and our collective vision for a better tomorrow. It also helps that every song and album from BTS comes packed with great visuals, music and dance moves, and more importantly, a great message for empowerment.

Hwang You have studied the political influence and the role of BTS in the Philippines, how great is it?

Murad In case of the Army for one specific candidate, their Facebook page was able to amass 94,980 followers as of July 10, 2022. We chose to study this Facebook page due to its high number of followers and social media engagements, which signals the strength of its influence on political engagement and participation of Filipino Armys who are also supporters of this candidate. The page was officially launched during the 2022 national campaign period to mobilize this candidate's presidential campaign bid and is operated by the supporting volunteers. The cover picture and welcoming statement of the Facebook page was containing the lyrics of "Not Today," a popular song from BTS, which serves as a battle cry for Army supporters: "All the underdogs in the world, a day may come when we lose, but it is not today. Today we fight."

Hwang You have mentioned that the Army gathered as BTS fans are showing reformist political moves. What are their reasons to participate in politics?

Murad One candidate's Army supporters' Facebook page reads - "United by BTS' music ... group of Filipino ARMYs advocating for good governance, inclusivity, and accountability." The reason why the Filipino Army rallied for was country's economic and sociopolitical welfare. Our deep desire for change to uproot the corruption that prevents Filipinos from fully enjoying their rights as citizens of this country seemed to be gathered under Army's rallies.

Hwang Beyond BTS, what kind of continuous efforts do we need to make for the Korean Wave to be sustained and developed?

Prakash I think people admire Korea not just for its pop culture but also because of its excellent infrastructure, technological advancements, efficiency and civility. Secondly, even though it can be uncomfortable, shows like "Squid Game," movies like "Parasite" and bands like BTS or artists like Psy and many, many others also succeed because they are honest and shine a light on both the good and bad in Korea. That honesty and independence is a strength and should be encouraged. Indeed, at its best, the Korean state has managed to promote and encourage culture without being heavy-handed, which is hard and to be admired. This should not change over time.

Murad The Filipino Army (fan group) is showing no signs of decreasing their support for BTS in spite of the temporary break. Our boys advocated for taking care of our mental health with their "Be" album during the COVID-19 pandemic, so as fans who understand what that means, we are 100 percent behind them whatever their decision might be. In general, the Korean Wave is not going to decline in the Philippines because there are so many other growing Filipino K-pop fandoms with the ever-increasing number of K-pop artists, girl groups and boy bands. The K-pop culture here is also increasing and the support will continue to come from fans and entire fandoms for album releases, music videos, brand collaborations, concerts and events and merchandise purchases.

Cho Even though K-pop is enjoying enormous global success, there is some criticism that K-pop is inauthentically manufactured. BTS' announcement that they will be taking a break also sparked a discussion about the darker side of the success of K-pop. As K-pop is increasingly being considered as a cultural content that serves to expand Korea's national brand and identity, the entertainment companies and their artists are feeling intense pressure to succeed overseas. The K-pop "idol" system that stresses methodical training and control has been regarded as an important component in its international success. However, it has also received criticism that this strict system is infringing on the musicians' freedom and creativity. Aspiring K-pop artists are scouted by various entertainment companies and put through a very strict training process from a very young age. This arduous process may ironically lead to a negative result of the wearing down the musicians' creativity and freedom. Many entertainment companies in the K-pop industry are working hard to survive in a very competitive global industry and protecting the artistic freedom and happiness of the artists may not be their priority. However, the industry needs to seek this very delicate balance between financial success and protecting the well-being of the artists in order to continue its sustainable long-term success.

The Korean entertainment industry's public diplomacy competitiveness

Oct 5, 2022

Kim Sooyeon

Professor, Department of English Literature and Culture at Hankuk University of Foreign Studies

Nan Zhang

Associate Professor, English Language and Literature Department at Fudan University

Kim Yunhee

Research Professor, the Hallym University of Graduate Studies

On Sept. 13, the Korean drama "Squid Game" won six awards at the 74th Emmy Awards, including those for outstanding lead actor and outstanding directing for a drama series -- the first non-English TV series to do so. "Squid Game" enjoyed explosive popularity internationally, made history, and received high praise at home and abroad. It seemed like an event that deserves to sweep the world at least once. In this sense, we cannot help but recall director Bong Joon-ho's "Parasite," Korea's first Oscar-winning film. The Korean entertainment industry has already attracted audiences around the world for decades. It has become a recipient of major investment and player on the stages of Netflix and Hollywood. Korean films and dramas are now a global trend as part of the Hallyu, or Korean Wave. What makes them so successful? Is it because K-dramas are the most "Korean" medium, or because they are in touch with global culture that goes beyond the ideas embodied in "K"? How can we use this soft power for public diplomacy? This week's discussion invites three experts from film studies and public diplomacy. Professor Kim Sooyeon at the Department of English Literature and Culture of Hankuk University of Foreign Studies, associate professor Nan Zhang of English Language and Literature Department at Fudan University and research professor Kim Yunhee at the Hallym University of Graduate Studies participated to delve into this topic further.

Hwang What is the significance of Korean entertainment, including films like "Parasite" or dramas like "Squid Game"? Also, what gives them huge success in relation to global K-culture?

Zhang The global popularity of K-culture, represented by things as diverse as K-pop, TV dramas, beauty products, food, lifestyle and so forth, remains one of the most impressive cultural phenomena in recent years. The worldwide success of Korea's entertainment industry has undoubtedly enhanced the status of K-culture and greatly contributed to its widespread reception. At the same time, the conceptual depth and artistic richness of Korean films and dramas raises K-culture up to a new level of excellence, troubling an easy divide between pop culture and high culture that somewhat shapes its image. If K-culture had sometimes been associated with what Max Horkheimer and Theodor W. Adorno have denigrated as the culture industry of global capitalism, then these visual contents at least encourage critical reflection, if not attacks, on the detrimental effects of such a socioeconomic system. Of course, there is no denying that the thriving of K-culture is inextricable from the development of the world capitalist market. Still, the visual contents' intellectually stimulating and aesthetically dexterous engagement with social issues that have transnational or global implications attests to the scope and vitality of K-culture, which can not only bring art to bear on consumerism, but cultivate a more nuanced understanding of culture in its global consumers.

Kim S. In the case of "Parasite," its accomplishment is especially welcome because it diversifies global K-culture. No Korean would want Korean culture to be represented solely by BTS or Blackpink. For all the positive global influence exercised by BTS, a boy band cannot embody the entirety of Korean masculinity any more than Psy could in the early 2010s. Nor would we want a national culture to be epitomized in certain commodities, such as cosmetics, or a specific miniseries, notably, "Squid Game." In short, these Korean films' success is significant insofar as it expands the realm of the "K" in K-culture enjoyed worldwide. Similarly, I am ecstatic about Lim Yunchan, the youngest person to win the first place at the Van Cliburn International Piano Competition recently at age 18. While Lim's breathtaking performances shown on YouTube add to the diversity of global K-culture with tens of millions of views, K-culture need not be confined to a small number of K-pop celebrities or musical prodigies. I hope that there will be multiple tiers of mainstream and arthouse, internationally acclaimed and lesser-known cultural products, which originate from Korea and are rejoiced globally.

Hwang What do you suggest to improve the East Asian entertainment industry's fture prospects and competitiveness in the global market?

Kim S. Selling well often translates to appealing to the masses at the cost of unfamiliar and uncomfortable truths. Hollywood fluff, feel-good movies such as "Singin' in the Rain" and "Forrest Gump," serve as a prime example. In this sense, East Asian movies doing well in global markets have little to do with their artistic growth or the creation of new perceptions. Calling new perceptions "aisthesis," the origin word of "aesthetics," Jacques Ranciere views the creation of new ideas and emotions, aisthesis, as the task of film art. In that East Asian movies are lesser-known than their western counterparts, I do wish that more people would watch Chinese, Japanese, and Korean films. An increasing number of East Asian movies are available on Netflix and other streaming platforms, but these movies are largely schematic and bland, far from creating new aisthesis. I suggest promoting heterogeneous sets of East Asian movies, such as classical and modern movies with cosmopolitan or local styles which surpass western audiences' expectations and which may attract a variety of new global audiences.

Zhang "Parasite" has set a good example -- and set the bar really high -- for East Asian movies. Its masterly treatment of social issues of global concern, such as inequity, unemployment, and poverty, coupled with deft use of local elements -- for example, symbolic objects, settings and experiences -- offers instructive ways to engage with audiences at home and abroad. Creativity knows no national or regional boundaries. When it is set free and deployed to confront thorny problems in a simultaneously ingenious and candid manner, it can manifest the unparalleled power of art to intrigue, inspire and move viewers, wherever they are. To be sure, given the inner diversity of East Asia, it is not always easy, or even desirable, to generalize about movies from this region. Directors and producers with transcultural perspectives and aspirations might be particularly sensitive to traditions and situations that vary from place to place. Some may have to negotiate between domestic and global markets that are governed by different tastes, demands, or standards. Instead of trying to please all, or to cater to specific markets, however, it might be more fruitful, as shown by successful cases like "Parasite," to aim for movies that speak to audiences in their own distinctive and melodious languages.

Kim Y. The way forward on K-movies in the global market is to fortify weaknesses and challenges in Korean Wave content. Although diverse people around the world are enthusiastic about Korea's soft power in the international community, scholars and specialists have pointed out one thing: the sustainability of K-movies and dramas based on the Korean Wave. It is a fact that "Parasite" was a worldwide box office hit and "Squid Game" recorded the highest viewing rate on Netflix. However, K-content alters its color easily to appeal to and attract global audiences. In this context, the K-movie industry needs to draw up measures that fit the varied and ever-changing global situation for a long-term strategy in the worldwide market. As an expert in journalism and mass communication, professor Lee Byungjong's opinion in his column wrote that K-content needs to discover its distinctive color reflecting its culture and values that other countries do not have. To find a shape in a long-term strategy and plan to lead the cultural industry by Korean soft power, the Korean government and the public continue to create the right environment in each position. The government supports establishing an infrastructure, platform, policy and system for K-content. It then connects this to fostering conditions for the public to create K-content of its own accord.

Hwang "Parasite" or maybe "Squid Game" presents a graphic portrayal of economic disparity in contemporary society. Can you share your ideas about the issue of class in your country or worldwide?

Zhang Economic disparity remains one of the most disturbing issues in both developed and developing countries around the world. Such disparity, however, isn't always visible or visceral to those who are inured to their own immediate environment. For example, in "Parasite," turning abstract concepts like class or hierarchy into graphic images can be more effective in motivating and energizing its audience. Visual representation may not overcome the effect of "out of sight, out of mind," but one can at least trust good art to leave a lasting impression.

Kim S. Economic disparity is truly worrisome and is intertwined with other global disasters faced by all humanity, such as climate change and food shortages. In Korea, economic inequality has ceased to simply mean an unequal distribution of wealth, and generates all sorts of resentment directed toward "other" groups. This is why generational, gendered, and class conflicts are proliferating and dividing Korean society now. Making better policies matter, but it should be accompanied by an awareness of the complex, and often psychological, workings of contemporary capitalism.

Kim Y. K-movies reflect the reality of Korean social problems vividly and plainly. The deep-seated issues depicted in these movies vary. Collusion between politics and business once seemed inevitable for Korea's economic growth, but now it poses a problem that needs to be resolved. They cover issues that connect to people's lives in Korean society, such as gender discrimination in the context of an androcentric community; unfair treatment of migrant workers; and difficulties for North Korean defectors to settle in South Korea. And finally, the inequality gap between rich and poor, which became more critical due to the pandemic. This came to the forefront as a serious matter that showed a disparity in education, employment rates, and health care.

Hwang The Korean Wave seems to be declining in China. Do you think Korean cinema still appeals to the Chinese?

Kim Y. Korea and China relations became estranged due to political issues in 2016; thus, the administration's order to ban the Korean Wave in China affected the Korean film industry. However, cultural exchange through movies between the two countries is still ongoing despite the tough situation. Although it is a different way of watching Korean movies or dramas, unlike before 2016, several Chinese movies that draw keen attention to its people are based on Korean content. For example, the remake of the Korean film "Veteran" has been a phenomenal success with the name of the Chinese movie "Big Big Man" in 2019. The recent Chinese movie "Moon Man," which captivated audiences in China is also based on a famous Korean webtoon called "Moon You" by the writer and illustrator Jo Seok. According to research by Korea's creative content agency in 2022, Korean content still made up the greatest portion of the adaptation film industry in China. Last year, the Korean movie "Oh! My Gran" got permission to release in movie theaters in China for the first time in six years since China's ban on the Korean Wave was carried out.

Zhang The answer is definitely in the affirmative. Korean cinema has a considerable following here, spanning various age groups, whose interest shows no signs of abating. The international success of movies like "Parasite" has further boosted the reputation of Korean cinema, winning more fans in China and beyond. Some might say that K-dramas are more popular than movies in general, but both are familiar topics in casual and academic conversations about films and TV series. One feels that Korean cinema is an integral part of K-culture, which continues to influence in fascinating ways the development of various domains of cultural life, ranging from music, dancing, cuisine, and variety shows to concepts of beauty and modern art.

Moreover, many would love to see further exchanges and collaborations on various levels between the two cultures.

Hwang What is your opinion about Korean media contents' role in Korea's public diplomacy?

Kim S. No popular culture product is free from the social and ideological roles it eventually comes to play, consciously or not. As a majority of films are commercially motivated, they tend to reproduce mainstream beliefs, rather than challenging the status quo, thereby perpetuating dominant social ideologies. If Korea's public diplomacy aims to communicate with foreign publics in a mutually respectful way in order to improve its own interests, Korean cinema may contribute to it -- not by inculcating a fixed national image and identity, but by constantly renewing itself and exerting soft power.

Kim Y. The government expects to advance Korea's reputation and diplomatic ties by earning trust and expanding its influence on the global stage based on three major public diplomacy activities – cultural diplomacy, knowledge-oriented public diplomacy, and public diplomacy on policy. The committee on public diplomacy held its sixth meeting last month, stressing the need to enhance Korea's global reputation on the basis of the Korean Wave, which will be the policy direction of public diplomacy for five years under South Korean President Yoon Sukyeol's administration as mentioned by the Minister of Foreign Affairs Park Jin. In that sense, the Korean film industry is a key mechanism for fostering Korea's cultural diplomacy in the international community. Korea's soft power is the core element of cultural public diplomacy, so movie content that reflects and includes Korea's soft power draws a positive image of Korea and disseminates its cultural value to the world. The content of Korean movies also sets a stage for forming a mutual understanding between the Korean and foreign publics, especially among Korean movie lovers abroad who embrace Korean culture spontaneously.

Hwang What challenges do you see for K-culture in general?

Kim S. Countless Korean movies and drama series show up on streaming platforms day by day. Despite the high number of productions and the skyrocketing budgets poured into them, there appears to be no match for "Parasite" and "Squid Game" in the last few years. I believe that it's due to a lack of original vision and storytelling. It's the same as Hollywood and other film industries, for that matter. Technology develops faster than the human imagination, and whatever you imagine can be meticulously visualized via state-of-the-art computer graphics now. The result is that spectacles and mise-en-scenes are more vividly rendered, but just barely remain new and interesting. While I have concerns for the rapturous ways in which "Parasite" and "Squid Game" have been received, these two succeeded in repeating universal themes reimagined in the context of contemporary Korea. Pursuing "original" ways through which to mix the global and the Korean is the key to the success of K-culture.

Dealing with North Korea in 2022, not very optimistic

Dec 20, 2021

Koh Yuhwan
President, Korea Institute for National Unification

Understanding the other half of the Korean Peninsula, North Korea, is literally arduous as its 'Arduous March' reminds. From the emotional 2018 when the peninsula was overwhelmed with the Panmunjeom Declaration to the disappointing meeting at Singapore, today we are standing in the middle of North Korea's impassiveness and indifference.

On the motionless circumstance, there exists a possibility of North Korea's provocation. It seems unpredictable but also might be doable to foresee how North Korea would react to the current state, when South Korea has only a few months of the Moon Jaein administration left and is ready to welcome the new one. As the Korean Peninsula is right around the corner to meet the new environment it is a timing to check out how North Korea would move.

Therefore, I have invited the president of the Korea Institute of National Unification, the most professional and authorized national research institution, for deeper insights.

In April 2020, Professor Koh Yuhwan from the North Korea department of Dongguk University was inaugurated as the 18th president of KINU. He has served as the Chairman of Peace and Prosperity in the Presidential Commission on Policy Planning and the Senior Adviser for the Office of National Security at Cheong Wa Dae.

Hwang You have attended the meeting hosted by Woodrow Wilson Center last December with the national policy think tank presidents. I wonder what impression or change you have felt from the atmosphere there.

Koh It was such a large conference with 30 to 40 American experts on the Korean Peninsula in the field. The impression I had the most was that the US is observing this Korean Peninsula situation on its own stance. In other words, it seemed quite difficult to persuade them with Korea's perspective and to move on toward the mutually agreed solution. It was clear that both Korea and the US has to check the respective national interest balance and compromise at a certain point. Additionally, I personally thought we needed to look back and think again about the way we have walked for the last 30 years to settle North Korea's nuclear issue.

Hwang It is commonly referred that North Korea's motivation in developing its nuclear weapon comes from the US' hostility toward North Korea. However, it surely must be more complicated than that.

Koh When it comes to solving North Korea's nuclear problem, we must consider various and numerous variations and approaches in a complex and comprehensive way. However, for the last 30 years, the US policy toward North Korea was either A or B. As a result, North Korea is still surviving with its 3rd generation inheriting the power, and what we are facing now is North Korea with nuclear power. In the beginning, the approach was based on anticipating North Korea's collapse, which eventually turned out to be a failure. Later on, the strategic patience which aimed to induce North Korea toward collapse by slowly isolating it through the rewards in exchange for the nuclear freeze, also could not make many outcomes. Moreover, the US did not powerfully step forth neither in resolving the hostile relations between the US and North Korea nor in developing the armistice regime into a peace regime. In between, the US also failed in taking advantage of using China leverage in terms of dealing with North Korea. Particularly, the US recognized that it is possible to restrain and control North Korea's threat that it has attempted to use North Korea's threat as one of the pillars in counteracting China, however, if we talk about what specific effort the US had made to denuclearize North Korea by using China leverage, probably the answer is not too positive. Lastly, the fact that both Korea's and the US' policies were inconsistent due to the government's replacement and that we were relatively ignorant to the special aspects of North Korea's leadership has played a critical and fundamental role in dealing with North Korea.

Hwang According to what you have mentioned, most of the American experts on the Korean Peninsula assert 'North Korea's responsibility' and Korea and the US are having different angles based on this assertion. Should we understand that the gap in perspective is leaving North Korea at the lower level of the US' foreign policy priority?

Koh Indeed. So far, the Biden administration's top priority is domestic politics. The following concern is China, and apparently, North Korea and the Korean Peninsula seem to be distant from the significances. Furthermore, the US is likely to put weight on analyzing what domestic political effect it will cause if the US chooses the end-of-war declaration, as the Korean government urges. This again represents that the Korean Peninsula concern is contemplated in the aspect of domestic politics when it comes to the US.

Hwang The current international politics seems steadily showing the transformation toward encampment diplomacy. I wonder how North Korea would respond to these flows. Shall we expect to see an ROK-US-Japan versus North Korea-China-Russia formation again?

Koh I assume that the current international community will not be divided into military and security terms like how it was back in the Cold War era. Also, since the states are all complicatedly interrelated under the so-called value chain, probably one single variable might be too weak to classify states into the camp. While the strategic competition between the US and China is going on, there must be spaces where they can either cooperate or confront and compete at the same time. Just as how it works to the US and China, one international issue must have multiple layers underneath and multiple angles to approach. Korea also might have a certain area where it can make the balance in the prior stance with its own value chain, rather than giving in to the international situation where Korea must choose either the US or China. Especially, Korea's capacity in semiconductor, IT, shipbuilding, and others are considerably high, therefore, we have a space where both the US and China must rely on us. In this sense, I presume that such a formation of the past Cold War would not necessarily appear in the New Cold War.

Hwang Since you have recently visited the US, what opinions on the New Cold War possibility did the American experts share?

Koh Not many experts were bringing the New Cold War situation to the table. However, they mostly agreed and emphasized building cooperation to counteract the complicated situation that we are standing in, because we are facing non-traditional security, unlike how traditional and military security were valid back in the Cold War era.

Hwang You have overlooked that North Korea's policy toward South Korea might change according to the following Korean Presidential election next year. I would like to hear how you prospect North Korea's policy toward Korea respectively when the conservative or progressive takes the power.

Koh North Korea issue is the major task for the next administration, regardless of whether the conservative or progressive government enters. In 2018, we all have contributed great effort to solve the North Korean issue with the peace and denuclearization process of the Korean Peninsula. Since then, the Korean government has established its own principle and guide map in dealing with North Korea, which is the frame of the Panmunjeom Declaration and the Singapore Declaration. Over this foundation, the upcoming administration will consider whether to develop the current government's principles and directions or to build new relations and policy accordingly. However, above all, it is obvious that making decisions to solve the situation with the balance of threat would not be easy for the next administration, no matter which one it is. Because taking the balance of threat kind of approach always risks a massive amount of price and cost. Additionally, taking into consideration that the Biden administration would sustain, the US itself would also cope with North Korea under the Singapore Declaration frame, fundamentally. In sum, it must not be so easy for the next administration to make a seismic change when it steps toward North Korea.

Hwang You mean there would not be a big difference in dealing with North Korea, regardless of whether the conservative or progressive comes to the power. Then, would Korea's further direction toward North Korea have a high possibility of change depending on which policy the US chooses toward North Korea?

Koh Exactly. However, unless the Biden administration makes moves to rapidly negotiate with North Korea without any conditions on the current agenda, I do not anticipate a great change in the US-North Korea relations to reach the point where North Korea desires, for a while. Ultimately the critical point is the fact that how long North Korea can stay still and be patient under this stalemate. Particularly, North Korea's attitude might change depending on what idea the US can provide to reactivate the current stalemate, along with what kind of mutual cooperation it will have with the new Korean administration. It is only that the Korean Peninsula issue is pushed backward from the US foreign policy priority, and it seems really tough to bring it frontward since the US itself is stuck with the domestic problems. Considering the overall calculations, two Koreas must also think of making efforts to play the main roles in leading and solving the issues in this Korean Peninsula.

Hwang Normally North Korea used to make provocations toward the US when there was a new administration entering. However, there was none for North Korea when Biden came to power. What could be the reason?

Koh North Korea's strategic status in the international society has changed a lot since it has practically completed the development of the nuclear weapon. North Korea is de facto recognized as a nuclear state and is still strategically developing nuclear power. In this sense, there is no essential need for North Korea to make additional provocation which will just give reasons for additional sanctions and restrains on North Korea to the US and international society. After all, we can interpret North Korea's break of provocation pattern in terms of its confidence that North Korea considers itself capable to control regional security and make the balance of power in the international society through nuclear deterrence.

Hwang Reminding so-called the 'North Wind,' would North Korea become the significant variable in the upcoming presidential election next year?

Koh Regarding the North Wind, unless North Korea does not make any direct and armed provocation or unless there is any progress in the declaration of the end of the war and holding summits, I assume North Korea would be the most decisive factor for the presidential election. For now, I guess Korean society has already overpassed the era that North Korea plays a large role in inducing the election results. Also, I personally predict the upcoming government transition period will focus on managing the state of affairs under the continuity of the current administration's policy toward North Korea, while the last transitioning period was clearly showing the differentiated approach in dealing with North Korea. As I have previously mentioned, it must be an enormous burden for Korea to resolve North Korea's nuclear problem with the balance of threat frame, therefore, the upcoming administration must be the important five years of settling down the policy direction together with the Biden administration. North Korea is also expected to well utilize this period for its own sake.

Hwang Some are saying that either Kim Jongun himself or high rankings from North Korea is attending the Beijing Olympics.

Koh In that issue, I guess the coronavirus situation will be high on the agenda. As Kim Jongun is seriously emphasizing coronavirus prevention, it would be difficult for him to personally visit China without the pandemic under control. Moreover, he might visit China under the formation of the bilateral talk, such as the Sino-DPRK summit, however, does not seem to attend the international events which is in fact a multilateral meeting. The absolute charisma is the core of North Korea's leadership (Suryong System), and the multilateral international event is not the perfect place where their dear leader can get the whole attention. However, it is possible for the high ranks like Choe Ryonghae or Kim Yojong to visit China. In this case, the high ranks from Korea's side might have the opportunity to meet and talk by high chance. Nonetheless, there are considerable variables to calculate, considering Korea's upcoming presidential election period.

Hwang If Moon Jaein administration suggests a virtual meeting before his time ends, would North Korea accept the proposal?

Koh There could be virtual summits between two Koreas, however, only the perfunctory agendas might be covered if it goes online. Rather than the virtual summit, it seems more meaningful if both Koreas discuss and come up with compromises with the hotline or another way of contact, then have a virtual summit with the announcing purpose. Though, North Korea will go through various considerations on what effect the summit would bring to the Korean government that is heading toward the end of the period.

Hwang How do you evaluate North Korea's current coronavirus situation? I would like to hear if there is any chance South and North Korea can cooperate to prevent further epidemics.

Koh So far, North Korea did not make any official announcement on coronavirus statistics. Personally, I believe North Korea has accepted the coronavirus pandemic as the inevitable obstacle and is considering vaccine as the ultimate avoidance strategy. North Korea claims that it is the 'coronavirus-free zone' due to the sanctions and containment policy, however, realistically it is impossible to maintain. Furthermore, the virus-free zone can be fatally hit once the blockade breaks down. In the end, we can say that current North Korea's responding policy against the coronavirus is just suspending the crisis, and the authority must be stressed with seeking how it has to overcome the situation. Under this flow, as North Korea's capacity in handling the coronavirus is very vulnerable, inter-Korean cooperation in further prevention and health care can contribute as the turning point to resolve the Korean Peninsula issue. Of course, finding the way that North Korea can accept the offer must come first.

Hwang How is North Korea's economy going on including its food security?

Koh North Korea's yield this year is around 4.5 million metric tons and it can be an appropriate amount till the end of this year. However, it will soon meet the need for supply of food by importing alternatives, while the trade under current conditions is not happening. The market is already facing the inflation of sugar, oil, and other daily life necessities. Moving on, North Korea is troubled with the marketization which grew some elites into the market powers as they held hands with the corrupted bureaucrats. Among these new powers, new conflicts are raising faces. Considering these aspects in a comprehensive view, we can see North Korea's economic status is very serious.

Hwang What stance would North Korea take between the preemptive action and the observation?

Koh For North Korea, there are numerous factors that it has to count in, such as Korea's new administration, its relations with the Biden administration, the coronavirus situation, strategic competition between the US and China, and so on. In North Korea's position, the simplest breakthrough against these complexities was to force the self-help revival under constraints. So far, it is watching the sanction versus self-help in the long term or all-out war, however, this model is infeasible in sustainability. If the US makes an approach and shows its will for the declaration of the end of the war, North Korea would make the following moves, but in case there are no big changes in the current circumstance, it seems North Korea would stick to observation due to complicated calculation.

Hwang It seems the declaration of the end of the war will be the hottest issue till the very end of the Moon administration. Some argue to implement only the defensive training in the US-ROK joint military exercise to drag North Korea to the table of declaration of the end of the war.

Koh I guess for North Korea, the matter of first step of defensive training or the second step of offensive training is not a big issue. What North Korea blames is the military exercise itself, regardless of the scale or the frame. Especially, North Korea is requesting Korea to cease the military exercises in exchange, since it has ceased nuclear tests and military exercises. Looking at the past flow of the Korean Peninsula till today, it seemed to have some signals of changes but meets the tension in March and August due to the US-ROK joint military exercise. This has repeatedly appeared for a long time. Indeed, as North Korea has succeeded in the nuclear test, Korea cannot give up the exercises because of returning the wartime operational control issue and so on. Nevertheless, if giving up and ceasing is impossible, reducing or combining two exercises into one can be an alternative.

Hwang When it comes to the Korean Peninsula security, the Moon administration has picked peace as the main initiative. I would like to hear your opinion on whether the next administration would value the peace or come up with a new dimension of inter-Korean relations.

Koh Today's Moon administration is emphasizing peace and talking only about peace since 2017 after the Berlin Peace Initiative. On the other hand, North Korea's priority card is self-help while the US is stuck with the idea of almighty sanction or sanction first. In other words, this means three countries are fundamentally having different positions that we need to find out the common interest for reconciliation. The upcoming administration must seek this common ground, breaking through fundamentalism. Most of all, if the active policy discussion and cooperation do not take place at the very beginning of the new administration, the policy momentum would run out very soon.

Hwang You have mentioned that the declaration of the end of the war would also be beneficial to China's national interest. Then how large of an effect would it bring to the domestic politics in the US?

Koh When we listen to those who oppose the declaration of the end of the war in Korea, they are mostly concerned about the withdrawal of the USFK and the weakened US-ROK alliance. These two are certainly the national interest to China. From China's point of view, the Korean Peninsula under the declaration of the end of the war would become a comfortable place where it can play its full influence. I see China as the revisionist power if the US is the status quo seeking state, when it comes to not only the Korean issue but also at the international level.

However, unlike how we expect, North Korea is not actively into the declaration of the end of the war and this is actually closely related to North Korea's preconditions. From North Korea's position, it cannot stop thinking about the possibility of betrayal unless the US makes a complete and clear promise, as the Moon administration is heading to the end. Also, from the domestic perspective, we see that Kim Jongun also needs to maintain a certain level of confrontation with the US to keep its charismatic leadership, therefore, is reluctant to the declaration of the end of the war.

From the US perspective, the number one priority is the strategy toward China. If the declaration of the end of the war is realized, then there will be discussions on the withdrawal of USFK, which goes against its plan to restrain and control China. In an extreme term, I can tell the relations of North Korea and the US is a hostile but dependent one. In this sense, we are standing at a stalemate as both countries are not making progressive moves.

The Geneva Agreement was signed in 1994, when President Koh was a professor at Dongguk University, yet we still could not solve North Korea's nuclear issue. President Koh saying that we have a lot to look back and reflect on as this issue could not meet a solution until one individual's life is facing the end, is lingering till now.

North Korea has bragged itself as the strong (kang 强) and prosperous (sung 盛) great (dae 大) state (kuk 國). Building a strong and prosperous state is North Korea's long will. However, the meaning totally changes by altering only two characters. North Korea is the strong (kang 强) nature (sung 性) fake (dae 代) state (kuk 國). This strong nature or self-esteem can be interpreted as the abnormal state that concerns the regime's survival as the ultimate priority. The thing is that North Korea's internal solidarity is amazing despite the worst conditions both from inside and outside. Nevertheless, it surely has a few vulnerable Achilles' heel.

Regarding the current Korean peninsula, the power can be distinguished into the status quo that is satisfied with the existing order or the revisionist that seeks to build a new order. The conflict between the two is natural, however, a new land form would appear and the tension between the two would rise depending on the new government's potential stance as the current government is trying to work toward the declaration of the end of the war and resolving the Korean Peninsula and North Korea issue. Despite it might not be very optimistic in 2022, we look forward to greeting the new opportunities from the new policies toward North Korea by the new government.

The End of Appeasing North Korea, Time to deal with its Fundamental Interest

Jul 4, 2022

Jun Bonggeun
Professor, Korean National Diplomatic Academy

Cho Hanbum
Senior Research Fellow, Korea Institute for National Unification

The recent Korean Peninsula had two situations going on in the South and North. The South was holding its first summit on May 21st with the US President Joe Biden in Seoul, just after 10 days of Yoon Seokyeol government's inauguration. Two leaders agreed on escalating ROK-US alliance into 'Global Comprehensive Strategic Alliance'. Korea has decided to participate the cooperation in high-tech fields and the Indo-Pacific Economic Framework (IPEF). In response to North Korea's nuclear threat, a high-level Extended Deterrence Strategy and Consultation Group (EDSCG) will be restarted. President Yoon, in his first media interview with CNN on the 23rd, said "The age of appeasing North Korea is over" stressing that "new talks" must be initiated.

Meanwhile, North Korean leader Kim Jongun visited Korean People's Army marshal Hyon Cholhae's funeral on Tuesday to express his condolences. On the following 23rd, Kim attended the Hyon's funeral ceremony to send off his mentor. The released photos showed Kim Jongun personally carrying Hyon's coffin at the very front line in grief.

On 23rd, Rodong Sinmun, the official newspaper of the Workers' Party wrote 'Comrade Kim Jongun is suffering from the great loss of a solid revolutionary who was his most respected senior in the revolution and an elder in our military'.

Two scenes made a subtle contrast. Amid two Koreas were under a power to power confrontation for more than 70 years, South is expanding its capabilities while North is losing it. And it is also bringing a strange atmosphere. President Yoon Seokyeol said, "The credit for inter-Korean dialogue depends on North Korean leader Kim Jongun". North Korea is calling for an absolute defense of its fundamental interests, along with the possibility of additional nuclear tests and missile launches. Will the two Koreas continue power to power even after the inauguration of new government? How should we understand these several ongoing situations in Koreas?

In this sense, this week's discussion invites two experts in North Korean issue who have dedicated long in major domestic think tank. Jun Bonggeun is Professor at the Korean National Diplomatic Academy, and was Secretary to the President for international security affairs at the Presidential Office. We also have senior research fellow Cho Hanbum from Korea Institute for National Unification, who is also a senior member of the National Unification Advisory Council. These two experts' research areas cover the North Korean nuclear issue, inter-Korean relations, nuclear policy, strategic studies, and so on.

Hwang How do you evaluate the ROK-US Leaders' Joint Statement overall?

Jun The ROK-US Summit was held amid a drastic deterioration in the diplomatic and security environment, including

North Korea's nuclear armament, intensifying US-China strategic competition, severance of the global supply chain, climate change crisis, and others. Two leaders agreed on the commitment for 'global comprehensive strategic alliance' in order to counter such diplomatic and security threats. This summit is particularly meaningful in that two countries confirmed the reciprocity and strategic complementarity of the ROK-US relations. From South Korea's stance, the United States has always been an irreplaceable diplomatic, security, economic, and scientific asset. The recent summit assured that Korea is also an indispensable asset to the US, in the same dimension.

Cho As mentioned, the ROK-US alliance has evolved into the 'global comprehensive strategic alliance'. It can be said that this agreement is a further developed version of the previous one, between president Moon Jaein and Biden on May 21, 2021. The ROK-US global alliance basically means that the spatial scope of the alliance has expanded from the Korean Peninsula to the region and the entire globe. What stands at the core of the comprehensive strategic alliance is the economic security and the value alliance. The essence of economic security is high technology and supply chains, and democracy and human rights are the most basic foundation of a value alliance. Due to the US-China strategic competition and Russia's invasion of Ukraine, a confrontation between the US-led democratic camp and the authoritarian camp centered on China and Russia is being formed. We can evaluate that South Korea, which leads the high-tech industry and entered advanced countries in 2021, has clarified its cooperative relationship with the ROK-US alliance and the democratic camp.

Hwang How do you see the agreement between the two leaders on the threat from North Korea?

Cho Two countries' positions are almost the same as the previous stance, as they are emphasizing the deterrence and dialogue under the purpose of North Korea's complete denuclearization. It is also noteworthy that the counter measures which were halted under Trump administration were resumed. That includes the confirmation of the extended deterrence pledges, operation of a high-level Extended Deterrence Strategy and Consultation Group (EDSCG), expansion of ROK-US joint military exercises, and deployment of US strategic assets. However, North Korea has declared that it can preemptively use nuclear weapons against South Korea, even if the situation is not under the nuclear war. In addition, North Korea has not yet equipped itself with nuclear capabilities against the US mainland, but the tactical nuclear weapon that is capable of attacking South Korea is estimated to be in the final stage. The Korean Peninsula's nuclear issue has shifted into a qualitative matter, and South Korea is a direct party that faces North Korea's nuclear threat. Compared to how the US has signed the Nuclear Sharing Arrangements with NATO, its extended deterrence policy on South Korea is quite insufficient. In the following future, the reliability of extended deterrence should be systematically improved, and securing a complete right on nuclear enrichment and reprocessing should also be considered, in case of an emergency.

Jun As North Korea's nuclear armament is actualized, establishing the military deterrence against it must be the priority in the policy toward North Korea. To that end, the leaders of South Korea and the US agreed on reaffirmation of their pledges to extended deterrence, normalization and expansion of joint military drills, early stage operation of Extended Deterrence Strategy and Consultation(EDSCG), and deployment of strategic assets in a timely manner. It is only that a cautious approach is needed to ensure that such a deterrent is not built to accelerate the arms race or to escalate military tensions between two Koreas. Otherwise, the effort to resume negotiations on North Korea's nuclear program should be doubled than expected.

Hwang As President Putin's warning toward Ukraine, Kim Jongun is also showing his willingness to use nuclear weapons in any situation where its fundamental interests are violated, although it is not in a war situation. To what extent do you see the possibility?

Jun Most nuclear-armed states deny the preemptive use of nuclear weapons and generally have a passive nuclear doctrine that they use nuclear weapons only to deter retaliation against other attacks. On the other hand, North Korea has been threatening with the preemptive nuclear strike card against South Korea since 2013, making it the world's most aggressive nuclear doctrine. Recently, North Korea is working on developing tactical nuclear weapons, which in other words means that North Korea will develop nuclear weapons that can be used in the actual combat situations, not just to deter the war. In today's world where nuclear taboo is prevalent, it is highly unlikely that an actual nuclear weapon will be used. However, as long as North Korea possesses nuclear weapons, it is necessary to prepare a multi-layered military response system such as preemptive strikes, defense, and deterrence of retaliation.

Cho In the case of North Korea, it tends to have a backlash against the growing internal difficulties due to sanctions and COVID-19. When we look into the Nonproliferation Treaty (NPT), it is based on an implicit promise that nuclear powers will not attack non-nuclear states under any circumstances other than nuclear war. In this sense, North Korea's warning is a dangerous move that shakes the whole foundation of the NPT system. If the nuclear threat against non-nuclear countries start to increase, more countries may attempt to possess nuclear weapons, which will fundamentally corner the status of existing nuclear powers in turn. Therefore, it is unlikely that nuclear states, including North Korea, will preemptively use their nuclear weapons unless they are in a vital situation of nation's survival.

Hwang The possibility of North Korea conducting nuclear tests and launching additional ICBMs is increasing. Do you think it will be implemented this year?

Cho North Korea's missile provocations, which began to be serious since January this year, can be seen as just fulfilling an already fixed schedule. However, it must not be so easy to carry out nuclear tests immediately, because it is a matter of political significance. In particular, North Korea has officially admitted the outbreak of COVID-19. Under such conditions, if a nuclear test is carried out when all transporting measures are limited, it will not only bring negative effects on support for North Korea as well as North Korean people's sentiments.

Jun The specific timing of North Korea's nuclear test and ICBM launch is difficult to predict. Since North Korea suspended its nuclear test and mid- to long-range missile tests in 2018, there is a military technical demand to test new nuclear warheads, advanced missiles, and mid- to long-range missiles before mass production and deployment. Within this flow, it is expected that North Korea will select the best timing that could maximize its internal and external political effects to conduct the actual test. For the time being, North Korea is unlikely to carry a nuclear test, as it is confronting a serious health and quarantine crises at the moment.

Hwang The Yoon administration is attempting to lead the relations with North Korea and promote policies to induce changes in North Korea. There are concerns about North Korea's resistance as it turned into the hardline and the arise of power to power in inter-Korean relations, in case the Yoon government's policies are specified.

Jun If the South Korean government raises human right issues and promotes a change-inducing policy, North Korea's armed provocation or 'strategic patience' is expected. However, whether North Korea pursues either a hardline or dialogue toward South Korea is generally due to its own needs rather than a response to South Korea's policy toward North Korea. In case a power to power confrontation comes, actively promoting inter-Korean dialogue to relied the tension must be held as well as building a strong military deterrence.

Cho Unlike the Moon administration, which stressed inter-Korean relations, the Yoon administration chose to lead the relationship with North Korea and to induce North Korea's change through cooperation with the international community. In particular, the inducement of change in North Korea is likely to conflict with the North Korea's policy which aims for closed and solidified system. The ROK-US Summit also focused on deterrence rather than dialogue. For a while from now on, a strong phase, so called the power to power is inevitable in inter-Korean and US-North Korea relations. However, there remains a room for dialogue and diplomacy as the escalation of the crisis on the Korean Peninsula is burdensome for both South and North Korea, and the US.

Hwang The quarantine situation in North Korea seems to be very serious. What do you think of the situation in North Korea?

Cho Kim Jongun himself described the current situation as a "the greatest turmoil since the founding of the country". Currently, North Korea is having difficulty in farming unless the urban areas provide "agricultural support", as it is going through the busy farming season. Nevertheless, the banning travels between cities, provinces, and counties means that the situation is considerably serious. Given that there has been no official COVID-19 vaccination reported in North Korea and that the medical system is virtually paralyzed, a nationwide damage is concerned. Moreover, as almost a half of the residents are under malnutrition, their low immunity is another concern. North Korea is evaluating that it is well recovering from the Corona situation, but the actual situation is presumed to be worse than the official announcement by the North Korean authorities.

Jun First of all, it is difficult to clearly figure out how the situation is going on in North Korea. The only channel is North Korean government's announcement. However, North Korea's capacity in public health and disease control is critically low. There are no COVID-19 diagnostic samples, inspection facilities, N95 or KF94 quarantine masks, and COVID-19 vaccines. From this context, it is estimated that there will be far more COVID-19 confirmed cases and deaths than the government announced. Furthermore, the nutritional status of vulnerable residents such as the seniors and children is very poor, that the number of deaths is expected to increase significantly as COVID-19 spreads more and more.

Hwang Do you anticipate quarantine situation in North Korea will bring a positive effect on inter-Korean relations?

Jun North Korea's health and quarantine crisis is an opportunity for North Korea to open up and improve the inter-Korean relations. However, if South Korea insists on inter-Korean dialogue and direct support between the governments to achieve results in its policy toward North Korea in a short period of time, North Korea is likely to choose to block again by high chance. Therefore, in consideration of North Korea's cautious position in the early stages, I would recommend to provide health and quarantine supplies through international organizations or private relief organizations.

Cho Given that Kim Jongun mentioned the importance of studying "the quarantine policies, achievements, and experiences from advanced countries", the possibility of accepting external support seems to be open. In fact, South Korea and the United States are the only countries that can provide vaccines and treatments at the level of achieving collective immunity for all North Koreans. The two leaders from Korea and the US reaffirmed their willingness to provide vaccine aid to North Korea at the summit.

Hwang At the inauguration ceremony, President Yoon Seokyeol used the term "complete denuclearization" of North Korea. What do you think the term complete) means?

Cho Given that North Korea's complete denuclearization will require at least about 20 years, a complete denuclearization within a short period of time through a package deal is physically difficult. Therefore, it will be tough to apply 'denuclearization first, promoting relationship later' model. Even if the complete denuclearization is not actualized, it would be a realistic alternative to parallel all measures, including the improvement in relations and discussion on peace treaty, in case there are some progress in practical denuclearization. Based on a comprehensive agreement on complete denuclearization, we can say that setting an entrance to denuclearization that involves specific actions might be the immediate goal at the current stage.

Jun During the last five years of the Moon Jaein government, inter-Korean and US-North Korea summits were held several times and there was an agreement on 'complete denuclearization of the Korean Peninsula'. In the meantime, however, North Korea has continued operating its nuclear facilities internally and has strived on strengthening its nuclear capabilities. Under the flow, the Yoon administration is demanding "verifiable denuclearization," not just the verbal one.

Hwang The president has emphasized 'freedom' for 35 times at his inauguration address. How should we interpret it in terms of inter-Korean relations?

Jun I anticipate that North Korean human right issues will be assertively raised both at home and abroad. Specifically, the launch of the North Korean Human Rights Foundation demanded by the North Korean Human Rights Act, permission of leaflets on North Korea in the context of freedom of speech, nomination of Ambassador for North Korean human rights cooperation by the Ministry of Foreign Affairs, and participation in the UN General Assembly's resolution on North Korea human rights are expected. I assume the military tensions between two Koreas will temporarily escalate as North Korea will strongly oppose and threaten political and military retaliation at that moment.

Cho The Yoon Seokyeol administration recognized the problem of unilateral inter-Korea relationship where North Korea stands superior and the entrenched practice of abnormal custom, that he set the normalization of inter-Korean relations as the main goal of his policies toward North Korea. The emphasis on freedom is related to the identity of the Korean system. There has not yet been a basic agreement between two Koreas that stipulates the provisional special relationship of the division system, so the Republic of Korea is the only legal government on the Korean Peninsula under the constitution. President Yoon's highlight on freedom seems to be related to these conditions. In other words, it can be interpreted as an intention to lead inter-Korean relations based on the ideology and values of the Republic of Korea.

Hwang Every government had different key points in their policy toward North Korea so far, like peace or unification. What would be Yoon government's focus?

Jun South Korea's goals and values in its policy toward North Korea can be summarized into unification, peace, and security. They are all mutually complementary, but at the same time, competitive. Park Geunhye government sought unification while Moon Jaein government pursued peace first, and Yoon Seokyeol administration mentioned that it values security. However, regardless of conservative or progressive, four tasks in North Korea policy, inter-Korean dialogue and cooperation, negotiations on North Korea's nuclear weapons program, building deterrence, and international sanctions, are always contained. While Moon Jaein government stressed the former two, Yoon Seokyeol government emphasizes the latter two, especially because North Korea's nuclear armament has become the reality.

Cho The new government's denuclearization task declared a 'complete and verifiable denuclearization of North Korea' and emphasized 'united and solidified leadership of the international community toward North Korea'. It is also notable that Yoon government specified the inducement of change in North Korea and proposed a 'developmental supplement' of Unification Policy for Global Korean Community on the premise of national consensus. In particular, given that President Yoon Seokyeol repeated freedom for 35 times in his inaugural address and emphasized liberal democracy, there is a possibility that he will seek to establish a unification plan based on the values of our system.

Scoping out forced repatriation of North Korean fishermen from various angles

Aug 4, 2022

Ko Gyoungbin
Former Chairman, North Korean Refugee Foundation

Yoon Yeosang
President, Database Center for North Korean Human Rights

During a speech at Victory Day celebrations on July 27, the North Korean supreme leader Kim Jongun criticized President Yoon Sukyeol, mentioning his name for the first time since his inauguration. Amid the dark days of inter-Korean relations due to Kim Jongun's strong criticism toward the current South Korean government, domestic political debate is still heated over the forced repatriation of two North Koreans who claimed to have killed 16 fellow sailors in 2019. Regardless of the legal aspects of whether this repatriation was compulsory or not, and regardless of domestic political powers' interests laid underneath the issue, we are keeping our eyes on the situation as the government's basic principles on North Korea, including human rights, can bring a certain impact on inter-Korean relations. In order to understand the implications of the incident, this week's discussion invites Ko Gyoungbin, the director of the Peace Foundation research committee and the former chairman of the North Korean Refugee Foundation (The Korea Hana Foundation), and Yoon Yeosang, the president of Database Center for North Korean Human

Rights, who is also serving as an adviser to the North Korean Refugee Foundation.

Hwang How do you basically interpret the recent forced repatriation?

Ko This forced repatriation did not happen in recent days but was in 2019. Therefore, today is not the first time it was controversial, and it was actually the same back in 2019 also. The faults and flaws of the Korean governmental system was pointed out as well. However, 2 1/2 years have passed since then and we are still repeating the same controversies we had in the past, which is basically about the matters of humanitarianism, legal process and procedure legitimacy, rather than efforts to improve or supplement the system. We have to put the things right once we recognize the problem. Otherwise, repeating the criticism stays as the criticism for criticism itself. No cow can be raised in a destroyed cowshed. We must focus on rebuilding and fixing the cowshed, not obsessing over the lost cow.

Yoon I would say that something that should not have happened in Korea had happened. As the repatriation happened forcibly against North Korean defectors' will, as they requested protection from the previous Korean government, this is an illegal action and a crime. Also, since it is highly likely that the defectors must have been executed, this is a serious violation of human rights at the same time. The Korean government back then seems to have determined a secret repatriation, firstly because the defectors had criminal charges laid against them, and secondly, because the decision was made in a political context with a lack of legal examination in order to promote inter-Korean relations and to suggest a friendly attitude to North Korea. Now it is waging a public opinion battle, stimulating public sentiment by using the term "brutal criminals," and not giving a clear explanation based on a legal approach.

The national institutes and civil servants who are in charge of official tasks must determine and implement them according to the laws and regulations. Making an excuse of public sentiment and deciding for political purposes that does not have a concrete legal grounds is a populist move and can be a shortcut to a dictatorship. Witnessing what has happened, it is regrettable that we could clearly see that political and ideological logic takes precedence over rules, regulations and human rights when it comes to issues regarding North Korea. I guess ideological camp logic can strongly influence people's decisions and life, compared to how North Korea weighs people's social classes and backgrounds.

Hwang Was there a similar case to this?

Yoon In fact, there have been hundreds of cases of North Korean defections via maritime routes since the 1990s, and the majority of them were repatriated after investigations. The government maintains that these defectors voluntarily clarified their will to repatriate, however, it is a fact that some must have been forcibly sent back for sure. Whether they were sent back by force or not can be made clear once the investigation documents written by the joint government investigation institute are made public. Therefore, the necessity of an investigation in relation to government or special inspection regarding repatriation is being raised.

Ko According to the spirit of the Korean Constitution, North Korean defectors are allowed to live in Korea after acquiring permanent residence just like other ordinary foreign refugees or by only verifying their nationality as a Korean citizen without a particular naturalization process. To this end, the North Korean Refugee Protection and Settlement Support Act has been enacted and implemented. Under the law, even North Korean defectors can be refused from requesting protection, if they have committed crimes against humanity, such as international terrorism and murder. However, even if this is a reason to refuse protection, in most cases, the protection is provided because the evidence cannot be obtained easily. The only case when a North Korean defector who requested protection was deported to North Korea under this provision was this controversial one in 2019.

Hwang So you mean that although these repatriated North Korean fishermen were charged with murder, the Moon Jaein government's decision to deport them is problematic?

Ko Actually, this remains legally ambiguous. It seems the case was problematic in that sense. The deportation of the North Korean fishermen rescued by South Korean military and police until now is also legally groundless. Their repatriation was based on considerations of inter-Korean relations and humanitarian reasons or common sense judgments, rather than legal ones, and if we have to mention legal issues, we have to explain it as an act of governance.

Yoon Yes, indeed. The South Korean government has no legal basis for deportation if North Koreans enter the country and request protection. Even felons cannot be screened and repatriated, at least under the law so far. In the event of a serious crime such as murder, the Korean government will still accept the defector as a citizen, but he or she will be decided as a nonprotected person during the screening process for the protection, conducted by the Ministry of Unification. In case the defector is excluded from the protection, it does not mean repatriation right away, but it means that the defector will be excluded from the government's settlement support service, normally provided for North Korean defectors.

Hwang President Yoon Sukyeol stressed Article 3 of the Constitution after receiving a report from the Ministry of Unification on July 22. Based on Article 3, North Korean defectors should be regarded as citizens, so it seems that the ruling camp has strengthened its claim that forced repatriation was an illegal process. What do you think?

Yoon Article 3 says "The territory of the Republic of Korea shall consist of the Korean Peninsula and its adjacent islands."

From context, Article 3 can only affect the legal status of people in North Korea whether they are citizens of the Republic of Korea, and has nothing to do with the legal status of North Koreans who entered the country and requested protection. According to Article 3, scholars may disagree on whether North Korean residents have the status of South Korean citizens, but there is no legal or academic disagreement on the fact that North Koreans who entered the country and requested protection are considered as citizens of the Republic of Korea or not.

Ko The president also mentioned that Article 4 of the Constitution should be realized and embodied at the same time. Article 3, in other words the territorial provisions, confirm the legitimacy of the Republic of Korea as the only legal government on the Korean Peninsula, and Article 4, the peaceful unification provision, recognizes North Korea as a partner to cooperate with peaceful unification. In reality, North Korea is an adversary that is hostile against us under the armistice regime, but at the same time, it is a partner whom we must talk to and cooperate with for peaceful reunification. The issue of bringing North Koreans to our courts, who are consulted on crimes in North Korea, should also be dealt with from a reciprocal perspective considering these two realistic aspects. Inter-Korean relations need to develop cooperatively and now we see the need for a criminal extradition agreement between the two Koreas.

Hwang How about if we look at the legal system regarding North Korean defectors?

Ko The current legislation is centered on settlement support once the protection is decided. On the other hand, the process before and after the protection is still remaining at the principle level, that the specifications are not stipulated. Again, the management and post-process of those who are excluded from the protection almost does not exist. The institution in charge of protection is also ambiguous. Under the current law, the minister of unification has the right to decide on protection, but he or she is only responsible for follow-up management of those who are determined to be protected, and he or she does not get involved in the investigation or the judgment process. In order to improve this institutional deficiency, in addition to human rights, considerations should be made at the level of anti-communist security and criminal policy. In our reality, the process of protecting North Korean defectors should be thoroughly prevented from being used as a safe invasion route for North Korean spies in disguise or as a refuge for inhumane felons. Moreover, there have been about 200 cases in the past 10 years in which the protections have been canceled in the middle due to serious crimes or smuggling attempts while these defectors were living in our society. In response, the legal system, such as accountability for follow-up management, is in a vacuum and still has problems in terms of human rights.

Yoon Discussing this case that we are talking about these days, I think the relevant laws should include the grounds and procedures for repatriation for the ones who voluntarily ask for repatriation, and if necessary, the criteria, procedures and regulations should be further discussed to cover repatriation of those who are difficult for the government to accept due to public sentiment. If the government's repatriation decision and procedures are unofficially handled by a limited number of government officials, there is a risk of forcible repatriation against their will. As such, there is a suggestion to form and operate a North Korean Defector Repatriation Screening Committee that involves both related government agencies and private human right experts.

Hwang To be honest, the domestic politicization of the North Korean issue seems quite excessive. Can we understand this case in this light?

Yoon Rather than judging whether the case and the act was illegal against the rule of law or not, it tends to be split into those who support and criticize it depending on which ideological camp people go for. This irrational social phenomenon is happening for sure.

Ko In democratic politics, people's attention to security and anti-communist issues is no exception. However, even if there are differences in perception between the ruling and opposition parties and even if political disputes are inevitable, there must be a barrier that should not be crossed. Especially, if politicians' involvement in the security and anti-communist sectors go excessively far, workers' morale would deteriorate for one thing, and then we must acknowledge that in the worst case they can come under pressure to work to suit those in power, not for the sake of national interest.

Hwang President Yoon also called for the launch of the North Korean Human Rights Foundation as soon as possible, saying that "peaceful unification based on the basic free and democratic order" stipulated in Article 4 of the Constitution means the unification process led by all the people of the two Koreas. What should the nature and function of the North Korean Human Rights Foundation be when it is established?

Ko There still is controversy over the pros and cons of the North Korean Human Rights Act, including the nature and function of the North Korean Human Rights Foundation. However, this law was enacted under the compromise between the ruling and opposition parties, and the nature and function of the North Korean Human Rights Foundation were also determined by compromise and agreement. Nevertheless, the delay in law enforcement is a problem in terms of compliance. I am just hoping the North Korean Human Rights Foundation to be cautious not to undermine private organizations' voluntary activities by eroding what they are already were doing for our society.

Yoon In order for the North Korean Human Rights Foundation to function properly, it would be reasonable to organize the functions centered on activities that support North Korean human rights and then include humanitarian aid in existing relevant laws, rather than including humanitarian aid alongside human rights issues, which North Korea has been reluctant to accept.

Hwang Stressing that individual human rights should be respected in the unification process, the president also mentioned that he would point out human rights issues which North Korea is sensitive to. How will this affect inter-Korean relations in the future?

Ko The establishment of the North Korean Human Rights Foundation was not intended to improve relations with the North Korean authorities. Of course, the North Korean authorities will feel provoked. I assume everything depends on what actually can be done under the pretext of human rights. North Korea will link the improvement of inter-Korean relations and the issue of human rights, but we have no other choice but to make a separate effort. This too, should be recognized in the context of a realistic need, not from viewing it as a contradiction in the situation on the Korean Peninsula.

Yoon Since North Korean authorities are reluctant to address its human rights issues, in case the problem is strongly raised at the government level, it would negatively affect future inter-Korean relations and cooperation. However, looking back at the inter-Korean relations and the exchange process so far, it is an excessive concern that the inter-Korean relationship will break down or a war will break out just by raising the issue of North Korean human rights. It is reasonable for the government to raise human rights issues at the theoretical level and make efforts to improve human rights in North Korea in the form of supporting the international community and private organizations, because the government still needs consultations with

North Korea in various fields, such as denuclearization, economic cooperation and humanitarian issues.

Hwang In what direction do you think the new government's policy toward North Korea, the so-called "bold plan," should head toward as it aims to come up with economic cooperation and security measures step by step in a response to North Korea's denuclearization measures?

Yoon First of all, the government needs to clarify whether it aims to completely denuclearize North Korea or to manage the denuclearization process. And if the "bold plan" basically means denuclearization, it should be definitely acceptable to experts and the general public, as well as to the North Korean officials. However, it is questionable whether there is a denuclearization plan that both sides would agree on.

Ko I theoretically welcome the new government's continued efforts to denuclearize North Korea through dialogue and its announcement that it will include measures to resolve not only economic issues but also the security threats that North Korea feels in its "bold plan" as a counterbenefit to denuclearization.

II

China's Diplomacy and Security

How China views the international and regional order

Nov 3, 2022

Zhang Tuosheng

Senior Research Fellow, China Foundation for International and Strategic Studies

The international community has been in an era in which "no one backs you up" since the Donald Trump's period. During the Trump era, US-China relations fell into a double trap of Thucydides and Kindleberger. Many in the international community believe that the international order has already entered the New Cold War between the US and China. Are we really in the New Cold War? Has the international order changed, or is it still changing? While the Cold War between the US and Soviet Union was apparently an ideological and military confrontation, US-China relations are politically and economically intertwined. It is not yet a conflict between civilizations, but a conflict of national interests and mutual distrust, therefore, we are more cautious about making any hasty judgments. China has not declared today as a New Cold War, although it says the current international order is becoming more unstable and indescribable due to US' unilateralism. Last week there was an important 20th Party Congress in China. There are many discussions on the direction and policy of Xi Jinping's third-term diplomacy. How does China view the current international order and the regional order? What kind of diplomacy will Xi Jinping's third term show in the future? It might be too early to judge, but predicting in advance is a must for the peace and development of the region in which we live. For a deeper discussion, this week's discussion invites authoritative strategy analyst Zhang Tuosheng. With military background, he is an Academic Committee Member of Center for International Security and Strategy at Tsinghua University as well as the Senior Research Fellow at China Foundation for International and Strategic Studies.

Hwang How can we evaluate the international order in this the post-Cold War period?

Zhang The collapse of the Soviet Union in 1991 marked the end of the Cold War frame of the US-Soviet Union's struggle over the hegemony, and the world entered a post-Cold War era. As a key feature of this new era, the trend of globalization, multipolarization, and informationization has accelerated, and peaceful development has become the main flow in the world. This great change in the international situation was most pronounced in the first two decades after the end of the Cold War. First of all, the acceleration of globalization and the interdependence of countries have been greatly strengthened. At that time, the World Trade Organization, various regional free trade zones, and multilateral economic cooperation organizations were established and developed one after another, and multilateral security cooperation dialogue in regions with different characteristics of military alliances was rapidly promoted as well. The development of global multipolarization is also evident, and major powers such as the US, Europe, Japan, China, and Russia have built some kind of a pattern. Many developing countries are entering the ranks of the strong powers, and their relationship shows a state of mutually coordinating cooperation and mutually constraining protection. As for the advancement of information technology, the Internet, mobile phones, and mobile computers, it has developed rapidly in the past years. The development of information technology has played an important role in promoting the development of globalization and multipolarization.

Hwang It has already has been 30 years since the end of the Cold War this year. We all seem to be facing a variety of changes since the end of the Cold War.

Zhang A number of disputes over ethnic, religious, territorial, and maritime rights that were overshadowed by the Cold War began to emerge, and became more pronounced by the so-called "human rights wars" conducted by the US and some Western countries, and the global anti-terrorism wars under the US. The end of the Cold War has taken mankind a big step forward, but it shows that it is still far from establishing a complete international political and economic order. Entering the 30th year of the post-Cold War era, three major events followed, including the global economic crisis caused by US financial instability, serious political instability in some countries in the Middle East and North Africa, and the US declaration of a pivot to the Asia-Pacific and implementation of its Asia-Pacific rebalancing strategy.

Hwang The international circumstance has changed significantly in the past few years since the outbreak of COVID-19.

Zhang First of all, the negative aspects of globalization have emerged rapidly due to the deterioration of governments around the world. The widening gap between the rich and the poor within the country, the imbalance in national development, the emergence of large-scale immigration, the deepening damages from international epidemics, growing transnational crimes, and the spread of WMD have intensively exploded. The environmental pollution and global climate change are also related to the above. As a result, the emergence of a counter-globalization trend, populism, protectionism, and unilateralism has prevailed in recent years, and pandemics in the last three years have exacerbated these trends of risks. Secondly, I would say there is multipolarization. As multipolarization develops, strong powers are facing a critical change in power and the geopolitical competition of the powers resumed. Therefore, the relationship between the strong powers has entered a period of high friction. In particular, the US-Russia and the US-China competition is the most prominent. Third, a rapid development of digitalization and technology has greatly promoted socio-economic development over the past 30 years, and the digital economy has become the most popular term in recent years. However, this development has also created a digital divide, driving polarization in international community and between countries. The development related to these trends has also brought growing uncertainty in recent years, due to the apparent logjam of relevant international laws and regulations. Information wars, cyber wars, and space wars have already become new topics in our world. Lastly, the existing international order is tending to falter and fall apart. Currently, Russia is openly proposing to completely change the existing international order. China has emphasized maintaining the international order based on international law, with the UN at the center, while the US and Western countries adhere to what they call a "rules-based international order." There is no longer a perception among countries that the international order that has been around since the end of the Cold War will continue.

Hwang Since the end of the Cold War, the Asia-Pacific has become the region that has the highest possibility of development. What changes have there been in the Asia-Pacific regional order during the last post-Cold War period?

Zhang Firstly, the objectives and principles of the United Nations Charter and the major international agreements were relatively well followed and implemented. Therefore, the Asia-Pacific region could maintain peace and security. Although there are still many security issues in the region, most have been well-controlled and we could avoid serious military conflicts and wars. Secondly, multilateral dialogue and cooperation organizations, other than military alliances, have been established and developed relatively quickly in this region. There are about a dozen multilateral cooperation forums that Chinese governments is participating in: The China-ASEAN Dialogue Cooperation, APEC, ASEAN Plus Three, Six-Party Talks, Korea-China-Japan Cooperation, East Asia Summit, ASEAN

Forum, ASEAN Defense Ministers Meeting, Shanghai Cooperation Organisation, Shangri-La Dialogue and the Beijing Xiangshan Forum. Thirdly, partnerships have been universally established to conduct comprehensive dialogue and cooperation in the political, economic, military, humanities, and other aspects of the region. The regional relationships between the countries are relatively balanced and stable. Fourth, many multilateral and bilateral free trade zones have been settled, and each country's economic interdependence has been greatly strengthened. Fifth, non-traditional security cooperation in the region has developed significantly, and lastly, as an emerging power, China has also begun to provide public goods to the region. For instance, China is promoting interconnection of the countries along the line through the Belt Road Initiative and is effectively building regional infrastructure through the establishment of the AIIB.

Hwang What are the greatest challenges that the regional order of Asia-Pacific is facing today?

Zhang Actually the imbalance in countries relations is getting quite serious. The US and Japan are forming an all-out confrontation with Russia, US-China relations have deteriorated seriously, and China-Japan relations have also retreated significantly. India has become an attractive target for the US and Japan. Even after the outbreak of the Russia-Ukraine War, the US accepted China as its main strategic rival and its most severe and long-term challenge. It is pressuring the Indo-Pacific, keeping China's key battlefields in check, attempting strategic competition with

China in politics, the economy, military, ideology, and other fields. For this reason, the US does not hesitate to pressure China by partially, or sometimes fully, excluding China from the economic and scientific areas, which will eventually bring major shocks and damages to the regional industrial chains, value chains and supply chains.

Hwang How is America's national strategy changing?

Zhang The US declaration of its pivot to the Asia-Pacific is an important sign that geopolitical competition among the powers that have disappeared since the end of the Cold War will return to the world stage. By the time Obama's second term began, friction between China and the US had escalated across the board, and Trump's election in 2017 was a turning point in the post-Cold War era. Since his inauguration, he has implemented America First, unilateralist, and protectionist policies, clearly designated China and Russia as strategic competitors, and has recognized China as the major strategic competitor. Trump's policies are the reaction to globalization, multipolarization, and informatization, and have brought major shocks and challenges to the world's peace development. Although some modifications and adjustments have been made to Trump's policies since Biden was elected in 2021, he basically continued Trump's economic and security policies, and further raised the confrontation between democracy and dictatorship, leading the world to a bipolar confrontation with an intensified ideology.

Hwang Please share some diplomatic examples with us.

Zhang The geopolitical strategic competition between the great powers shows that not only does it cause a heated war in Europe, but it has also reached a dangerous point in bringing the Cold War to an all-out resurgence in Europe. In August, the House Speaker Pelosi openly violated the One China Principle and visited Taiwan, causing a serious crisis in the Taiwan Strait. At the same time, the Korean Peninsula is pregnant with a new nuclear crisis, and the possibility of military conflict or a cold war in Northeast Asia under the new international situation should never be underestimated.

Hwang Can you tell us in detail from the aspects of security and military?

Zhang The multi-faceted economic security dialogue and cooperation organizations, the ones that were established after the end of the Cold War, have been devastated by US's massive military build-up including Five Eyes, QUAD, AUKUS, exclusive Indo-Pacific economic partnership, and Chip 4 alliance. Partially, the regional dialogues and cooperation are even tied up and are making no progress at all. Due to the difficult situations, some are in tight position to reach an agreement, and some are even put under a risk being suspended. Additionally, conflict zones are overheating, crises and the possibility of military conflict are growing, and regional peace and security are threatened. One of the most prominent issues in East Asia today is the Taiwan strait and the second one is the Korean Peninsula. Not long ago, there was a serious crisis in the Taiwan Sea and in the case of the Korean Peninsula, the deterioration of US-China-Russia relations has significantly weakened international cooperation in denuclearizing the Korean Peninsula, facing the risk of a new nuclear crisis. The strategic stability in the region is also facing serious challenges. In addition, the arms race has already been repeated in the region. Many countries in this region are standing in front of an enormous pressure from the US to choose their border areas. Governance in this region and non-traditional security cooperation between countries have been seriously disrupted accordingly.

Hwang How do you foresee China's foreign policy?

Zhang According to the report of the 20th Party Congress, China's foreign policy can be interpreted like the following compared to the 19th Party Congress report. Firstly, I would emphasize the continuity of China's foreign policy. China does not seek hegemony or promote competition with the US, and stresses the continuity of its diplomatic stance, such as peaceful coexistence, cooperative development of relations, and mutual respect. The second aspect is that although China did not particularly mention the US, but in fact, it implies that the security challenges coming from the US have intensified. According to the National Security Strategy, announced by the White House recently, China was described as a country with the capability that can put everything into the competition with the US. Nevertheless, China still hopes to stabilize US-China relations through dialogue mechanisms and crisis management rather than confrontation. We do not want a new Cold War, and it would be nice to hold a US-China Summit during the upcoming G-20 Summit to discuss further about it.

Hwang What can countries in the region do with regard to the great changes in the international circumstances and serious challenges to the Asia-Pacific region?

Zhang Although there are serious challenges to the international circumstances and the regional order, we should not take it in too pessimistic perspective. We must work together to overcome the depression and uncertainty of globalization, multipolarization, and informatization by strengthening global and regional governance. This should further ensure that the new Asia-Pacific order formed during the post-Cold War era can be integrated and led to new developments, so that the elements of the above fields can be exercised and the world's peaceful development flow can be maintained. Today's great flow will pass us in the end. In recent years, we had the establishment and development of CPTPP and RCEP, the expansion of SCO, the continuation of ASEAN+ dialogue cooperation in this region. Furthermore, China is absorbed in promoting its relations with the US in terms of mutual respect, peaceful coexistence, and mutual benefit, while the China-US, China-Korea economic and trade cooperation is developing at the same time. Most of the countries in the region do not want to be placed in a situation where they have to stand by either the US or China. Moreover, the recent crisis in the Taiwan Strait could have been eventually managed without such tragedy as the Russia-Ukraine War. This is what we can call the hope is.

Halifax International Security Forum, glimpse of United States' determination for leadership

Nov 25, 2022

Hwang Jaeho

Professor, Division of International Studies at Hankuk University of Foreign Studies

There are some influential security dialogues around the world where, once you attend, you will be able to see the flow of international circumstances. The Shangri-La Dialogue is a collaboration between Britain and Singapore, where the United States and China openly engage on their Asian agenda. The Munich Security Conference is the windmill for European security, Russia's Primakov Reading and China's Xiangshan Forum are their own platforms to raise voices under the purpose of countering the US. And the Halifax International Security Forum in Canada is the essential security dialogue to read into the US' strategic thoughts.

This HISF, which has developed for more than a decade, clearly shows the reason and presence behind the existence of American leadership. A number of US House of Representatives and Senate members participated, and around 300 officials, politicians, journalists and experts from the US, its allies and partners gathered to discuss pending global issues. From Nov. 18-20, Halifax covered a wide spectrum of issues, from the war in Ukraine to climate change, energy, disinformation, food security and technological innovation.

By far, the war in Ukraine was the overwhelming topic. Ukraine's President Volodymyr Zelenskyy, his wife and Ukraine's security chiefs were all attending online, and former President Petro Poroshenko participated in person. They strongly set forth that the war in Ukraine is not just a war for Ukraine itself, but a war for global security, and that the reason it has to win lies in its sense of mission for democracy. US Defense Secretary Lloyd Austin also made this point clear in his speech. Russia's militancy in Ukraine has not ruled out the possibility of using nuclear weapons. He stressed the need to "defend every inch of NATO territory" under a rules-based international order, as Russia shows the "justification for the use of force" -- just as China does -- when national interests collide.

Sen. Jim Risch, R-Idaho, pointed out that China is economically outpacing unstable areas while democratic countries falter. Rep. Michael McCaul, R-Texas, noted how challenging it is to unravel the complex web of tyranny, and the risks of competition between powers beyond time and region. Canadian Defense Minister Anita Anand echoed the necessity to actively deal with Russia's invasion and maligning China in the Indo-Pacific region to protect the rights and values of democracy.

The consistent theme of the forum was support and solidarity for democratic values. The threat to democracy is becoming more diverse and growing larger. Global democracy has fallen into a recession, and the Ukraine war is a serious case that proves it.

How will the US and its allies and partners save democracy? There are numerous democratic countries around the world, but unity is weak.

Tyranny, on the other hands, shows its strength in solidarity. If not for the US and Western Europe, democracy is still weak in self-sustainability. Ukraine is now praised as a fighter for democracy, yet it had flaws in its system before the war, and as we have already seen in Afghanistan, a system without the will to stand on its own feet does not last long.

The US was clearly an attractive model as a value of freedom and a market economy, and as a preferred option for many countries in terms of choosing their systems.

However, amid the recent confusion in leadership, it is necessary to restore its competitiveness and confidence. Many countries are still not so happy with the "America First" agenda, but they have not deserted expectations for American leadership.

The US must believe in its own solid alliance infrastructure and the tight networks it has built for more than 70 years. As many HISF participants have emphasized, unity may be the best answer. And above all, as HISF President Peter Van Praagh said, "Don't be afraid."

Now the US must prepare for another competition. The US has surpassed the Soviet Union in military competition and Japan in economic competition. However, China, which has chased the US to more than two-thirds in terms of total power, is an unprecedented non-Western competitor that is qualitatively different. As seen in the embarrassing scene where President Xi Jinping and Prime Minister Justin Trudeau's bilateral talk was exposed in the media, the difference in communication, expression and cultural and civilization distance is great between Western countries and China. Now, a real battle with China awaits the US as it overcomes Russia with the war in Ukraine.

The NATO Summit recognized China as a systemic threat, and the White House's National Security Strategy sees the next decade as a strategically critical period.

China's emphasis on Chinese-style modernization suggests that the Western style is not the only path for modernization, but that China also can be an alternative. The fierce competition between the US and China has already begun, as the US tightly tied up its shoelaces and showed its temper at the HISF.

What is more important along with the unity between the US' alliance is that the US itself has to prove its vision as a leader and its capability in providing public goods. Only then will the unity of the democratic camp become more solid and the middle ground be more attractive. But for now, I could catch a glimpse of US' will and determination in Halifax.

Strategic Puzzles left after Biden's Asia Tour

June 2, 2022

Choe Wongi

Professor and Head of Center for ASEAN-India Studies, Korea National Diplomatic Academy

Wang Junsheng

Professor, National Institute of International Strategy at Chinese Academy of Social Sciences

On May 20 to 24, the international attention shifted to the Indo-Pacific region from Ukraine, where a power struggle between the US and NATO against Russia was taking place in mid-February. President Joe Biden attended the QUAD Summit in Japan after visiting Korea in May. It was only 10 days after the inauguration of Korea's new government of President Yoon Seokyeol. As President Biden selected Korea for his first visit in Asia, he certainly attracted Korea to its side, considering how Korea was making a neutral stance between the US and China.

Continuing, at the QUAD Summit in Japan, he re-tuned the harmony between participating countries since they still have spaces to fill in, and established QUAD's frame as the core engine of Indo-Pacific Strategy. In addition, Indo-Pacific Strategy's economic plan, the IPEF, was launched with including more countries from Southeast Asia and others. How should we look at this United States' Indo-Pacific Strategy and cooperation with its allies? Among all those words and implications, what are the feasible or not feasible ones, and what will end up as the wind bill and what will actually attract further investments? It is necessary to put the puzzle pieces together on Biden's spectacular Asia tour.

This week's interview asks to two diplomatic experts from Korea and China. Firstly, Choe Wongi is a Professor and Head of Center for ASEAN-India Studies at Korea National Diplomatic Academy in Seoul. And Wang Junsheng is the Director and Professor of the Department of China's Regional Strategy, National Institute of International Strategy at Chinese Academy of Social Sciences.

Hwang How would you evaluate the US-Korea summit held on May 21?

Choe I think the new South Korean government and Biden's government managed to closely coordinate their priorities and strategic directions on major issues such as the North Korea policy, the economic, technology and supply chain cooperation, and their joint response to the Indo-Pacific geopolitics. In particular, the two allies seem to have achieved a strategic consensus on the need to expand Korea's regional role and its coordination with the US in Indo-Pacific. I think the most notable and important outcome of this summit is the fact that the US and Korea have overcome the gap in the strategic perceptions and priorities between the two countries, which have been disclosed during the previous Moon administration, especially when it comes to dealing with North Korea's nuclear weapons and the alliance coordination in Indo-

Pacific regional affairs.

Wang This summit has achieved Yoon administration's goals of further strengthening relations with the US, reinforcing cooperation with the US Indo-Pacific strategy, and enhancing Yoon Sukyeol's own leadership image. The United States has gained even more. The Biden administration has successfully incorporated the foreign policy of the Yoon administration into the broader framework of U.S. foreign policy. In contrast, South Korea's diplomatic flexibility has reduced due to the damage of Sino-ROK relations, but Biden administration has further increased its leverage in the strategic suppression of China.

Hwang Please share us your perspectives on evaluation of four leaders' QUAD summit in Tokyo on May 24.

Choe The most notable achievements of the QUAD Summit are, first, that they managed to dispel some perceptions of a crack among the QUAD member states stemming from India's neutral stance on Russia's invasion of Ukraine, and second, that they reaffirmed the bond and strengthened internal solidarity among themselves. India is often said to be the 'weakest link' of the QUAD, but the successful conclusion of Tokyo Quad Summit shows that India's QUAD strategy is a subset of its China strategy, and that the strongest glue that solidifies the unity among QUAD countries is their shared strategic perception of China. As long as India feels serious security threats from China's assertive expansion as it does right now, India will never be the weakest link, but the most important strategic member of the QUAD. Given China's assertive behavior and attempts to change the status quo by force in many parts of the Indo-Pacific, India's threat perception of China won't change but will only grow even stronger, and QUAD is likely to be able to maintain its strategic focus and internal solidarity, and also to expand areas of cooperation among its members.

Wang This summit was the second time that the QUAD leaders met face-to-face. The summit adopted a joint statement covering a wide range of regional and global issues such as the North Korean nuclear issue and the response to the pandemic, which increased the institutionalization of QUAD. But at the same time, due to the different interests of the US, Japan, India and Australia, the summit has achieved less substantive results and more general discussions. The fact that China was not mentioned at the summit shows that the four countries also have different views on jointly putting pressure on China.

Hwang What could be the reasons, achievements, and limitations of President Biden's trip to Asia?

Choe I think Biden's Asia tour this time is part of his efforts to put his Indo-Pacific Strategy into practice, and mobilize support from allies and partners in this part of the world. If you look at what Biden administration has been doing for the last couple of weeks, I mean, US-ASEAN Summit, the ROK-US Summit, the QUAD Summit, the official launch of IPEF with a total of 13 members including 7 ASEAN countries, and Secretary of State Blinken's announcement on the Biden administration's China Strategy, you can see what Biden is aiming for. I think Biden administration was quite successful in maintaining and even strengthening the internal cohesion among the QUAD members in spite of the apparent discord with India regarding the Ukraine War as well as the change of Australian government from the Liberal Party to the Labor Party. While the main reason Biden traveled to Asia was the third QUAD summit held in Japan, his stop in Seoul and meeting with the newly inaugurated President Yoon of ROK was no less significant. Given the fact that the previous Moon administration quite broke away from Indo-Pacific coordination with the US even though ROK is the 'linchpin' ally to the US, it is quite an achievement for Biden that new conservative government in Seoul pledged to put priority in strengthening ties with the US not only at the bilateral level but also with regard to the regional affairs in the Indo-Pacific.

Wang Biden's visit to East Asia obviously pays more attention to the economic vitality and strategic importance of this region. It can be argued that Biden's visit has achieved its purpose, which is to incorporate the foreign policies of the South Korea's new government and the Japanese government into the framework of the US Indo-Pacific strategy, and at the same time launched the IPEF and held the QUAD summit. Of course, for Biden administration, isolating China will not help address America's difficulties and global issues, including those in the Asia-Pacific.

Hwang President Yoon Seokyeol has vowed to come up with a Korean version of Indo-Pacific Strategy. How do you see the new Korean government's further diplomacy would be like?

Wang The Yoon Sukyeol administration's Indo-Pacific strategy is still being formulated, but such a policy is obviously not a regional strategy, but a global strategy. Considering that South Korea's economy has entered the top ten in the world and has become a developed country, Yoon administration's new strategy will further amplify its expectation to become "global pivotal state" and exert global influence.

Choe President Yoon Seokyeol is very critical of the former Moon administration's 'balanced diplomacy' that endeavored to strike a balance between the US and China. The basic stance that the Yoon government pursues is to set the US-ROK alliance as the axis of Korea's foreign policy and to strengthen cooperation with the US bilaterally, regionally as well as at the global level. He has pledged to seek for "free, open, and inclusive Indo-Pacific" through cooperation with the US and also stressed ROK's responsibility that is commensurate with its international status as the 10th largest economy in his recent interview with VOA. At the Yoon-Biden Summit, President Yoon announced that he would formulate ROK's own Indo-Pacific strategy as its comprehensive regional strategy. However, it is quite uncertain to what extent and at what level President Yoon will turn his pledges and commitments into actual policies and actions, especially with regard to the Indo-Pacific cooperation with the US, Korea-US-Japan trilateral cooperation, and cooperation with the QUAD in the days ahead. For example, Yoon repeatedly made pledges to uphold the fundamental values of freedom, democracy, and human rights in his foreign policy approaches, but it is highly likely that he would confront many challenges as well as constraints in pursuing his 'value diplomacy'. I think, for the time being, Yoon's administration is expected to focus mostly on economic and functional areas, such as the QUAD working groups, in his engagement with the US and other like-minded partners.

Hwang What do you think are the similarities and differences between the previous Moon administration's New Southern Policy and the Yoon administration's Indo-Pacific Strategy?

Choe Given his publicly stated positions and strategic orientations, just like Moon did, Yoon administration is also likely to put priority on strengthening ties with ASEAN countries and India. However, it looks like Yoon will be more active in regional security affairs and also try to expand ROK's regional role in the Indo-Pacific region. In managing relations with China, Yoon is expected to take a clearer stance on bilateral as well as regional issues compared to Moon who took an approach of "strategic ambiguity". For instance, the Yoon administration is more likely to make a clearer voice when it comes to maritime security in the Indo-Pacific, especially the freedom of navigation in the South China Sea, etc.

Wang The New Southern Policy of the Moon administration is a regional strategy, mainly promoting cooperation with Southeast Asia. The Indo-Pacific strategy of Yoon administration, on the other hand, is a global strategy. Moon Jaein has been committed to promoting the cooperation of the New Southern Policy with the U.S. Indo-Pacific strategy, while Yoon administration directly launched the its own Indo-Pacific strategy, which is likely to be highly similar and overlapping with the U.S. Indo-Pacific strategy.

Hwang Despite South Korea's expression of willingness to participate in QUAD, the US implied its intention to maintain the current system. Do you see there still is a possibility of scaling to QUAD plus?

Wang There are many reasons why the United States does not want South Korea to join QUAD for the time being. The most important one is that the mechanism is just running and not mature. The US is well experienced in building mechanisms and is well aware that expanding the mechanism at this point of time will not necessarily help its development. The US needs to take into account the bumpy Japan-South Korea relations and how the US will coordinate with Japan once South Korea joins in. However, considering that the U.S. purpose of constructing QUAD is to serve as the great power competition, and the importance of South Korea in the achievement of U.S. strategic goals, it is only a matter of time for South Korea is accepted as QUAD member.

Choe The US does not seem to be interested in expanding QUAD beyond the current four countries for the time being. I think the Biden administration is more interested in strengthening the solidarity among four QUAD states rather than expanding the QUAD's membership. Of course, they will promote cooperation with countries other than the current QUAD members through working groups in such areas as climate change, advanced technologies, and vaccine supplies, etc. In this regard, you can say that ROK would be the most important potential 'partner for QUAD'. On the part of ROK, Seoul will not seek a QUAD membership, but strengthen its cooperation with QUAD states without membership.

Hwang What are the outlooks of Indo-Pacific Strategy that you consider?

Wang After the Obama administration, the Trump administration and the current Biden administration, the U.S. Indo-Pacific strategic goal has become more and more clear, which is to maintain the U.S. leadership in the Asia-Pacific region, and that QUAD and IPEF are fundamentally aimed at this. The US Indo-Pacific strategy is not conducive to the stability and prosperity of the Asia-Pacific region, as it is committed to shaping a divided and confrontational environment, which is contrary to the development of the Asia-Pacific region.

Choe In addition to QUAD and IPEF, it looks like that the US is making efforts to establish multiple mechanisms in support of its Indo-Pacific Strategy. Besides QUAD and

IPEF, you have a host of diverse minilateral arrangements, i.e., AUKUS, Korea-US-Japan cooperation, NATO, as well as bilateral partnership with some key countries in ASEAN, such as Vietnam, Singapore, and Indonesia. It seems the US is working very hard to organize an Indo-Pacific cooperation network based on various issue-based coalitions as well a number of bilateral partnership with regional countries. As Blinken recently stated in his China Strategy speech, the Biden administration is now focusing on "shaping the strategic environment that China operates in" rather than "engaging China itself". However, we never know how much this Indo-Pacific Strategy going to achieve its intended goals. For example, to date the US is not so successful in mobilizing support for its Indo-Pacific Strategy among ASEAN countries. In addition to the Indian Ocean, and the South China Sea in particular, where China has been aggressively expanding its maritime foothold in key areas, the US is not in a position to garner much support from South Asia except for India. Also, as seen from the recent China-Solomons Security Pact, China is now making inroads into the West Pacific, where the US has traditionally maintained a military primacy.

Hwang Do you assess that Indo-Pacific Strategy has its purpose in containing China?

Wang This is obvious. All these mechanisms of the United States are closed in nature, because US sees China as a specific adversary. When the US considers China as a strategic competitor and is committed to suppressing China's surrounding areas, the purpose of the United States to build relevant mechanisms to pressure and contain China is obvious. This is also in line with the institutional hegemony built by the United States after World War II.

Choe In the early days of the Biden administration, you seemed to have two different schools of thought within the administration regarding its strategy against China. The first one is that the US should pressure China to bring behavioral change in its revisionist and expansionist moves; and the other one is that since the US cannot change China's external behaviors, it should keep on pressuring to eventually weaken China's power. I understand some internal debates were going on, but based on what I get form Blinken's China strategy speech couple of days ago, I think Biden administration has now completely abandoned its approach of 'putting pressure to change China's behavior' and moved on to the latter approach.

Hwang From your point of view, does the Ukraine crisis strengthen or weaken Indo-Pacific Strategy?

Choe It is true that the US was distracted a bit by Russia's invasion of Ukraine, and there are some concerns that US's attention to and focus on Indo-Pacific Strategy might have been weakened, as India is remaining still as neutral unlike other Western countries. Nevertheless, I think the core of US's foreign policy is still the Indo-Pacific Strategy. There are absolutely no disagreements on this among the US, India, or European countries for that matter. In short, I don't think the Ukrainian war is not a significant enough factor that would dilute Biden's focus on Indo-Pacific Strategy.

Wang After the outbreak of the Ukraine war, the United States has to invest some resources, but it did not weaken the US Indo-Pacific strategy. From the perspective of the United States, it has always believed that China and Russia are two competitors, investing resources to contain both countries at the same time. But it is worth noting that the United States believes that China is a more serious competitor than Russia, which has not changed since the outbreak of the Russian-Ukrainian war, as evidenced by Biden's recent visit to East Asia.

Hwang 13 countries in total decided to participate in the launch of IPEF. What could be the reason that explains such a number of countries are joining, although specific directions and contents have not been settled yet?

Wang There are 13 countries have joined the IPEF of the United States, and most of them maintain close economic and trade relations with China. It's worth pointing out that the goals of these 13 countries and the United States are likely to be different. By joining IPEF, most countries hope to develop their economies through regional cooperation and achieve stable supply chains and industrial chains, while the United States uses them as a tool for great power competition. Therefore, these 13 countries that join the IPEF should avoid becoming a tool of the U.S. foreign strategy while try to achieve their own economic development goals.

Choe A total of thirteen countries joined the IPEF. All of the ten ASEAN countries participated except Myanmar,

Cambodia, and Laos, which are under China's stronghold. The main reason why ASEAN countries joined the IPEF can be understood in terms of their hedging strategy. For example, Singapore has expressed its support for China's bid to CTPPP membership while participating in the IPEF, and also has supported the GDI that President Xi Jinping recently announced. Also, ASEAN countries as well as ROK have nothing to lose by joining the IPEF because it is an 'empty shell' at the moment. The stated goal of the IPEF is to "set new standards" in such areas as the digital economy, climate change, and anti-corruption, etc., but nobody knows exactly what will become of the IPEF since it lacks any substance or clear operational directions. Moreover, the IPEF is not going to be a binding agreement like any trade agreements. In short, contrary to China's strong objection to the IPEF and its official position that it is another new arrangement that the US devised in order to contain China, it is quite uncertain whether or not the IPEF is going to develop into a substantive mechanism to play such a role in the coming future.

US and China Neck to Neck in a New Cold War Long Race

Jan 10, 2022

Shi Yinhong

Director, Center on American Studies at Renmin University of China

US President Joe Biden and Chinese President Xi Jinping had their first summit on Nov. 16. Although the summit was an online-only meeting, the whole international society paid serious attention, since it was the first bilateral talk since the Biden administration was inaugurated 10 months ago. During the main discussion, Biden pinpointed everything he had to from the US' point of view for its own national interests. This includes human rights issues in Xinjiang, Tibet, and Hong Kong, unfair trade, a free and open Indo-Pacific, Taiwan defense, and others. In response, President Xi has criticized the US's politicization of trade and human rights issues. On the Taiwan issue, he issued a warning: "Those who play with fire will get burned."

On the other hand, it seems both leaders shared an implicit consensus about US-China conflict and competition staying within controllable limits. President Biden has said, "Our responsibility as leaders of China and the United States is to ensure that competition between our countries does not veer into conflict." He added that the US needs to establish a "commonsense guardrail." Xi has also said that China must "stabilize the rudder" so both the US and China can "move forward against the wind and waves without yawing, stalling or colliding."

What is the true face of US-China relations? Is the New Cold War no more than rhetoric, or is it an actual feature? To discuss these things further, The Korea Herald invited professor Shi Yinhong, a renowned Chinese expert in American Studies. He is currently a professor of International Relations, chairman of Academic Committee of the School of International Studies, and director of the Center on American Studies at Renmin University of China in Beijing. He has served as a counselor for the State Council of China since February 2011.

Hwang First of all, I would like to hear how you would evaluate the US-China Summit.

Shi In despite of few instances of concrete cooperation, all of which were quite limited, indecisive and likely temporary, the summit online on Nov. 16 Beijing Time has in fact demonstrated how wide the disagreements between China and the United States are. Also, it showed how difficult it is for both countries to achieve a remarkable and lasting rapprochement on any major area of their rivalry. It showed how easily several of them (areas) could deteriorate even further from an already high level of tension.

The issue of Taiwan of course is the most prominent and significant hot spot. The White House made a statement four days before their first bilateral summit. President Biden said that he would not seek concrete results on the issue. Rather, he said he was primarily concerned with setting up the conditions for effective competition. So the two heads of state would discuss how to responsibly deal with competition between the two countries. This was in line with the general principle repeatedly declared by the Biden Administration. As National Security Adviser Jake Sullivan said on Nov.11, "stiff competition" is the US' fundamental tune while doing its best to prevent a US-China military conflict through both deterrence and diplomacy. This means that on the issue of Taiwan in particular, and the US-China strategic-military rivalry in general, the Biden Administration strongly pursues a situation where the US can safely broaden and deepen the almost comprehensive support given to Taiwan, including military support. This goes with broadening and deepening the rivalry against China in the Indo-Pacific region and even beyond without risk of military conflict.

Hwang Continuing our discussion on the summit, do you think the two countries have at least got onto the right track? Or would we expect greater competition between the two in 2022?

Shi Such a guideline (of "stiff competition") has been so prominent in President Biden's statements during the summit and even more so afterward by his administration's words and actions. The administration's words and actions feature both an unprecedented increase in frequency and some remarkable escalation on some issues. The permitted time for this interview restricts me from going into any detail, which is well-known to every expert. Moreover, during a short time span of about 1 1/2 months, the Biden Administration displayed a very hardline approach. It was more hardline than almost ever before, on the issues of Xinjiang, realignment of supply chains mainly against China, high tech "containment" toward China, and the Indo-Pacific regional rivalry.

Hwang Do you consider US-China relations as a New Cold War?

Shi I have repeated again and again in the past few months that I personally believe a New Cold War has been emerging between the United States and China, if it has not yet definitely emerged. It is a New Cold War, of which one's perception depends on whether one puts emphasis on the word "New" or on the phrase "Cold War." If one emphasizes "New," of course one could find numerous differences between US-Chinese relations and the former US-USSR Cold War, though so many people today incline to overstate those. On the other hand, if one emphasizes "Cold War," one can easily see that the current rivalry and confrontation between Washington and Beijing already have some major essential features of the old Cold War between Washington and Moscow. We can see it even more so in world history between two antagonistic great powers. We have already seen increasing severity between Washington and Beijing in many respects. There have been more hostile geopolitical and geo-strategic actions, an intensifying arms race, intensifying ideological rivalry, and increasingly severe struggle in the areas of high tech. These have aggravated hostile and more nationalistic public opinion in both countries against each other, while restraining political leadership on both sides.

Hwang In that case, what definition would you suggest to describe relations?

Shi From this perspective respecting both the current situation and historical experiences, what is "New" is mainly the critical "decoupling" from critical economic interdependent relationships. This leads more and more critical areas into fragmented and group-oriented separations, just like the strategic stalemate in Europe before the 1980s. This has been replaced by the ominous strategic dynamics and fluidity now in East Asia and the Pacific and beyond. This is a situation which sharply challenges intellectual and other capabilities of the present political and strategic leaderships for every major power. Not only that, the pandemic and other imaginable climate-change related disasters complicated things much further and often stunted leaders' capacities in a broad sense. Also the "New" is a much more high-tech approach to great power warfare or parawarfare which dramatically increases the dynamics of the rivalry, making it very difficult to control. The "remnants" of economic interdependence and liberal globalization are likely not stronger than all the forces against stabilization.

Hwang Some are saying that national competition between the US and China comes from technological competition. What do you think the fundamental reason is?

Shi People are more often than not inclined to easy and simplistic explanations. Among a few of the most prevailing ones throughout history is so-called One Cause Theory. Although the technological competition has been a very important causal factor in the national competition between the US and China, it is extremely difficult to suppose that the historic rivalry between two huge powers like them comes only from a single factor, no matter how significant it is. The so-called fundamental and continuing "power transition" matters matter a lot. Domestic political and social systems, or essential ways of organization at home, with domestic political requirements in terms of both power and ideas, also matter a lot. Closely related to this is ideological competition, differences of adamant political and even cultural traditions, major domestic vested interests of various powerful groups, etc. And finally, ominous interactions between rival major nations, especially in an environment characterized primarily by "jungle politics" and a shortage of critical resources, broadly defined, as is increasingly the case now. The above five or six, together with technological competition, are fundamental reasons. It is difficult or even impossible to make a strict order of importance among them, I believe. This is one of the major reasons why the present rivalry between Washington and Beijing is far from easy to deal with, let alone to solve.

Hwang A number of countries are concerned with China's assertive diplomacy. Does this come from the leader's tendencies, or people's nationalism due to generational change?

Shi China's "assertive diplomacy" is certainly something positive and, more importantly, something it is entitled to, as seen by the majority of the Chinese public. And it is less significant and harmful than China's assertive strategic-military actions, as seen by strategic and political elites in the US, its allies and close partners. These two things are closely interconnected, together with China's much increased economic clout. People, especially in China, might doubt that any major nation which experienced such a drastic rise of strength like China did would behave much differently. Besides, I would guess that the Chinese political elites at large rather strongly prefer it. And more so, perhaps, the overwhelming majority of the Chinese public who are influenced by them. By the way, the prominent malfunction of the US and most of the other advanced Western industrial countries in the face of all the major challenges at home was what greatly encouraged an over-triumphalism in China in the first place. Generational change is of course an important reason for all the above, like that in other countries for their current political, social, and international behavior.

Hwang The United States' aggression toward China is obvious. What is China's core interest?

Shi Some of China's core interests are most prominently and repeatedly declared by the Chinese political leadership. They teach and guide perception of the most critical interests to the Chinese public. The most paramount one is the leadership of China by the Chinese Communist Party. Or in leaders' repeated words, "political security," the No.

1 for national security. Secondly, the absolute prohibition of the independence of Taiwan, especially the de jure one. And the realization of unification across the Taiwan Strait as soon as possible, which was recently declared by China's top leader as indispensable to the "great rejuvenation of the Chinese nation." For both of these core interests on Taiwan, the Chinese leadership has declared repeatedly that China refuses to make any commitment to no use of force while it will continue to do its best by peaceful means. Thirdly, among the core interests of China according to the country's leadership are economic, social—and I believe international--development. They have a formally declared time schedule in terms of decades, and general standards for a few stages of "high quality development." Then there are other core national interests such as the South China and East China Seas. China has claimed territorial sovereignty of islands and 12 nautical miles of adjacent waters. Along with territorial sovereignty of these areas, they have claimed any Chinese-claimed territory's administrative integrity and fundamental security as among its national core interests. As such, I believe the objective of their military buildup is aimed at making the Chinese armed forces one of the two or at most three strongest national armed forces in the world within a few decades.

Hwang Does the Korean Peninsula also fit into China's core interests?

Shi I have to point out that in my firm belief a few implicit facts are held by the Chinese leadership as the core national interests, including at anytime no tolerance toward any major military threat, at least an imminent one, that comes from the Korean Peninsula.

Hwang How do you anticipate the security environment of Northeast Asia in 2022?

Shi Since the Biden Administration's stampede from Afghanistan, its posture toward China has revised to some degree. Its drastic political predicaments, domestic priority, and strategic difficulties have forced it to freeze as it were the level of high tension between itself and China. This means (1) there would be temporarily no longer at large escalation of tension comparing with its first eight months; (2) At present and in the predictable future there also would be no remarkable and lasting mitigation of tension with China in all major issue areas of rivalry and confrontation. The numerous ominous developments pointed out in my answer to question 1 has begun to make me seriously doubt whether the bilateral relationship would continue to freeze the level of high tension and not reverse to its escalation.

Also, primarily important in predicating the security environment of Northeast Asia in 2022 is the Japanese strategic/military posture toward China throughout 2021: The Japanese government whether under Yoshihide Suga or then Fumio Kishida has definitely destroyed the bottom line on Taiwan, which for many years after the government of Yasuo Fukuda constituted the political basis of the bilateral political relationship -- i.e., in practice the Japanese

Prime Minister and his major subordinates never publicly in words and deeds touch the issue of security of Taiwan. Moreover, it is becoming a Japanese fundamental national policy that in the event of major military conflict broke out between the two sides of the Taiwan Strait Japan would launch with the US a joint massive military intervention to prevent the fall of Taiwan.

There is no indication that the above developments in 2021 will probably or even possibly be reversed in 2022. A deterioration of the already tense East China Sea dispute between China and the Japan-US military alliance cannot be excluded, and so too a major drastic development of the DPRK nuclear and missile program.

Hwang The following year is the 30th anniversary of diplomatic relations between Korea and China. What is the most significant agenda in this relations? Is sticking to "Three noes and one limitation" our crossing point?

Shi For the relationship between ROK and China, besides the unsolved and unsolvable dispute over THAAD, which has dented the bilateral relations so much with a lasting effect, there are several other developments that happened in 2021that I believe will have a negative impact on China's perception of the ROK under President Moon Jaein, though he and his administration have taken a quite friendly attitude toward China in despite Washington's pressure and disadvantageous domestic opinion about China.

Under the implicit but strong American leverage over

provision of COVID-19 vaccines and over continued permission to use American technology to produce semiconductor chips, together with the very seductive American offer to abolish the severe restrictions imposed upon ROK missile development, President Moon decided and then declared during his visit to Washington for the summit with President Biden that ROK would partially participate in Quad, the four power Indo-Pacific strategic alignment with non-strategic and para-strategic aspects. And that ROK (indirectly as he did through for major Korean cooperation's huge investments in the US) would also partially join the realignment of critical supply chains primarily targeting China. More seriously, he stated in the joint statement issued by his summit with Biden that he would cooperate with the US on peace and stability of the Taiwan Strait.

Hwang Do you have any other comments to share regarding the relationship between Korea and China?

Shi A problem even bigger than the above is the lasting prevailing negative public opinion about China since 2017 when the THAAD dispute spoiled whole of the bilateral relations. China's de facto comprehensive sanctions lasting several months, combined with other elements, leave President Moon no domestic public basis for a friendly posture toward China, and there are powerful forces both in the US and ROK to maintain and aggravate that. I have to frankly state that in the face of the 30th anniversary of the diplomatic ties between ROK and China, the political environment is regrettably not so advantageous for further remarkable warming up of bilateral relations, and economic ones less so, because of, in the first place, high tech decoupling under American pressure. For we Chinese and President Moon, there is a regrettable gap between what should be and what can be, though both have to do something for better.

If there is any criterion in deciding the national interest in between the US and China, it must be having the nation's "own principles." The very foundation of this "own principle" is the capacity in reading the flow of the international order. So far, there are a number of voices that accepts today's US-China competition as the New Cold War. However, standing at the "entrance" of the New Cold War, as the former Secretary of State Henry Kissinger has mentioned, might be a more accurate description. Today's US-China competition is not the same as the US-Soviet Union Cold War, which was mostly about competition. The current one can be said to have competition in 7 out of 10 areas with cooperation in the other 3. If we believe that we are standing in the middle of the New Cold War, we must define the New Cold War.

In other words, is Biden's next four years going to follow a Trump-ish foreign policy? Is China going to become more opaque and assertive? Is the international society going to lose the multilateral mechanism and its function? Will the powers flock to either one of these two superpowers and be hostile to each other? Will ideology and cultural conflicts float up to the surface? Are we entering into an era of anti-globalization or non-globalization? We are only able to define the international order after the COVID-19 pandemic and in the further future, when we clearly and comprehensively can answer to the questions above. The US's China bashing seems set to continue due to the mid-term elections. However, because of the two sides' economic closeness, they will still have gray areas of cooperation.

Seeking a crack for cooperation amid the tension between the US and China

Jul 3, 2022

Choi Wooseon

Professor, Korea National Diplomatic Academy

Yu Tiejun

Professor, School of International Studies at Peking University

US-China relations are the most critical bilateral relations among numerous others in the international community.

Since Xi Jinping became the supreme leader of China in 2012, China has been shaping its own diplomatic color, instead of "taoguang yanghui" (keep a low profile and bide your time, while also getting something accomplished). Although there is still a lack of sophistication and detail, it is clear enough to shock and give tension to the US, since the US has enjoyed an exclusive status in the international community with its authority and capabilities.

The White House published its Indo-Pacific Strategy Report in February this year, and Secretary of State Tony Blinken's speech at George Washington University in May de facto revealed the US' ideas and direction toward China. Despite the emphasis on the need for cooperation between the two countries, the inevitability of competition was reflected.

Nevertheless, the situation is never easy, because it is difficult and impossible to eradicate inconvenient and dissatisfying supply chains even though the two have been intertwined over the past few decades. An uncomfortable relationship between the two makes it uneasy for the countries in between. They have to endure the irritation from the US and China, but they also have to seek national interests at the same time.

Where are US-China relations standing now? What are these two countries' thoughts and where are they heading to?

To find the answers, this week I invited two experts from Korea and China. We have Choi Wooseon, a professor at the Korea National Diplomatic Academy, and Yu Tiejun, a professor at the School of International Studies in Peking University.

Hwang How would you evaluate the current US-China relationship?

Choi My assessment is that the US and China are standing at the early stages of real competition. Some say that the US-China relationship has already entered a cold war, but I think it's a bit exaggerated. I think it is a competitive relationship in which there is still a certain amount of cooperation between the US and China.

The critical trigger that intensified this competition between the US and China was the emergence of the US' tough posture toward China in 2017. Before then, US policy toward China was largely focused on cooperation, and its attitude toward China's rise was engagement rather than balancing.

However, in 2017, US policymakers began to converge to the consensus that this policy had helped China grow while failing in inducing it to become a status quo power and that stronger constraints on China in military and economic areas were in need. Fundamentally, this consensus resulted from the changed power relations. The US now considers China as a near-peer competitor. So it is stepping up its balancing of China.

Hwang What is the Joe Biden administration's purpose in its China policy?

Choi It is mainly about maintaining America's superiority as long as possible and retarding China's growth, but it is unlike the Cold War in the past in that America does not totally contain its opponent with the aim of collapsing it. Although the recent Russian-Ukraine war has made Russia the US' new rising trouble, the US is still keeping its focus on China. Accordingly, Asia's strategic priority is staying at the top of the US foreign policy. And the US' main course of action is to pursue competitive economic policies toward China while strengthening its economic vitality. In particular, the US emphasizes eliminating unfair practices and selective decoupling in high-tech areas. It also stresses accelerating military innovation, upgrading alliances and partnerships, and restoring US leadership in international multilateral organizations. Further, we now see the competition of values that president Biden highlights.

Hwang Do you think we can say that the Biden administration is basically continuing the previous Donald Trump administration's stance on China policy?

Yu Actually there are several different characteristics in the US-China strategic competition. First, the Biden administration is trying to expand the alliance front to strengthen its alliance system and to constrain China. Biden's expansion is through the US-Japan alliance, the US-ROK (South Korea) alliance, the US-Philippine alliance, NATO, AUKUS, the Quad, Summit for Democracy, and so on. Additionally, the US has set the Indo-Pacific as the strategic competition ground between the US and China, especially focusing on the Taiwan Strait and the South China Sea. The US and China continuously have disputes on international order, socioeconomic systems, development models and ideologies. The so-called superpowers competition' between the US and China is being prolonged.

Hwang What do you think about alliance policies like the Quad and AUKUS?

Choi I think the US is making long-term efforts to form multilateral alliances in the region in gradual and flexible ways. Due to China's limited military threat, the US' military superiority and geographical distances between countries, most countries in the Indo-Pacific region will likely continue a certain level of buck-passing to the US for a while. American policymakers recognize the reality.

Hwang What is the overall US policy toward China, including military aspects?

Choi I think that, in the near future, China will pursue neither an earnest arms race nor military confrontation.

US policymakers also presume that China's threat is not imminent. However, it is true that military competition between the US and China is intensifying, and the US considers China's development of precision strike capabilities and cyberspace electronic warfare capabilities as serious challenges to the US' superiority, especially in airspace and battle network. Also, China's navy is increasing its potential to take control of the Western Pacific, which could be the greatest threat to US position in the long run. As a result, the US has been shifting to the military strategy that focuses on great power conflict, especially with China, since 2018. And the US is accelerating its military innovation to overcome Chinese challenge, focusing on the development of new operational concepts and investments in future capabilities.

Hwang What is the Xi Jinping administration's policy that counteracts these US moves?

Choi I think that Xi government still maintains a defensive and conciliatory posture. It seems to be avoiding direct military challenges under US superiority, and tends to favor easing tensions with the US to focus on economic development.

On the other hand, it is true that it has maintained an active stance in foreign policies and territorial disputes with the neighboring countries since the late 2000s. And China is making long-term efforts to reshape the regional order in its favor through the Belt and Road Initiative and other measures. Certainly, American policymakers consider these as challenging behaviors to the US.

Hwang What is the general perception of China's security situation in the region?

Yu From China's perspective, it is worth noting that the security situation surrounding China, such as the Korean Peninsula, the South China Sea, and Taiwan, is getting serious. The instability of the Korean Peninsula is prolonged due to the failure of establishing the peace regime, which mainly was about North Korea's nuclear issue, and the South China Sea issue is still in conflict with the Philippines and Vietnam.

Lastly, Taiwan has long been the core of the US-China Strategic competition and crisis management. Although both the Trump and Biden administration claim a "One China" policy, it seems the "strategic ambiguity" is steadily changing into "strategic clarity." For one example, the US mentioned Taiwan seven times in the Indo-Pacific report in February 2022, and is conducting arms sales, military education and military connections with Taiwan.

Hwang How does China view the Russia-Ukraine war?

Yu The ongoing Russia-Ukraine war is not making any progress through negotiations and is in a stalemate. This is making a major impact on the security situation around the world and is causing problems in various areas such as the economy, trade, finance and energy. The Russian-Ukraine war is a big challenge for China, since China is having friendly relationships with both Russia and Ukraine.

Hwang The issue of nontraditional security is increasingly emerging in the international community.

Yu Yes, especially as new pandemics such as COVID-19 hit the world hard, it has had a profound impact on global politics and the economy, and the importance of environmental security, such as climate change, is sustainably growing. However, under the circumstances where international organizations have failed to play their role, the global governance is facing serious challenges. I am saying that this era is the era of peace and development, but it is also true that at the same time we are facing the crisis and challenges that I mentioned earlier. In the future, I wish three countries -- China, Korea and Japan -- continue on cooperating as much as possible in areas where they can to promote the development and peace of the international community.

Hwang What are the prospects of US-China relations?

Choi The trend of increasing competition between the US and China is not reversible because it basically the result of the changing balance of power. This trend shows that economic interdependence has limitations in controlling competition. Rather, security competition is now making significant negative impact on economic relationship. And, despite the Russian-Ukraine war and the necessity to invest significant resources and energy in Europe, the US will stick to its Asia-centric policy to compete with China. It is because China is its real competitor. Russia will be weakened over time through the war and sanctions. And the US will be able to keep naval and air capabilities required in Asia while deterring Russia in Europe.

Yu Since President Trump took power in 2017, the US has considered China as its biggest strategic competitor. Ever since then, the US-China relationship has entered a full-scale competition. Many experts are now concerned what if the US-China relationship enters the "New Cold War" or Cold War 2.0. On the other hand, while the US-China competition is escalating in terms of politics and security (and sometimes even confrontation exists), a close relationship is still going on in the economics. For example, US-China trade reached more than $755.6 billion in 2021. In other words, unlike the past Cold War, the current US-China relationship is very economically interdependent, which is a big difference from the past Cold War. Basically, the strategic competition between China and the US is expected to intensify, not diminish. This is because the power gap between the US and China is narrowing down in terms of the balance of power and both are mutually recognizing one another in a negative view.

Additionally, the ideological and domestic political

situations are also heating up the competition. The US-China strategic competition will last in the long term, for more than a decade. It will expand beyond political security to economic security and high-tech areas, and will focus on the Asia-Pacific region, particularly Taiwan. Of course, both the US and China will try to prevent a fierce confrontation at the front line, and the two countries will maintain this situation where they "keep the competition but avoid the collapse." In order to do so, it must be necessary to refer to the deterrence and crisis management experiences and cases from the past in terms of national security.

Hwang What could US-China relations be in long-term perspectives?

Choi There are different scenarios such as a cold war, limited cooperation, cooperation, military conflict and condominium. I personally think that there will likely be limited cooperation between the US and China until the mid-2030s. When I imagine their relations in the longer term, however, there will be a competition like the Cold War because it is probable that at some point after the mid-2030s, China will seek to dominate the region for its own security, attempting to exclude the US from the region. Then the US will respond by containing China to prevent it from becoming a regional hegemon. Nonetheless, I expect that we can see the balance of power and stability based on the US' military superiority and grand alliance in the region.

Hwang It seems that we can understand the US strategy toward China over the last few years through President Biden's recent visit to Korea and Japan.

Yu The official launch of the IPEF (Indo-Pacific Economic Framework) must be one instance of what you mean. In the face of intensifying competition between the US and China, the fact that the US did not have any position in the Comprehensive and Progressive Trans-Pacific Partnership with the RCEP (Regional Comprehensive Economic Partnership) must have been the reason why it had no choice but to make efforts to strengthen cooperation with Korea and Japan.

Choi President Biden's trip to South Korea and Japan was pretty successful as it was a sign that the US' focus was on the Indo-Pacific region amid the ongoing Ukraine war. The Moon Jaein government achieved a significant level of improvement in relations through the ROK-US Summit in 2021. However, there still was a gap in China policy of the two allies. The Moon government basically pursued a kind of balancing between the US and China while the US was stepping up its balancing against China. In contrast, the ROK-US Summit this year showed a greater synchronization when it comes to China policy. If you read through the statement, there is one very important change that you can see between the lines.

In the past, the cooperation on the Korean Peninsula and global issues was emphasized under a comprehensive development of US-ROK alliance. However, cooperation at the regional level was largely avoided because it could be interpreted as targeted at China. This time, the statements or the remarks are clearly pointing at ROK-US cooperation in the Indo-Pacific region. The statement contains an active posture of the Yoon government not only about joining IPEF, but also about working with the Quad. In addition, a more positive attitude toward Korea-US-Japan cooperation, including security cooperation, was expressed.

In the same context, it seems that a coherent stance toward maritime security and Taiwan has begun to be established. So these changes must be a sign that the current government has shifted from a so-called "balancing" between the US and China to a policy that clearly prioritizes the alliance with the US. However, it should not be predicted that this will lead to a hostile policy against China. Although the new government's foreign policy can be seen as strategically prioritizing the US, it is obvious that it will also continue to pursue a constructive relationship with China.

China will not side with Moscow to engage new Cold War

May 18, 2022

Zhu Feng
Director, Institute of International Relations at Nanjing University

At Bloomberg's New Economy Forum in Beijing back in 2019, the former United States Secretary of State Henry Kissinger mentioned that the US and China were still in the "foothills of the New Cold War," which basically meant that we had not entered it yet. From my personal view, there must be a few objective criteria before determine that the New Cold War has begun: Will Biden's 4 years also present Trump-ish foreign policies? Will China become more opaque and assertive? Is the international community losing its multilateral mechanism and function? Will the powers gather around two great pillars and form a mutual hostility? Will the ideological and cultural conflict float up to the surface? Are we stepping into the era of anti-globalization or non-globalization? We will be able to convince ourselves that we are standing in the middle of the New Cold War only after we can clearly answer all these questions.

Despite the heated US-China competition, I still believe the relationship is about 70 percent competitive and 30 cooperative. However, Europe is in a time of critical trouble, when it is one of the two poles in the United States' international strategy, along with the Indo-Pacific. We are witnessing indexes that accord with the New Cold War. Although China is reluctant to even use the expression "Indo-Pacific," and is using the term "Asia-Pacific," how is the Indo-Pacific doing? As the storm of New Cold War approaches, what strategic decisions is China making? Additionally, as the Korean Peninsula is one of China's core regions in its national strategy, how is China interpreting and planning its relations with both South and North Koreas? This discussion invites professor Zhu Feng, who is the Director of Institute of International Relations in Nanjing University. He has been researching the above issues for a very long time. One of his prominent publications was America, China and The Struggle for the World Order, co-edited with professor G. John Ikenberry and professor Wang Jisi in 2015.

Hwang What does the Ukraine war indicate in terms of the international order? Are we heading to the New Cold War, or maybe toward multipolarity?

Zhu The Ukraine war is an unexpected subversion of the international order which has originated in the collapse of Soviet Union and embedded on globalization. Despite a lot of uncertainties with the endgame of the war in Ukraine, there are a couple of things we could confirm from now on: the first is that an iron curtain is descending once again on Europe, and there is no way that Russia and the EU can converge economically and politically. Instead Europe would be divided into two separate parts with fewer interactions. It is the EU which is heading toward "decoupling" from Russia, and the others are Russia and its Eurasian brothers like Belarus. Furthermore, geopolitical tensions will last for years, as the US and Europe would never allow Russia to escape charges for war crimes and compensation to Ukraine for its reconstruction. In this regard, there is no hope that Ukraine war will eventually end in diplomatic concessions between Russia and the West. The New Cold War is becoming a ruthless reality in the Europe. But I don't think that a new Cold War could extend into the Asia-Pacific. The scathing reality is that China has no interest in siding with Moscow to engage in a new Cold War. It would be fatally detrimental to China's national interests. Furthermore, exclusion of Russia from the European community would keep Moscow isolated and damage its innovation of science, education and national governance. I am quite skeptical of the factual implications for Russia of the Ukraine war. Will it be more autocratic, or less stable due to growing domestic dissatisfaction? Anyway, post-Ukraine-war Russia might revert to a Stalinist model, and its internal tensions would sour. That sort of Russia is truly not what Chinese want to see. And a Russia in an uncertain transition could also be less helpful and even disruptive to the regional security in East Asia.

Hwang What implication does it have for China's national strategy?

Zhu The Ukraine war has given an unexpected thrust to China's national strategy. Beijing and Moscow relations have been warming in the past 10 years, and Joint Declaration of Feb. 4 between Putin and Xi might signal new intimacy between two countries. But ironically China did not have any idea of the upcoming war program by President Putin. Otherwise, China needed to step back from the high profile of Putin-Xi summit early February. Actually Beijing's attempt to build up strategic ties with Moscow is simply based on an idea that China and Russia could team up against hegemonic United States, rather than threaten or harm any European states. China has been Ukraine's biggest trade partner since 2016, and Kiev plays a key role in China's push for the Belt and Road Initiative (BRI). Train connections throughout China to Europe go through Ukraine. Sadly, the Ukraine war has delayed China's BRI project to link China's Chongqing and Amsterdam, and suddenly put a halt to Chinese trading volume of more than $11 billion annually with Ukraine. Furthermore, Beijing's reluctance to part with Moscow suffers a lot of criticism from the European community, and is likely to damage China-European political and economic relations. Last year, the EU regained its position as China's biggest trading partner. To be honest, the Ukraine war's negative effect on China's national strategy is immense.

Hwang Is the Ukraine war making the US-China relations more competitive -- or can it be an opportunity for cooperation?

Zhu The Ukraine war of course made China-US relations more competitive and volatile. The reasons behind that are multiple. First of all, the US desperately hopes China will distance itself from the Moscow, as Washington is highly aware that China might be the biggest backup behind Putin's Russia if the flurries of western sanctions do not weaken Russia as much as they can. Thus, Washington has seriously warned China not to provide Putin government with any military and financial assistance. If not, the US openly threatens to take heavy-handed action against China immediately. And second, American high-ranking officials remind China that the Taiwan issue could risk turning into an Asian version of the Ukraine war if Beijing is intent on militarily coercing Taiwan back. It means that Taiwan is a time-bomb for "Ukraine" in Asia. But Beijing fully rejects such analogy, as it makes it clear that Taiwan is not a sovereign state as Ukraine is, and use of force against Taiwan's independent move is legitimate according to China's domestic legislature. But Washington is apparently taking the opposite view by assuming that the US would defend Taiwan from China's military coercion. Last but not least, the Biden administration stresses that the main purpose of American global security endorsement is to lead a "democratic bloc" in the world to confront the "authoritarian bloc" headed by China and Russia. The Ukraine war seems proven for that proposition. Of course, China fully disagrees with such labelling by the US. Expectably the Ukraine war now is actually exacerbating Beijing-Washington relations.

Hwang When it comes to the Korea-China relations, what are the common points and differences between Moon Jaein and Yoon Seokyeol's government?

Zhu To envision the Yoon Administration's China's policy, I am confident that there would hardly be a big distraction and even remarkable divergence from his predecessor. President Moon insists that the Korea-US alliance is definitely working on the Korea Peninsula-centered military and security collaboration, while President Yoon unambiguously emphasizes his policy priority of fully enhancing South Korea's military alliance with the US. Therefore, many Chinese are suspicious that President Yoon would finally choose sides between Beijing and Washington and hereby decisively lean toward the US amid their great power competition. Yes, I believe that the Yoon Administration would bet more on Korea-US military cooperation, and push deeper within American arms-holding. But it does not automatically mean that the Yoon Administration would pursue an anti-China, or confronting China, policy reorientation. Keeping the delicate balance between the US and China would serve Korea's interests best. Nevertheless, considering the diplomatic stalemate between the South and North on the peninsula, the Chinese should adopt a understanding view on President Yoon's policy option to seek closer ties with Washington. Even more missile defense deployment in South Korea would not be much harmful to Chinese strategic striking capability, considering the new technology proceeding so fascinatingly. But Korea should be aware of what China is truly watchful of. To be honest, staying out of the Quad is a fundamental requirement for Beijing. Seoul embracing the Quad will definitely upset China, as it has been defined as a rudimentary plan to establish an Asian version of NATO. Beijing of course is not willing to see China-Korea relations harmed by a contentious military camp.

Hwang During the campaign, Yoon mentioned that China does not respect Korea. How do you see his remarks?

Zhu I think such a complaint is quite misleading. He referred to a couple of things, such as China's selected commercial sanctions on Seoul in 2015, when President Park Genhye decided to authorize missile defense deployment in South Korea, and a local media outlet in China stupidly noting that Kimchi originated in China. But personally, I consider that such arguments might not ease down between the two neighbors. Beijing's selected sanction after missile defense deployment also caused a lot of debate in China. To be honest, I was one of a few Chinese scholars who did not back any retaliation to missile defense disputes because I assumed that any retaliation would cause unpredictable reactions from South Korea. Thus President Yoon has this sort of impression, and even his open expression of his desire for China's respect are understandable. But hopefully, President Yoon will abandon such bad detachments. Meanwhile, Beijing should be equally aware of Koreans' China psychology. Actually no matter how China and Korea solidify their ties, mutual respect and benign accommodation are absolutely necessary.

Hwang Is there anything you consider the new Korean government should be discreet about besides THAAD in its policies towards China?

Zhu I just picked up on the Quad issue. Additionally, I would really love to see Beijing and Seoul reinforce their communication and dialogue on how we could break the blackmail from Pyongyang on inter-Korea relations by endless provocations in the region by launching missile tests. Particularly, we need work together, hand in hand, to push for the restoration of nuclear disarmament talks which have been stuck in a quagmire for more than a decade. Nuclear dismantlement and peaceful engagement of the two Koreas serve China's long-haul interests. On the other hand, China could be a trustable partner for South Korea to engage North Korea and seek normalization of inter-Korea relations. The Six Party Talks formula has proven to be the only workable mechanism to achieve a periodic breakthrough in denuclearizing North Korea. In addition, I always assume that the best way to break down the North's hard shell and change its nuclear aspirations and belligerent policies is to firmly but gradually draw North Korea out of its isolation. Beijing and Seoul could have a lot of common ground to stand on, and a lot of options we could stand for.

Hwang As seen in President Xi and President Yoon's phone call and Chinese Vice President Wang Qishan's attendance at Yoon's inauguration ceremony, China's efforts to Korea's new government seem to be clear. What are the reasons behind this?

Zhu The most important reason is that South Korea is a country that deserves Chinese respect and emphasis. Both Beijing and Seoul have tremendously changed in the past decades. Beijing should encourage Seoul to exploit its diplomatic activism as a leading middle power, and play a constructive role to mitigate regional security tensions and smartly soften the great power competition between Beijing and Washington. Actually, South Korea is a leading trading partner and import source of high-tech parts.

China is Seoul's biggest trading partner. No one could deny the reality that Beijing and Seoul are increasingly and fundamentally indispensable on almost all fronts. But the surging challenge is that the Biden administration is desperately heading toward "de-coupling" from China, even with supply-chain restructuring. The US is always bent on a "chip alliance" with Japan, Korea and Taiwan to insulate China from acquiring a high-tech semiconductor industry. The purpose of the US is to dampen China's innovative competition and dwarf Beijing's efforts to catch-up with the US in terms of power. But such actions would inevitably bring a new Cold War to regional and global supply chains. It is horribly against the interests of Seoul and Beijing. President Yoon should pass through such tests from Beijing's "pull" and Wasington's "push." Globalization and rules-based openness are keystones of East Asia's economic sustainable growth.

Hwang We are greeting the 30th anniversary of Korea-China relations. How do you anticipate the further improvement of this relationship? What sort of cooperation do you recommend?

Zhu this year marks the 30th anniversary of Korea-China relations. Simply looking back and taking a quick glimpse of our ties during that time, I have to say that it has been a history-changing 30 years, and history-remaking 30 years. Now our societal penetration has never been stronger and more powerful. Cross-border travel also reached a historical height. China and Korea have become so interdependent. We love and respect each other. On the other hand, Korea is a leading force on how China could finish off its domestic transition. Both of us are equally convinced that liberty, democracy and prosperity are the underlying factors for a country to ensure people's happiness. Looking to the future, Chinese and Koreans need to respect each other, compliment each other and match each other. Even if what happens is even irritating, we are fated to stick to each other forever.

Hwang Kim Jongun emphasized North Korea's fundamental interest at the celebration of the 90th anniversary of North Korea's army.

Zhu North Korea's new militarist movement is worth of noticing. In the past 30 years, the country and its leadership have remained intact and unchanged. The family control-centered power system, personality cult-based ideology and persistent economic and social lockdown from the outside actually means Pyongyang never exiting the Cold War. The Ukraine war and China-US strategic competition seem to revitalize N. Korea's cold war mentality. It wishes that great power rivalry would force Beijing and Moscow to take it in their arms once again. That's what North Korea truly wants. But I have to say it is a miscalculation by North Korea. 30 years ago, when Beijing decided to brush off Pyongyang's opposition to normalizing relations with the South, Beijing has made the strategic decision already -- China chooses the South over the North in pursuit of China's national interests. Now and in future, nothing would detach it from this strategic decision.

Hwang President Yoon stressed the substantial denuclearization in his inauguration speech. How can the term "substantial" be interpreted from China's perspective?

Zhu "Substantial denuclearization" definitely means, in my understanding, a full, irreversible and complete nuclear disarmament of North Korea. It has been clearly declared in the Joint Statement of the Six Party Talks in 2005. Such principled consensus should be insisted on without any condition. But mapping out the path to realize "substantial denuclearization" needs bilateral and multilateral cooperation and coordination. China and Korea now are working on providing COVID-19 assistance to the North. Engaging North Korea, rather than perpetually sanctioning and pressuring it, remains a significant option to change North Korea.

What China learned from the Russia-Ukraine War

Jun 15, 2022

You Ji

Professor, Department of Government and Public Administration at the University of Macao

Right before the Russia-Ukraine War broke out, Russian President Vladimir Putin hurried to attend the Beijing Winter Olympics. Putin's visit was a show of his consideration to China, and many have analyzed that the Russia-Ukraine War would have broken out faster if it was not for the Winter Olympics. As shown, China was a critical factor to consider. All of international society, including the United States and Europe, looked to see whether China supported Russia -- both physically and emotionally. This was due to concurrent factors such as the uncertain prolonging of the Russia-Ukraine War; intensified competition between the democratic camp of the US and its Western allies standing at the center versus the authoritarian camp of China and Russia; the US and China's strategic competition; and the possibility of additional "provocations" from countries confronting the US like North Korea. In this light, the strategic weight and portion China's correspondence and response takes in the current international order are significant. How is China observing the Russia-Ukraine War? How is it interpreting the situation in terms of its national strategy? How does China see the People's Liberation

Army (PLA)'s military strategy and power in light of the conflict? How does China see its neighboring region's security? To seek answers to these questions, I invited professor You Ji, who has researched this area for decades. He is currently a professor of international relations in the Department of Government and Public Administration at the University of Macao. Previously, he was a reader (professor) in the School of Social Sciences at the University of New South Wales.

Hwang Despite Russia's military superiority, what would be strategic military reasons for Russia's failure to achieve its goal in the short term, as it heads into a long-term war?

You An assessment of Russia's war performance as a success or failure depends on one's subjective judgment. First, we do not know Putin's war objectives in the first place. He set limited goals for the war: no occupation, no regime change and no elimination of the Ukraine armed forces. As such, the war is not a traditional one, but a kind of special military operation. These "three noes" have in fact created an exit for Putin to end the war after claiming that he has taught Ukraine a lesson, like what the Chinese did to India in 1962 and to Vietnam in 1979. As this is a highly politicized war, failure or success cannot be judged by battlefield indicators. Putin may have achieved a positive outcome.

Hwang What does a positive outcome for Russia mean specifically?

You The very act of war is an indicator of Putin's great zeal, who dared the entire West and stimulated Russian patriotism at home. NATO avoided direct combat engagement with Russia, not even attempting to set a no-fly zone. Ukraine announced its neutrality and non-NATO membership, although it is now hesitating under the West's persuasion and military aid. Putin has forced a new fait accompli onto Ukraine on the independence of the two "people's republics" in the Donetsk and Luhansk regions. With the decisive weakening of Ukraine's defense and industrial capabilities, Russia has struck back at Ukraine's Azov Battalion, driving it out of eastern Ukraine. Certainly judging by the standard of recent US wars, Russia has endured enormous casualties and equipment losses. Yet Russia has no such culture of body bags in comparison to that of the US. The drawn-out war demonstrates the Russian military's deficiencies. Yet Russia still has the upper hand. To Russia, the physical cost may not apply to conventional criteria for a military victory -- only Putin's immediate political objectives do. Of course, he may have misjudged the long-term implications of this war to Russia.

Hwang US Secretary of State Antony Blinken mentioned that what the countries Russia has attacked --- including Ukraine, Georgia and Moldova -- have in common is that they are not NATO members. He added that countries can avoid invasions from Russia if they belong to NATO, and that it is Ukraine's basic right to decide its own future and fate. Do you see this as persuasive?

You Envelope-pushing is always a dangerous act of confrontation, especially when it is leveraged against a nuclear power such as North Korea. This can be suicidal if the opponent is pushed to the point of pursuing mutually assured destruction (MAD). The lesson of the Russia-Ukraine War is that top powers must reserve a space of ambiguity in confrontation to avoid a showdown. Under this simple reasoning, the defense of Ukraine, Georgia and Moldova may be enhanced if they join the NATO. But what about security for Russia, as John Mearsheimer asked? How will Russia respond to Blinken's promise to recruit the three countries to NATO? Will Moscow swallow such a reality? And is NATO ready to confront Russia militarily, or just use Ukraine as a proxy to weaken Russia? After the Russia-Ukraine War, Russia will certainly be crippled. As a result, it may not be able to wage another war against, say, Georgia, for a long while. But if it gambles not to swallow this bitter fruit, the world will be insecure for a long period of time. Despite that, Ukraine, Georgia and Moldova may feel more secure. The world community needs to reckon with the consequences of when the East-West rivalry becomes a zero-sum game. The sensitive and sensible approach of Northeast Asian countries towards North Korea is an example to follow. "Live and let live" is still a principle of peace for the world. Unfortunately, the age of MAD has returned in the advent of the Russia-Ukraine War.

Hwang Can we say the world has entered into a New Cold War?

You We definitely can, although the specific definition of the New Cold War may not match the old one. The Russia-Ukraine War either creates or enhances new realities of Cold War power confrontation. The West's ideological campaign will intensify, repeating the great East-West Schism of the 11th century. It is forging an ideological foundation for a New Cold War of the West vis-a-vis the rest. To many Chinese analysts, a new "end of history" crusade is in the making against the West's rivals, especially China and Russia. The West will accelerate forming its bloc. Not only will NATO's eastward expansion continue, but its Asian expansion will also become more conceivable. This will coalesce NATO and Indo-Pacific security more organically.

Hwang How do you foresee the New Cold War to be?

You The militarization of the New Cold War will deepen, raising it to the level of reinvigorating nuclear MAD threats in multiple regions. This includes especially the Korean Peninsula, where renewed confrontation will resume sooner than later. Central Asia may be thrown into new internal crisis following weakened Russian capacity to intervene. All the regional sovereignty disputes involving China would be structured into global geopolitical strife under the US Indo-Pacific Strategy. The West's economic decoupling will double down in certain key high-tech and IT sectors in the aftermath of the Russia-Ukraine War. Eliminating China from the critical value chain will be stepped up. These may differ from the original Cold War specifics, but both Cold Wars will share one fundamental feature: containment against identified adversaries such as China and Russia.

Hwang How do you envision future battlefields and what would be at the core of the wars?

You Because this is the first scaled European war fought by a top military power in the post-Cold War era, a nuanced analysis of the Russia-Ukraine War could shed new light on future warfare. First, this war proves that traditional warfare is not yet out of date. Russia was overly optimistic about its precision strike capabilities at the beginning of the war, and hoped to achieve a quick victory on this point. Thus, it did not concentrate enough manpower and firepower to overwhelm Ukraine's resistance. Combat-style special force operations worked for Russia in the past -- for example in Georgia -- but it could not be a general rule. Meaningful victory has to be won by battlefield engagement at the campaign level in scaled wars, based on at least 3-to-1 personnel and equipment superiority. Secondly, a war of attrition is still a basic way for victory, as elaborated by the late Chinese leader Mao Zedong's theses of people's war and protracted war. The US' military power was depleted from recent wars, and Russia is bleeding in a similar fashion -- especially as it fights the entire West which is standing behind Ukraine.

Hwang Is the Russia-Ukraine War a crisis or an opportunity for China?

You Yes or no, depending on how long the war lasts. In the short term, despite all the war's negative impacts on China, such as huge pressure on Beijing to condemn Russia and a sharp rise in energy prices, many Chinese commentators believe that the Russia-Ukraine War may have somewhat diverted America's obsessive focus on China. This may impact the US' Indo-Pacific initiative against China. If this is true, it is certainly a positive outcome for Beijing, no matter how temporary this diversion may be. With the entire Western world devoting a bulk of its leadership attention, material resources and military redeployment against Russia at the moment, Beijing may have somewhat obtained an enlarged breathing space for maneuvering in Asia. This would help it tackle more urgent challenges at home, such as the new COVID-19 outbreak in key Chinese cities and the unprecedented domestic pressure of economic slowdown. Even if the Russia-Ukraine War is not a replica of the US' war on terror in the early 2000s, which allowed for China to rise in its aftermath, it could still be an opportunity that should not be missed.

Hwang Aren't there any threating aspects for China?

You According to the Chairman of the US Joint Chiefs of Staff Mark A. Milly, Russia is the West's primary target, but China is its "pacing challenge," meaning that the US will not sideline China as a primary adversary. Chinese leaders are not really so naive that they believe the Russia-Ukraine War would substantially distract the US from the Indo-Pacific region. Washington has its own pace for implementing containment measures against China at each phase. When Russia is fundamentally crippled, the West will be better able to concentrate its power to deal with China in the next phase of East-West contention, which will make it harder for Beijing to manage its already adverse geopolitical environment.

Hwang What are the implications of the Russia-Ukraine War for the PLA and its military strategy?

You The implications of the war in Ukraine for the PLA are profound. Many new concept weapons and combat methods have been tried in this war with great effect. To the PLA, this may herald a new revolution of military affairs in conceptualizing future wars. For instance, future tank warfare may take a new form. Tank swarm combat may be partially replaced by contests between tanks and anti-tank missiles. The javelin is a very cost-effective weapon that was used to frustrate Russia's army offensive, as well as sting anti-aircraft missiles. Furthermore, the wide use of drones opens a new horizon in future warfare. The Ukraine military has extensively employed AeroVironment Switchblades for a variety of battlefield objectives, such as decapitation operations. The PLA has seriously studied these new developments, and sees them as game changers to the rules of combat engagement in future warfare.

Hwang Among several points, what do you expect the PLA to learn from the Russia-Ukraine War?

You Russia's employment of battalion-sized battle clusters is also what the PLA has emphasized in its army restructuring in the latest round of military reforms. Russia's defects in pursuing such tactics sounds an alarm to the PLA, which will likely reassess its combat methods in campaign warfare. After all, the use of battle clusters is different in an all-out war versus that in special force operations. Last but not least, battlefield transparency on the basis of advanced command, control, communications, intelligence, reconnaissance and surveillance and human intelligence are still the keys to final campaign success. The Russian military paid a heavy price in confronting the superior NATO chain of soft-kill capabilities, which is a profound lesson to the PLA.

Hwang It seems quite difficult to conclude the Russia-Ukraine War with any one side's complete victory. Some say the divided Korean Peninsula model is a solution. What do you think about this idea?

You "Complete victory" is out of the question for either side, as neither can achieve their desired political and military objectives. Also, they have endured devastating damage. But interestingly, both sides could claim victory on their own terms. As mentioned earlier, Putin could find a quick exit from the battlefield like what former Chinese leaders Mao Zedong and Deng Xiaoping did in 1962 and 1979, respectively. That is, if Putin is sensible enough not to allow US tactics of slowly but fatally crippling Russia to materialize. And then Ukraine could announce victory over the Russian invasion. Barring these two ends in the victory-defeat spectrum, there are other scenarios, some of which resemble the Korean reality of division. For instance, an armistice could be negotiated based on the map of current combat lines. Russia could claim the lands where it has expanded its presence, in the two "people's republics" of Donetsk and Luhansk and in some of Ukraine's richest areas with Russian-speaking populations. If this cease-fire could not be achieved, it is likely that Ukraine would sustain military pushback against Russian occupation. NATO will be firmly behind Kyiv. In such a case, the war will be long lasting. Then not only Russia but also Ukraine will bleed. Europe and the US will encourage Ukraine to fight on, and the whole world feel the consequences.

Hwang Then what are the military and strategic implications of the Russia-Ukraine War for the Kim Jongun regime in North Korea?

You From China's standpoint, the Kim Jongun regime shares many dilemmas that Beijing faces in observing the Russia-Ukraine War. North Korea maintains good relations with both Russia and Ukraine, although Russia is more helpful to Pyongyang. North Korea would have stayed neutral if the US were not in the equation. The nature of the issue is different when Russia is fighting the West alone for states identified by the US as "others," which is what Ukraine represents to the West. It is not too difficult to imagine that Kim Jongun's heart is more with Putin. Like China, North Korea would not want to see Russia fall, even though it cannot do much to help.

Hwang Logically speaking, what military lesson can Kim Jongun learn?

You Probably it must be the practical value of nuclear weapons, with which Russia withstands the more powerful West. This is especially the case since Russia's conventional weapons are qualitatively inferior to those of NATO. Putin's threats of using nuclear weapons in "critical moments" have worked, as seen from the US' determination to not directly engage Russian troops. This guarantees the Russian military an edge against Ukraine on a one-to-one basis. Now Kim Jongun may conclude, watching the unfolding of the Russia-Ukraine War, that if North and South Korea engaged in any military clash, he would face an integrated offensive by all US allies, including NATO member states. Denuclearization will therefore be further off his agenda, under the New Cold War order of irreversible two-camp confrontation.

Hwang What do you think are the implications of the Russia-Ukraine War that the new South Korean government should take into account for its foreign and defense policies?

You Beijing would be wary if South Korea's new government draws implications of the Russia-Ukraine War in a way that worsens China's security concerns. For instance, Seoul may become more vigorous in leveraging the blocs' confrontation, either propelled by the US or out of its own willingness. There is a logic for the new administration to do so in the sense that, as reflected by the Russia-Ukraine War, a powerful coalition is the best guarantee for deterring and defeating any foreign invasion. A sensible guess on Seoul's new foreign and strategic policies encompasses, among other things, practical entry into the Quadrilateral Security Dialogue Plus' activities; a shift towards improving relations with Japan; siding with US efforts against China more willingly; and so on.

Hwang In light of the Russia-Ukraine War, South Korea is expected to strengthen cooperation with its allies when it comes to policies toward North Korea. What are your thoughts?

You China will likely worry about Seoul's toughened North Korea policy, which would squeeze North Korea's strategic space through increased sanctions and joint war drills, while diminishing North-South contacts. What Russia has experienced is a step-by-step escalation of tension. The lesson of the Russia-Ukraine War is that although Russia has been severely sanctioned and its soldiers killed in large numbers, it is no comfort for Ukraine because the latter suffered a lot more in terms of human casualties and an economic loss of $600 billion. Many cities have been bombed back to the "Stone Age." Hopefully the conservative government in Seoul could strike a sensitive balance in supporting allied security and ensuring its own national interests. Despite all the current instabilities, peace on the Korean Peninsula deserves to be retained. Even with a negative stance toward the North, the new administration needs to recognize the fact that it has an unpredictable nuclear foe.

Japan's China Policy, between firmness and flexibility

Jul 4, 2022

Zhang Yong

Research Fellow, Institute of Japanese Studies at the Chinese Academy of Social Sciences

Mie Oba

Professor, Faculty of Law at Kanagawa University

Madoka Fukuda

Professor, Department of Global Politics at Hosei University

Since China has overtaken Japan in economy volume back in 2010, Japan's vigilance and checks against China have been rising on the surface and materialized. Mostly, two countries are having a wide gap regarding the issues surrounding East China Sea, South China Sea, and Taiwan Strait. The Ukrainian War re-emphasizes the importance of traditional Japanese geopolitics. In addition, the technology competition, which is the core of supply chain and future hegemony, intensifies Japan's foreign and security policy by strengthening its alliance with the US. As seen at Biden's attendance at QUAD Summit in Japan this May, Japan is generally observed to continue playing its role as the first pillar of US's Asian alliance and to stand at the forefront in containing China. However, Japanese diplomacy will not be unconditionally tough. Japan not only first conceived and contributed to developing the Indo-Pacific Strategy but also has the flexibility to replace the sensitive and misleading term 'Strategy' with 'Free and Open Indo-Pacific'.

Considering the international relations, economy, and security, China is never a country that Japan can be unconditionally hostile to. They are countries that cannot move away from each other and has to cooperate together. This week's discussion invites two experts from Japan and one from China to figure out Japan and China's complicated thoughts and realities. Here we have Research Fellow Zhang Yong from Institute of Japanese Studies in Chinese Academy of Social Sciences (CASS), Professor Mie Oba from Faculty of Law in Kanagawa University, and Professor Madoka Fukuda from Department of Global Politics in Hosei University.

Hwang How do you see Japan's diplomacy under Kishida administration?

Jang First of all, I can say Japan is maintaining Abe administration's diplomatic route even after Prime Minister Kishida came to the power. From Japan's point of view, the current international order is in a period of change that the 'rules-based international order' has undergone drastic changes and is facing serious challenges. Under this upheaval of international order, Japan continues to advocate stability, prosperity, and value, and actively supports the establishment of peace under US control, strengthening the dollar as the key currency, maintaining a free trade system under the General Agreement on Tariffs and Trade (GATT) and World Trade Organization (WTO), the expansion and ripple of the liberal democratic governance model, and the revitalization of the market economy. These international principles and norms of the international community have become the most basic principles pursued by Japanese diplomacy. In other words, I would like to say once again that Japanese diplomacy values "rules-based international order".

Hwang Please continue about Japan's diplomacy under rules-based international order.

Jang I would say there are three particular reasons why Japan chose the rule based diplomacy. The rule based diplomacy can avoid uncertainty in this period of changing international order, can compensate the weakening hard power, and on top of that, Japan has the will and capability to expand the rule based diplomacy. Specifically, Japan's rule based diplomacy is only partially mitigating the uncertainty, emphasizes partnership as the diplomacy that can explicitly respond to crises, and seeks to decide parties' behaviors through rules and clear provisions. In addition, Japan's rule based diplomacy is always related to consultations and discussions on multilateralism, and by spreading rules under the multilateralism, a "quasi-alignment" can be formed to deter common threats.

Hwang What efforts is Japan making for its rule based diplomacy?

Jang There can be two approaches that I can think of. The first is to expand the rules based through internal supports, primarily to enlarge the perspective of multilateral free trade and market economic factors. The second is to limit exclusive rules and to diversify bilateral issues through the liberal democratic governance model and the structure of

Hub and Spoke. This is evident on multilateral platforms such as QUAD and FOIP, and Japan continues its efforts to export and guide rules at the regional and global levels through these approaches.

Hwang What does President Biden's trip to East Asia mean to Japan?

Jang As imbalance is growing and an exclusive international order is being dominant in terms of security, President Biden's trip to East Asia would have been a great help to implement Japan's new rules based diplomacy. I see these US's summits with Korea and Japan were a process to meet respective countries' needs and behind it had its own national interests. In the end, the US, Korea, Japan, these three countries have found the biggest pledge through cooperation for their national interests, especially in the sense that Japan is trying to achieve the strategic purpose pursued by Japan with the support from the US.

Hwang What are the prospects for Korea-China-Japan cooperation?

Jang Korea, China, and Japan have achieved a lot through cooperation despite the heightened strategic competition between the US and China. I think that the current moment when the conflicts are intensified can be rather a very historic period for bilateral and trilateral diplomacy between Korea, China, and Japan, and it can be a very strategic time to strengthen the foundation for cooperation. In this respect, Korea, China, and Japan should look back on history and develop new strategies while looking forward to the future, and build trust in various fields through cooperation between the private and government in traditional and non-traditional security. On that basis, mutual respect is critically necessary, and we will have to use the wisdom by putting ourselves in others' shoes.

Hwang How is the economic relationship between China and Japan?

Fukuda Currently, Japan's dependence on China is quite high. According to Japan External Trade Organization (JETRO), despite the Corona pandemic, the decline in trade with China has been relatively small, with China accounting for the largest share of all Japanese trade in 2020. Also, Japan's tourism industry has been hit hard as the number of Chinese tourists has decreased due to the Corona pandemic. As witnessed, the need to maintain friendly relations with China from an economic point of view is very high, however, Japanese awareness of economic security is escalating. As shown in what happened during attracting Japan's TSMC plant, Taiwan and Taiwanese companies have become more important as we are trying to reduce the dependence on China since last year. Considering these situations, it can be interpreted that the pro-China and pro-Taiwan parties are compatibility standing apart, regardless from the politics and economics.

Hwang How do you expect the Kishida government's further policy toward China?

Fukuda I consider Kishida government aims to build 'a constructive and stable relationship' with China and to maintain its position to continue talks with China regarding the situation in Ukraine and security issues in East Asia. In addition, when it comes to the Taiwan issue, there is no particular action that goes beyond expressing an interest in the importance of peace and stability in the Taiwan Strait, which seems to be drawing a line from Abe's remarks. However, we still have to take a cautious look at how the different values and potential security confrontations between China and Japan will bring a significant impact on future China-Japanese relations, as the gaps have become apparent due to the situation in Ukraine.

Hwang What is the Japanese government's stance on Ukraine?

Fukuda As Russian invasion of Ukraine broke out in February this year, the Kishida regime, along with the US and NATO countries, imposed economic sanctions on Russia and implemented support for Ukraine. China basically supports Russia and considers the US is creating a confrontation. In the similar sense, there is a growing sense of crisis in Japan over the Taiwan Strait due to Russia's invasion of Ukraine. During the recent Japan-China online foreign ministerial meeting, the Kishida government has stepped up its call for China's responsible response and Beijing has expressed its wariness in the case if Japan's cooperation with the US violates China's national interests, including the Taiwan issue.

Hwang Then what could be Japan's stance on Taiwan?

Fukuda As the international political environment changes, the Abe administration was very active in seeking to improve relations with China during its second half, while its policy toward Taiwan was very restrained. Then, as the strategic competition between the US and China intensified, Japan's position in China-Japan relations has changed, and after the inauguration of the Kishida administration, Japan's policy toward China has shifted to make a more active policy on Taiwan. However, Japan's active involvement in Taiwan is a problem that must be analyzed through changes in the international environment or structural factors, which means that there is a limit to seeing it as a difference in the regimes. However, I think that Japan will take a more active approach toward Taiwan when military tensions continue to rise in the Taiwan Strait like how it is going today. But still, when it comes to the stability of the Taiwan Strait, Japan has maintained its official stance to engage through US-Japan alliance from the past, so I would like to express a very cautious stance on this.

Hwang What are your thoughts on the current Indo-Pacific Strategy?

Oba From the 2010s to today, strategic area we call the 'Indo-Pacific' have become increasingly important, and many countries are announcing their strategies for the Indo-Pacific from their respective positions. And the countries at the center of this flow are QUAD and we have made further progress amid the Corona pandemic. In addition to QUAD, in September 2021, there was an announcement that a new strategic framework called AUKUS by the

United States, the United Kingdom, and Australia would provide technology for building nuclear submarines to Australia. Then in 2019, ASEAN version of Indo-Pacific Strategy the 'ASEAN Indo-Pacific Outlook (AOIP)' was established. The United Kingdom, France, Germany, and the EU are also in ready to deepen their involvement in the region with their respective Indo-Pacific Strategies and policies.

Hwang What is the background and nature or character of the Indo-Pacific strategy?

Oba The establishment of this new strategic regional concept called the Indo-Pacific, and the direct impetus behind the various flows to strengthen ties in this strategic region, must be precisely attributed to growing concerns about China. The increasing need to respond to the growing uncertainty caused by the fluctuation of international and regional order is the essential reason why countries around the world are attempting to seek and strengthen their Indo-Pacific Strategy or their new links based on it.

Hwang How much weight do values and norms have in the Indo-Pacific Strategy?

Oba There certainly are confrontations between powers, but there also are conflicts between values. What the Free and Open Indo-Pacific(FOIP) and QUAD specifically emphasize are the universal values, which are the democracy, rule of law, freedom of navigation and aviation. These are related to the core interests of desirable political systems, values, norms, and national sovereignty. China, of course, strongly opposes the moves to increase pressure on China under these values. Moreover, due to the influence from the Russia-Ukraine war, which is continued since February till today, the advanced countries and other countries around the world are taking strong measures such as economic sanctions against Russia. Meanwhile, as China is attempting to defend Russia, advanced countries are raising their voices on criticizing China as well as some are pointing out the 'friendliness' of China-Russia's political system. Summing up, the confrontation of values is drawing more attention than before.

Hwang How would you evaluate the cohesion of QUAD countries?

Oba Above all, it is the fact that globalization of the economy must be dealt when we discuss. However, even on top of that, four QUAD countries that have agreed to promote FOIP are all having various point of views, including their respective approaches toward the relationship with China. There is a tendency to pursue a stable relationship and refrain from excessive provocations, and for Australia, economic relations with China are significant for the stability and prosperity of its own economy.

Hwang I would like to ask you other countries' stances, besides QUAD, toward Indo-Pacific.

Oba ASEAN's AOIP highlights inclusiveness, including not only the United States, Japan, Australia, India, but also China and even Russia, and it particularly draws a line with the

US-led FOIP in terms of containing China. France's India-Pacific Strategy has a quite clear tendency to contain China, but Germany's India-Pacific policy focuses on maintaining a balance by strengthening relations with other Asian countries as well as China, since it has been tightening its relations with China so far. The United Kingdom, which also participates in AUKUS, shares a consensus on the way it faces China with the United States and Australia to some extent, however, as it is geographically located far from the Indo-Pacific, we can say it is understandable to take an ambiguous stance against China.

Hwang What are the prospects for the Indo-Pacific Strategy?

Oba While respective countries' directions of policies and the desirable order are not necessarily consistent, QUAD and other links are striving to strengthen the solidarity. The US will advocate IPEF and I expect Japan, Korea, Australia, Singapore, and Thailand will participate accordingly. Changes in the regional order caused by changes in the balance of power between the US and China lead to the formation of a strategic region called the Indo-Pacific, where new cooperation is sought and strengthened. What kind of cooperation will be achieved through this process and cooperation between the countries will eventually affect the further shape of the Indo-Pacific regional order.

Hwang The underlying competition between the US and China is unlikely to be resolved.

Fukuda It is impossible for Japan to be equidistant between the US and China, and it is clear that the US alliance will be more important and Japan's options will be limited as the Biden administration is willing to confront China with its allies. In other words, Japan is expected to ultimately choose to increase its deterrence against China in line with the US and like-minded countries, and will emphasize the importance of "peace and stability of the Taiwan Strait" if necessary, and may further promote cooperation with Taiwan.

Chinese thoughts on Belt and Road Initiative, its shine and shade

Jan 30, 2022

Qian Feng

Director, Research Department at the National Strategy Institute at Tsinghua University

Huang Yunsong

Associate Dean, School of International Studies at Sichuan University

Lin Minwang

Professor and Assistant Dean, Institute of International Studies at Fudan University

The Belt and Road Initiative (BRI), formerly known as One Belt One Road, was first initiated as Chinese President Xi Jinping presented "One Belt" in Kazakhstan in September 2013 and "One Road" in Indonesia the following October. One Belt represents the Silk Road Economic Belt that connects all the way from Central Asia to Europe through an overland route, while One Road stands for the Maritime Silk Road that stretches its branches to Southeast Asia and beyond.

It has already been almost a decade since BRI was presented and now has become incomparably the strongest diplomatic mechanism in China's diplomacy, and a major national and international project. On the other hand, it is Xi's most representative brand. Ever since he came to power, the

New Type of International Relations was running at the front line of his foreign policy slogan and BRI was a practical measure that backed it up. It is not only massive in scale, but also supports and cooperates a lot with numerous neighboring countries.

However, its approach to cooperation has room for improvement and has perhaps lacked skill, leading to mistakes and causes problems. The BRI is basically showing two faces, both the bright and dark aspects of China's thoughts and actions on foreign exchanges. Continuing the discussion to comprehensively understand China's ideas, this interview invited three Chinese experts who are conducting research on BRI.

We have Qian Feng, the research department director at the National Strategy Institute, Tsinghua University, who also is a senior research fellow of Taihe Institute and a member of the China-South Korea Future Relations Development Committee; Huang Yunsong, the associate dean of Sichuan University School of International Studies, as well as the coordinator at China Center for South Asian Studies; and Lin Minwang, professor and assistant dean of the Institute of International Studies at Fudan University.

Hwang What is the most remarkable outcome of the BRI?

Qian In the past nine years since the BRI, I think the biggest achievement is not at the material level, but at the spiritual level of people-to-people connectivity. From the international perspective, it has expanded China's circle of friends and increased the communication between the world and China. From the domestic perspective, this is not only China's new round of reform and opening up, but also deepens the pattern of all-round opening up. The BRI has expanded the vision of the 1.4 billion Chinese people, made the Chinese people more aware that to achieve better development, China must embrace the world with a more inclusive and open mind.

Huang Professor Qian mentioned the way China engages with the world. It enhances China's position and role in the international community, especially among the developing countries, and fulfills China's responsibilities as a major global power. As a participant and facilitator of global economic and social development, China has been widely recognized and accepted by the international community.

Hwang What would be the most successful case of cooperation in the BRI?

Huang The China-Europe freight trains under the flag of BRI through Central Asia, as well as the infrastructure and industrial cooperation in South Asia have achieved breathtaking results so far. However, ASEAN may be the most successful region for the BRI in the long run. Among them, the most outstanding is the China-Laos railway that is destined to promote bilateral trade, people-to-people exchanges, and ultimately the comprehensive integration between China and ASEAN.

Qian In this case, Nepal previously imported more than half of its electricity from India during peak power demand. But now with the completion of the Upper Tamakoshi Hydropower Project, Nepal has not only historically solved the chronic problem of power shortage, but also realized the "transformation" from power importer to exporter, starting to sell hydropower to India -- the former largest aid country.

Hwang From China's perspective, what is the toughest challenge against the BRI? And what is the most critical problem within the BRI itself?

Huang Using ideology as a boundary, the US has divided the world into the democratic and nondemocratic camps, effectively compromising cooperation between China and the West under the framework of the BRI. Due to the intensified competition between China and the US, a considerable amount of resources have been diverted to the field of defense and security, resulting in the reduction of financial sources for the BRI.

Lin Many major powers view the BRI from the perspective of strategic competition, which has led to a high degree of politicization of this cooperative initiative. However, due to geopolitical considerations, many countries did not support it, but proposed the opposite initiative to undermine it.

Hwang How do you assess the criticism on "debt trap diplomacy"?

Qian That kind of accusation is not a new topic in recent years. Under the manipulation of public opinion in US and other countries, the … "debt trap theory" was quickly constructed and became the basis for open slandering and smearing China. In fact, these claims are highly politicized and completely untenable. Take Sri Lanka for example.

In terms of total foreign debt, 54 percent of Sri Lankan external loans come from international capital markets and only 9 percent of loans are from China. According to Sri Lanka's central bank, loans from China's share of total Sri Lankan sovereign debt is currently about 3 percent, with bilateral loans far lower than Japan and less than India.

Huang Its fundamental motive is to curb China's international influence and stigmatize its economic, trade and investment cooperation with the developing countries.

Hwang How do you see or imagine the BRI in maybe two to three decades?

Qian China has now signed more than 200 cooperation documents on jointly building the BRI with 145 countries and 32 international organizations. Following this trend, it is conceivable that BRI will achieve more and more results across a wider coverage in 2050.

Huang By 2050, it may not be odd to see that China and the US finally let go of the burden of great power competition and reach an understanding on various issues including the BRI.

Lin There is no deadline for cooperation under the BRI. By 20 to 30 years later, the connectivity between China and neighboring countries will be greatly improved, and will truly realize the "same breath and common destiny," and the economic and cultural ties will be very close.

Hwang How much does the BRI contribute to China's grand strategy?

Huang China's grand strategy is to realize the great rejuvenation of the nation, instead of becoming a global hegemon like the US. The BRI will only allow China to more deeply integrate into the international community in terms of economic and social development. This may cause the US and the other Western countries to engage in more intense geopolitical struggles against China. In this sense, the BRI is a double-edged sword that enhances China's capability to realize its grand strategy and exacerbates the confrontation between China and the West in the next few decades.

Qian To add to that, the fundamental purpose of China's diplomacy is to safeguard China's sovereignty, security and development interests, creating a more favorable international environment for its rise.

Lin China does not consider the BRI to be its grand strategy, but due to China's economic influence and its size, the initiative must have certain geopolitical implications.

Hwang Do you think B3W (Build Back Better World), suggested by the US, could be the US and its allies' version of the BRI?

Lin The geopolitical intentions of B3W are obvious, once again showing that the US plays a negative role in promoting regional economic development. If the US really wants to promote regional economic development, it should join various initiatives for regional economic development and provide more substantive infrastructure projects instead of empty appeals.

Huang If B3W can meet the needs of developing countries in terms of infrastructure, industry, technology and finance, then it should be welcomed and supported by the international community. However, if it is only for the purpose of geopolitical and great power games, which forces the developing countries to take sides between China and the US, it is difficult to imagine a sustained, far-reaching and substantial impact of B3W.

Qian B3W can exist together with the BRI, to make a greater contribution to the world. However, B3W is an ideological plan, marking the so-called "democratic" and "nondemocratic," excluding the BRI. There are many beautiful slogans now, but Washington has shown a reluctance to invest in real money. And its domestic political split will also bring a series of obstacles to realize the B3W.

Hwang How do you foresee the cooperation between Korea and China in terms of the BRI?

Qian China and Korea will mark the 30th anniversary of the establishment of diplomatic ties this year. The BRI and "New North" and "New South" policies have practical conditions to connect. In particular, the concept and vision, promotion path, regional scope, cooperation areas and content are highly consistent. If successful docking is achieved, it will become a new opportunity and platform for China-ROK cooperation.

Lin I am very optimistic about the cooperation between China and South Korea under the BRI. South Korea has maintained its own strategic autonomy in diplomacy. At the same time, the cultural and geographical ties between China and South Korea have no reason not to promote the continuous deepening of economic cooperation between the two sides.

Hwang Would a BRI cooperation that includes North Korea be possible?

Huang For a long time to come, the DPRK's primary concern will still be sovereign and political security. The space for cooperation between the DPRK and China in the fields of economy, trade, industry, and infrastructure needs to be further explored. The cooperation between China and the DPRK on the BRI may only be a matter of time and conditions.

Qian As North Korea's largest neighbor, the door is always open to it. Looking ahead, everything is possible. China has no reason to refuse it.

When we look back at one particular country's economic cooperation with its neighbors, BRI is obviously incomparable in scale in terms of financial, physical, and policy aspects. Moreover, it is a fact that the BRI has had massive results. During the interview, the three Chinese experts generally were proud of what the BRI has cultivated so far, and had positive expectations of BRI's future. Regarding the challenges that BRI is facing, they mostly acknowledged them as errors that could happen in the process, while emphasizing the bright side and being quite passive and cautious in mentioning the shade.

Nevertheless, we cannot purely accept BRI as a simple economic project. If "China First" dominates BRI, if Indo-Pacific countries actively respond to BRI, it might be difficult to be too optimistic about the future. The experts in the interview were discreet in reading BRI's security and military aspects, but checks against China are coming from the US, US allies or friendly countries, as well as from some countries that are cooperating in BRI but are unsatisfied.

These are critical matters for BRI's further expansion. Korea has so far expressed its interest in Korea-China BRI cooperation, however, it cannot take practical steps forward since inter-Korean relations have not made big progress. Furthermore, although Korea is geographically and culturally close to China, there is a systemic gap between the two countries and Korea is geopolitically, geo-strategically, and geo-economically exposed to a dilemma between BRI and a "free and open Indo-Pacific" amid the rising tension between the US and China. In the end, the improvement of conditions on the Korean Peninsula will be the biggest facilitator of Korea's entrance to the BRI.

Is a new monetary world emerging?

Mar 16, 2022

Benjamin J. Cohen

Professor Emeritus, Department of Political Science at the University of California, Santa Barbara

Chey Hyoungkyu

Associate Professor, International Political Economy at the National Graduate Institute for Policy Studies in Tokyo

The US dollar has been at the center of the global monetary system for more than seven decades since the end of World War II. The dollar-dominated international monetary system has shaped the postwar world political economy by significantly contributing to US power, both economically and politically, as well as lubricating the wheels of the global economy. However, in recent years there have been some notable growing developments that might shake the dollar's global supremacy.

China has been endeavoring to promote the international use of its own currency, the renminbi, since the outbreak of the global financial crisis of 2008. Cryptocurrencies such as Bitcoin have also grown considerably, with their aggregate market capitalization reaching almost $3 trillion last November, a staggering jump from a mere $14 billion five years ago. The growth of stablecoins is likewise remarkable, as shown by the rise of Tether's market capitalization from around $4 billion in January 2020 to $80 billion this month.

Meanwhile, the majority of central banks are currently exploring central bank digital currencies, with China at the forefront among major economies, already piloting a digital renminbi with a large population. Will these new monetary developments challenge the current dollar-led global monetary order and transform the monetary map of the world? This is undoubtedly one of the most salient questions for the future of the global political economy, given that such developments could affect the state's capacity to manage its economy, the operation of the world economy and the distribution of power in the globe.

Two experts joined a discussion on if a new monetary world is emerging. First is Benjamin J. Cohen, a distinguished professor emeritus at the University of California, Santa Barbara. He is a prominent specialist in the political economy of international money and finance, and also is the author of 18 books, including most recently "Currency Statecraft: Monetary Rivalry and Geopolitical Ambition" (2019) and "Rethinking International Political Economy" (2022).

Chey Hyoungkyu is an associate professor of international political economy at the National Graduate Institute for Policy Studies in Tokyo. Prior to joining the institute, he worked as an economist in the Economic Research Institute at the Bank of Korea. His new book "The International Political Economy of the Renminbi" was published by Routledge last November.

Hwang Do you think that the current dollar-centered global monetary system will face significant challenges in the coming years?

Cohen There will no doubt be challenges. The question is: How significant will they be? The US dollar's central role was formalized in the Bretton Woods agreement of 1944. But almost immediately the greenback came under pressure, as US liabilities grew to exceed the supply of gold stored away in Fort Knox. The demise of the dollar-based system has been predicted ever since. Two challenges stand out. Some observers anticipate the rise of powerful alternatives to America's currency, such as the euro or the renminbi. Every international money in history has ultimately met its match and gone into decline. Why not the greenback, too? Others point to America's persistently growing debt, which jeopardizes US financial credibility. Once the world's largest creditor nation, the United States now is history's greatest debtor. Sooner or later, many fear, this massive "overhang" of debt could shake the market's faith in the dollar.

Chey There are certainly challenges to the dollar emerging. They include both internal challenges, such as the recently growing inflationary pressures in the United States, and external ones like the efforts of some states including China and Russia to build nondollar international payment systems.

That being said, I think that overall the greenback's global supremacy is likely to remain solid for quite a while, given the many critical incomparable advantages over other currencies that it holds, including the depth and liquidity of the US Treasury market and the US supremacy in military power, a very important ultimate source of confidence in the dollar. In short, there is at this moment no visible strong currency to rival the dollar.

Hwang How do you assess the internationalization of the Chinese renminbi over the past years?

Cohen The renminbi (RMB) has not lived up to expectations; nor do I expect it to do any better in the years to come. Fifteen or so years ago, when the RMB first emerged on the world stage, a bright future for it was predicted by many. China was on its way to become the largest economy in the world, as well as No. 1 in trade. So why shouldn't the RMB surpass the dollar as well?

Yet in actual practice China's currency has made little headway, accounting for less than 3 percent of turnover in the foreign-exchange market (against 45 percent for the dollar) and no more than 4 percent of global monetary reserves (against 60 percent for the dollar). The biggest problem is China's Great Wall of capital controls, which discourage foreign investors and central banks alike. So long as Beijing resists opening its financial markets, the appeal of the RMB will be limited.

Chey Despite the considerable efforts by Beijing to promote renminbi internationalization, its actual progress does not match many early rosy forecasts for it. Since reaching a peak in mid-2015, the renminbi's internationalization has retreated somewhat and remains largely stagnant.

That being said, there are some noteworthy signs that have positive implications for it. The renminbi's global share as a reserve currency has continued to grow until now, albeit gradually. Moreover, its use as a global payment currency has begun to rebound since late last year, and it has overtaken the Japanese yen again. The saga of renminbi internationalization is still ongoing.

Hwang Do you think that the introduction of a digital renminbi will lead to a significant increase in the renminbi's international use?

Chey Beijing is exploring how a digital renminbi can be used for cross-border payments, working with Hong Kong, Thailand and the United Arab Emirates on a project to build a multiple central bank digital currency platform for international payments. In this regard, one key issue is achieving technical interoperability across central bank digital currencies. It should also be noted, meanwhile, that a digital renminbi is essentially still the renminbi. Therefore, even if the technical hurdles to its international use are fully overcome, the currency's internationalization may still not increase significantly without resolution of the renminbi's major disadvantages as an international currency, including the limited capital account convertibility in China, the underdevelopment of the Chinese financial markets and the nation's authoritarian political regime.

Cohen The answer will depend on what other governments do. Other things remaining the same, a digital RMB would enhance the appeal of China's currency for payments and other purposes. International use of the RMB would certainly be encouraged. But other things are unlikely to remain the same.

Digitalization will surely be pursued by other monetary authorities as well -- most notably, by major actors like the Federal Reserve and European Central Bank -- largely neutralizing any advantage the RMB might have as a first-mover. And of course there will also be many privately issued digital currencies out there adding even more to the competition. In this context, China's renminbi will not enjoy any special advantage.

Hwang Will the launch of a digital renminbi pose a substantial threat to the United States or the dollar?

Cohen My answer here is much the same as my answer to your previous question. Digitalization is attractive to market actors because it offers the promise of anonymity as well as fast and efficient settlement of transactions. In effect, it represents an updated, modern equivalent of cash. In the absence of any reciprocal initiative by the Federal Reserve, a digital RMB could indeed pose a significant competitive threat to the dollar.

But as I suggested, I do not expect Washington to sit quietly on its hands. Quite the opposite, in fact. The Fed recently issued a research paper outlining the advantages and disadvantages of digitalization -- the first step toward a digital dollar, which I am sure will come into force in the next few years. A principal motivation will be to ensure that any early advantage enjoyed by a digitalized RMB will be temporary at best.

Chey Since the mere digitization of the renminbi will not necessarily lead to substantial growth in its internationalization, the digital renminbi will not necessarily threaten the dollar's global supremacy either. However, if it helps China to construct an international renminbi payment system, especially with countries burdened by US financial sanctions such as Russia and North Korea, it could be utilized as a conduit enabling them to circumvent those sanctions, and accordingly undermine Washington's capacity to achieve its foreign policy goals. But this impact will be limited given the US implementation of "secondary sanctions" also, as long as the dollar retains its status as the dominant international currency.

Hwang Do you think the international standing of the euro can ascend further in the future?

Chey The euro area has traditionally maintained a neutral stance toward the euro's internationalization. Recently, however, European discontent with the dollar's dominance has grown, due largely to the Trump administration's "America First" policy and its imposition of "secondary sanctions," which have coerced European firms to comply with the US primary sanctions.

As a result, the eurozone does now have the will to promote the euro's international roles. But the euro's chief weaknesses, such as the absence of a central political authority in the eurozone and the fragmentation of the euro capital market, remain largely unchanged. They will likely hinder any substantial further internationalization of the common currency.

Cohen Today, the euro stands as the world's second-most-important international currency, but is still far behind the dollar. It is best understood as a regional money, used mainly by countries in Europe and parts of Africa but not much beyond.

Many Europeans would like to see the currency rise in standing. But that is unlikely to happen for two reasons. First, the center of gravity of the world economy is shifting to Asia, where the euro is less useful. And second, the appeal of the currency -- particularly as an investment medium or reserve asset -- will remain limited so long as there is no genuine fiscal and banking unification among the euro zone's 19 sovereign members. The monetary union offers nothing so attractive as the vast market for US Treasury obligations and other dollar-denominated claims.

Hwang Do you see more promise or peril from Bitcoin and other cryptocurrencies?

Cohen Cryptocurrencies offer both promise and peril. On the positive side, as I have said, they offer the promise of anonymity as well as the possibility of speedy and efficient settlement of transactions. Through so-called "blockchain technology," market actors have access to decentralized payments systems that are independent of both governments and private banks. But there are also three major dangers.

First, competition among cybercurrencies could lead to greater risk-taking by their sponsors, leading to the modern equivalent of old-fashioned "bank runs." Second, as Bitcoin demonstrates, there is a risk of unrestrained price volatility, limiting the usefulness of cybercurrencies as a medium of exchange. And third, there is the possibility of a real threat to state authority in monetary affairs, threatening macroeconomic instability.

Chey The blockchain technology underlying cryptocurrencies appears to benefit global finance in various ways. The benefits of cryptocurrencies themselves are more questionable, however. Despite their spectacular growth in popularity as virtual assets, the use of cryptocurrencies as money is still extremely marginal, owing largely to the roller-coaster volatility in their prices, which hinders the establishment of confidence in them. Moreover, in the case of Bitcoin, the so-called "king crypto," transaction fees have risen significantly, weakening its advantage as a means of cross-border payments or overseas remittances. At present the use of cryptocurrencies appears to be limited largely to transactions in them as speculative assets, or for illicit financial activities. This may not be the world that crypto enthusiasts have envisioned.

Hwang Do you think that the use of cryptocurrencies will grow significantly?

Cohen Yes, I do. Demand for cryptocurrencies is bound to grow precisely because of the advantages offered -- anonymity and the possibility of lower-cost payments networks. In response, cryptocurrencies are multiplying like rabbits. My feeling is that for now we are in the equivalent of a "bubble" -- a frenzy of experimentation and risk-taking -- that is going to end badly for many. In reality, cryptocurrencies have come to serve primarily as a vehicle for risk-loving investors. But eventually, with consolidation and the introduction of proper public supervision, the market for cryptocurrencies is likely to settle down just as similar eruptions of financial innovation have done in the past. There is no reason why privately issued cryptocurrencies cannot function efficiently alongside central bank digital currencies, just as Mastercard and Visa credit cards function alongside cash today.

Chey The wild fluctuation in cryptocurrencies' prices is attributable primarily to one of their core attributes: the absence of a central authority that manages and protects their values. Therefore, the feasibility of cryptocurrencies ascending as major money is not likely to be high. It is of course true that mainstream investors have recently begun to include crypto in their portfolios, and a growing number of major financial institutions offer crypto-related financial services. And these developments may heighten their use as assets. But, unlike other assets, cryptocurrencies have no intrinsic value at all. There may thus be a possibility of their markets collapsing when a big shock occurs.

Hwang How about stablecoins? Will their use grow? How will they affect the global monetary system?

Cohen Stablecoins are simply one species of cryptocurrency. The earliest cryptocurrencies -- beginning with Bitcoin, the granddaddy of all cryptocurrencies -- were backed by little more than flimsy promises. Trust was supposed to be cultivated by delegating verification to a public consensus mechanism managed through a peer-to-peer network that alerts participants to every transaction in real time.

For some, that was not enough. Thus stablecoins like Tether or USD Coin were introduced, intended to reinforce trust by promising full backing with conventional reserves. Unfortunately many stablecoins are quite lacking in transparency, increasing their risk and so limiting their appeal. That is why I suggest the need for proper public supervision, to assure that backing will indeed be adequate.

Chey In contrast to traditional cryptocurrencies such as Bitcoin, the values of stablecoins are pegged to other assets, such as the dollar, and are accordingly supposed to be "stable." This is a great allure of stablecoins, and they have in fact grown remarkably during the pandemic, in terms of both market capitalization and trading volume.

However, their actual redeemabilities have been called into question, as shown in the case of Tether, the largest stablecoin, which overstated its reserves. They can also face liquidity problems. Therefore, stablecoins carry with them significant potential risks to financial stability.

Hwang Besides China, a large number of other countries are also considering introducing central bank digital currencies. How do you think they will affect the global financial system?

Chey Central bank digital currencies will likely become public digital money having more safety, more resilience and greater availability than cryptocurrencies, which are private digital money. They have strong potential to enhance financial inclusion, to make possible more efficient financial services, and to strengthen their governments' capacities to manage the economy. They may open a new chapter in the history of money.

However, it is also true that CBDCs involve notable latent risks, including the possibilities of their becoming "panopticons" to monitor and control citizens. How to balance the pros and cons of central bank digital currencies must therefore be carefully considered.

Cohen As I suggested earlier, I fully expect that many monetary authorities will pursue digitalization. Those central banks that do introduce their own version of a cryptocurrency will enjoy an advantage relative to those who lag behind. Being backed by the "full faith and credit" of their sovereign governments, they will also enjoy an advantage relative to privately issued cryptocurrencies.

My guess is that eventually most if not all central banks will join the game, if only to defend their own currencies against encroachments by others. In turn, a network of central bank digital currencies will provide the infrastructure for a global payments system that could be much cheaper and swifter than anything we have seen until now

Hwang There are voices saying that the United States should issue a digital dollar to defend the dollar's global status. Do you agree?

Cohen Yes, I most certainly agree. As I have already noted, the dollar faces serious challenges – not least, the possible rise of powerful alternatives. The threat to the greenback will grow to the extent that other major central banks succeed in introducing a genuinely attractive digital currency.

If the greenback's long dominance of the global system is to be sustained, Washington will have no choice but to counter with a digital version of its own beloved greenback. Otherwise, decline beckons. If monetary history teaches us anything, it is that international currencies like the dollar may flourish for a long time. But they do not last forever.

Chey The US decision on whether to issue a digital dollar will obviously depend upon whether Washington assesses this to be in its own interests. While neither cryptocurrencies nor a digital renminbi are likely to challenge dollar supremacy immediately, they could cause some crack in the current dollar-centered international financial system, by facilitating the creation of nondollar international payment networks for some countries as I mentioned earlier. It seems that concerns about such geopolitical and financial risks have grown in Washington recently, as shown by President Biden's March 9 executive order that includes strong support for exploring the idea of a digital dollar.

What makes China so committed to winning the international technical standards battle?

Aug 13, 2022

Lee Heejin

Professor, Graduate School of International Studies at Yonsei University

Ping Gao

Senior Lecturer, Global Development Institute at University of Manchester

The international economy and industrial world are entering a revolution. The competition between nations and between corporations is escalating over industrial and technological competitiveness, and technological hegemony has emerged as the determinant factor in reorganizing the international order and maintaining the world great power's status.

The United States is continuing its strong stance on China policy, even after the Biden administration took over, and China is also setting up its technology independence strategy. Under the flow, the technical standard to secure the nation's industrial competitiveness for the future is becoming more essential. In that sense, the world of international standards is going through a silent war. In the second half of 2022, the International Telecommunication Union (ITU) and ISO (International Organization for Standardization) are holding elections for their leaders.

The US and Russia are fielding candidates to head the ITU, while candidates from Korea and China are competing for leadership of the ISO. These upcoming elections are critical in the sense that they are part of a process where the US-China competition over the technological hegemony continues, and as an influential effect on the further drifts. What is the fundamental reason that these international standard institutes' elections are drawing attentions from the entire industrial world, international strategies and diplomacy, and geopolitical experts? What opportunities and meanings would it bring for Korea? This week's discussion invites two experts from Korea and China to seek for the answers. We have professor Heejin Lee from the Graduate School of International Studies in Yonsei University, who is also the director of the Center for Converging Industries and Standardization in the same university. We also have Ping Gao, a senior lecturer at the University of Manchester's Global Development Institute. He specializes in information technology innovation and development policy, especially in China.

Hwang What exactly are the technical standards and the international standards? Please give us more details.

Lee Rather than giving a definition, some examples will be helpful to intuitively understand what they are and their functions. Let's think of electric plugs and USBs. The former is an example of an unstandardized item; the latter shows the value of standardization. Whenever you pack for overseas travel, you may have at least once imagined how convenient it would be if we could have a global standard for electric plugs. That's what we see in USB. In the past, there were so many different shapes of plugs to connect different computing devices such as PCs and printers. Now we can enjoy the convenience of globally standardized

USB. We also imagine that the company that developed the USB technology dominates the market where the standard is widely and inevitably used by users, and can control the development path of related technologies in its own favor. In short, technical standards provide interoperability, and most of all, reduce costs, particularly in trade. They can also influence the trajectory of future technologies to the technology owner's advantage.

Gao From the viewpoint of standardization scholars and practitioners, a standard for a technology system defines its overall technical architecture and specifies interfaces among its components and subsystems. A technical standard provides a legitimate choice for the market. An international standard refers to a standard accredited and published normally by SDOs (standards development organizations) such as ISO, ITU, and IEC (International Electrotechnical Commission). It is used in international markets. The role and characteristics of standards are recognized by Chinese state leaders. President Xi Jinping underlined "standards have become the common language of the world." So developing and owning an international standard means that your language is used across the world.

Hwang What could be China's thoughts underneath its active involvement in international standardization organizations?

Lee China has been successful in becoming a world factory. It was achieved by being integrated into the global supply chain. Chinese firms learned "standardized" modules designed by global firms and made products accordingly. They found out that this way they ended up in a so-called "technology trap." Once they pay license fees for intellectual properties, the margin is too thin. Behind standards often embedded are patents, called SEPs (standards-essential patents). Once you become a standardized module producer of the global supply chain, you are locked in and can only earn razor-thin margins. One of the ways to get out of the trap is to develop (your own) standards along with intellectual properties. For this reason, China has been actively participating in international standardization activities since early the 21st century. The core of the idea is concisely expressed in a maxim often mentioned within China's policy and business circles: "The third class firms make products; the second develop technology; the first set rules, that is, standards."

Ping Gao, senior lecturer in the Global Development Institute, the University of Manchester, specializing in information technology innovation and development policy, especially in China.

Ping Gao, senior lecturer in the Global Development Institute, the University of Manchester, specializing in information technology innovation and development policy, especially in China.

Gao The owners of a standard have an advantage over others when competing in the market. Standards and their adoption contribute to economic growth and promote trade. China is well aware of the economic importance of international standards. Given the size of its domestic market and the advancement of its technological capability, China is in a position to challenge the international standardization landscape. China will increasingly seek to shape international standards that serve its own interests, and work hard to bring its indigenous standards to the international market. As a part of this strategy, China is active in becoming the organizers and publishers of international standards. China's position on standards and international standardization is reflected by the address of President Xi Jinping to the 39th ISO General Assembly in Beijing in 2016 September: in a globalization context, international standards are the technical foundation of the development of the global governance system and economic and trade cooperation. International standardization plays a fundamental role in facilitating business transactions, supporting industrial development, and regulating social governance. He described China's strategy of international standardization as to promote innovative, coordinated, green, open and sharing development with the support of standards.

Hwang Could you explain more about the development of China's national standardization policy?

Gao China's standardization policy has three stages: the follow-up stage (1978-2000), the catch-up stage (2001-2014) and the upgrading stage (2014 forward). In the following stage when China had limited R&D funds and relied on foreign technologies in economic development, the government controlled the adoption and standardization of foreign technologies. The catch-up stage started after China acquired a certain level of technological capability, which allowed the government to support the development of indigenous standards owning independent IPRs (Intellectual property rights). Through the catch-up stage, China gained substantial technological capability and entered the upgrading stage, when China focused on international standardization. In the whole process the Chinese government continued offering policy support, but tended to relax its control over standardization and rely on the market in standardization.

Hwang How high have Chinese standards reached so far?

Gao For a long time, international standardization has been dominated by a few industrialized countries. However, this situation cannot (continue indefinitely), and China cannot always be an adopter of foreign technologies and standards. In recent years, China has emerged as a leader in key ICT such as 5G mobile communications systems. While the US and the EU remain the driving force for international standardization, China has begun to challenge the situation, especially in the field of ICT. As Tian Shihong, director of the National Standardization Administration of China (SAC) said: China has created brilliant achievements in international standardization. China has adopted more than 10,000 international standards, and is also actively submitting proposals for international standards to ISO and IEC – the number of proposals has grown 20 percent every year.

Lee Not just taking the leadership positions of SDOs like ITU, IEC and ISO, the number of technical committees (TCs) chaired by Chinese experts is increasing a lot. TCs are the front line where standards are actually made in each industry or technology within those SDOs. The number of submissions by Chinese firms and experts has also rocketed over the last decade. There are different views on Chinese standards. One says that despite the high numbers of Chinese participants in international standardization venues and of those submissions made by them, the quality is low. As they are funded by the government and evaluated by quantitative measures, they just submit as many proposals as possible. The other argues that it is a process of learning, and that some of the standards proposed by Chinese firms/experts reach high quality. 5G is a good example. After almost 20 years' efforts in ICT standardization, China made an achievement at last by overtaking the US. in mobile communication technologies. China's lead in 5G is attributed to leading 5G standardization; about one third of SEPs are held by Chinese firms like Huawei. China's lead in 5G standardization alerted the US and other countries. Unless something is done, it might be repeated in other emerging technologies.

Hwang What's the link between China's rise and international standardization? In other words, what's the role of standardization for China's rise as a global power?

Lee For China, technical standards are not just a tool of competitive advantage in industrial and economic levels, but a strategic vehicle for setting a new geopolitical order. China aims to become a rule maker, not just following rules made by others. In the Belt & Road Initiative, standardization is a key pillar. China tries to promote Chinese standards in the countries along the road. Due to the power of standards, they will be able to lock-in the economies once they adopt Chinese standards. The famous project called "China Standards 2035" -- though its report is not published -- reveals a clue of China's vision for standardization. It is a sequel to "Made in China 2025." While the 2025 pursues dominance in the production of goods, the 2035 aims to control the rules of production and trade systems. Reportedly it envisages a national strategy to set standards in emerging technologies. China aims to become the designer of the whole system that makes governing rules for technologies, not just a module participant.

Gao According to Tim Ruehlig at the German Council on Foreign Relations, technical standardization is a crucial arena of rivalry between China and the US, China's ability to shape technical standardization is increasing, and technical standardization carries influence in terms of economics, legal, political, and discursive implications. I share these opinions with him. To understand how China uses standards to support pursuing its economic and political ambition in globalization, we can see China's international standardization strategy in its Belt and Road Initiative (BRI). China released the "Action Plan on Belt and Road Standard Connectivity (2015-2017)," which is updated and extended by the "Action Plan on Jointly Establishing

Belt and Road Standard Connectivity (2018-2020)." The objective is to support the construction of interconnection and interoperability in relevant countries, internationalize China's domestic technical standards, improve the "going out" of Chinese standards, promote the joint formulation of international standards, and enhance the international influence of Chinese standards.

Hwang I wonder how the other countries are responding to China's active engagement in international standardization?

Lee To begin with the US, it considers China's active approach to international standardization as a threat to the international order. They say that China is "dominating" international SDOs. Among the three biggest international SDOs, the heads of ITU and IEC are Chinese. China has applied for the president of a third SDO, that is, ISO, where a Korean candidate is also competing. An increasing number of TCs, where standards are actually made by experts typically representing their country, are managed and chaired by Chinese conveners. They may influence one way and another the processes and outcomes of standardization. If the dominance is left unattended, standards and global rules are made by China. The US "securitizes" technical standards, particularly in digital technologies; China's dominance in the international standardization regime which has been traditionally ruled by the Western bloc is a threat to national economic security. For this reason, the US returns to the international SDOs. For example, Biden strongly endorses the American candidate for the ITU Secretary-General. The position has been maintained by the Chinese SG for the last 8 years.

Hwang What could be China's response to these different views?

Gao Yes, for both the US and Europe China's active engagement in international standardization is regarded as a threat to international order. They think the growing Chinese footprint in international standardization is not just a source of influence for Chinese companies but empowers the party-state. I do not think they are fair. China is opening up and keen to collaborate with foreign technology giants, but will not stand by watching them to dominate Chinese or international markets. You cannot blame China's ambition of being a key international player and becoming a rivalry to the US. at the same level someday - this will be China's response to the US.

Hwang Are there any particular move that China is taking domestically?

Gao Chinese policymakers are described to protect national interests in technology in the face of global powers, adopting techno-nationalism which nurtures domestic innovation. It involves promoting domestic technological advancement along with globalization in pursuit of independence from foreign technologies. However, this is the strategy for catching up. China's domestic standardization system is undergoing reform. My research also found China is decreasing the state control on standardization, and changing from state-control, to state-support, and finally reliance on market mechanism.

I agree that more involvement of China is still needed in the future, due to its huge market, strong technological capability and high standardization level.

Hwang What was the motivation that triggered China to apply for the ISO president election, given that it already has held the president in the past and the head positions in other SDOs like ITU and IEC?

Gao I am sure China will not give up opportunities to support its nationals taking high offices in important international organizations -- I assume every country including Korea will do so. This also applies to the standardization sector. Like in Korea, Chinese people and also the government considered the presentation of Chinese nationals in high offices of important international organizations as a national pride and a symbol of its success in catching up with technology superpowers. I read a report by SAC on China's standardization development, which lists Chinese being elected as ISO and IEC heads as key events. Chinese official media proudly reported that Chinese took leadership in three key international standardization organizations -- ISO, ITU, and IEC. Moreover, being a leading player and having more decisive power usually owned by the US in international standardization are a strategy or target of China in international standardization. It is understandable the Chinese government expects the elected Chinese will help it in doing this -- you know someone's decision is always impacted by his personal background.

Hwang Given the circumstances surrounding the geopolitical competition for technical standards, what is the significance if the Korean candidate is elected?

Lee The coming ISO presidential election gives us a new opportunity of an unprecedented nature. It is often said that Korea now, as a developed country, should contribute to, and even lead in, global rule-making. In international SDOs like ISO, a substantial portion of global rules are made. That is why China is keen to take the leadership and many other countries concern whether the international standardization would be controlled by a specific state. The countries need to cooperate to renew and/or form multilateral practices for rule makings and standardization, particularly in emerging technologies. In that sense, we will be in a good position to initiate such endeavors because we are leading in some of those technologies. Having an ISO president will give us advantages in stepping out the first step towards a global rule maker.

Hwang What is Korea's current stance under the competitive flow? And what could be done by the Korean government after the election?

Lee The inclusion of "Open RAN cooperation" in the Korea-US summit statements in 2021 and 2022 in a row symbolically shows a delicate situation of Korea in the standards rivalry between the US and China. Open RAN is a kind of standards project designed to weaken China's dominance in 5G, which basically means that the project is politically motivated. Compared to how the 2022 US-Japan summit statement includes a whole separate Open RAN section, the fact that Korea-US summit statement mentions it in one sentence represents the reality. Moving on, in terms of ISO/ITU election, it seems that its meaning is not fully recognized in Korea. Technical standards are a key pillar in national technology strategies and have been upgraded to a theme for geopolitics. Therefore, an integrated approach across the government is necessary because it is not a matter of an individual agency or ministry any more. We need to understand why the entire US government officially and expressly endorsed the US candidate for the ITU Secretary-General since June last year, when the election is coming this October. At the same time we need to pay attention to why China makes another attempt for the ISO presidency despite the concerns of the international standards community.

III

Global Issues and Views

Europe will not detract from US focus on Indo-Pacific

Mar 30, 2022

David M. Finkelstein

Vice President and Director of China and Indo-Pacific security affairs, Center for Naval Analyses

The White House in February announced its Indo-Pacific strategy in what seems to be its most inclusive and comprehensive report yet. The report makes no doubt that China's presence is of utmost importance when it comes to the US' Indo-Pacific strategy, which was initiated in the Trump administration.

In the report, the US looks to seek ways to contain China's rise, but also maintain a somewhat amicable and cooperative relationship with Beijing. The Indo-Pacific strategy initially which was largely focused on the military aspect, however, is steadily extending to other domains to include politics, economy, security, and culture. The US' intentions and will are quite obvious, although the measures and approaches are still uncertain. While the US is constantly stressing the significance of the Indo-Pacific strategy, nevertheless, we still need time to see where it stands in the US' overall security policies.

We cannot easily judge at this point whether the situations in Europe, including the war in Ukraine, would have an influence over the strategy or not, and if so, whether it would be a positive or negative one. Above all, the Indo-Pacific strategy is the US' version of China's Belt and Road Initiative, while the Belt and Road Initiative is China's Indo-Pacific strategy. We are witnessing the spears of the Belt and Road Initiative against the shields of the Indo-Pacific strategy.

Under such complicated and suddenly changing global security circumstances, we need to understand the US' strategic thoughts and military strategies since the US is the one who is leading the changes and responding to it. In this sense, this week's discourse we invited one of the representative Chinese military experts from the US, Dr. David M. Finkelstein, and had a deep discussion regarding the Indo-Pacific strategy. He is vice president and director of China and Indo-Pacific security affairs at the Center for Naval Analyses, a nonprofit research institute in Arlington, Virginia. He is also author and co-editor of several Chinese military-related books. The views expressed herein are strictly his own, and do not reflect those of CNA or any of its sponsors.

Hwang While Europe is in conflict with Russia, do you see the Indo-Pacific Strategy having any kind of momentum?

Finkelstein Russia's unprovoked invasion of the Ukraine has radically shifted the discussion of security affairs and national defense among the nations of Europe, between Europe and the United States, and beyond in some cases, for obvious reasons. At the same time, my own view is that events in Europe will not detract from Washington's long-term focus on the Indo-Pacific region. There are a host of traditional and nontraditional security challenges in the Indo-Pacific that are neglected at the peril of the US and its allies and partners in the region. There is no question that the long-term economic security of the US resides here in Asia.

So, while the current crisis in Europe has the headlines, I have every confidence that the US will continue to push forward key initiatives under this Indo-Pacific strategy. One data point to underscore this assertion is that during public Congressional testimony on March 9, in the midst of Russia's invasion of the Ukraine, the assistant secretary of defense for Indo-Pacific security affairs told the House Armed Services Committee that the Indo-Pacific region remains the priority theater for the Department of Defense.

Hwang The US and China are competing in earnest, and the military area is not an exception. Previously, the US has mainly focused on preventing terrorism and a "Two-War Strategy," and now moved on to a "One-War Strategy" that concentrates on the strong powers such as China and Russia. Do you see this trend continuing?

Finkelstein One of the remarkable but likely underappreciated aspects of the history of the US armed forces is that since the late 19th century and early 20th century the American military has had to constantly adapt — and not just to changing technologies. It has had to adapt to ever-changing security threats, to shifting geographic theaters of operations, to different types of conflicts and modes of war, different adversaries, and different allies and partners. Thinking back in time, the US military has not had the luxury of being a one-theater warfighting military since World War I — and even in that case the US armed forces were still deployed globally on other missions, not just in Europe. And of course, at times, the US armed forces have had to prosecute operations in multiple theaters of conflict simultaneously. This is a long way of offering that the historical record would strongly suggest that the US military will adjust its focus and capabilities as conditions change. But I feel compelled to point out that the US military has maintained significant military forces in the Indo-Pacific region since the late 19th century, and that is something I believe will remain a constant given enduring American interests in the region.

Hwang Given that the Indo-Pacific strategy report seems to excessively concern China, it is expected that the US is going for the "value" alliance, to pressure China by concerting all its allies and friendly countries.

Finkelstein The Interim National Security Strategic Guidance issued by the White House in March 2021 was quite direct in articulating the administration's concerns about how the People's Republic of China is pursuing its national interests, and the implications for the US and other nations. It is not surprising, therefore, that the new Indo-Pacific strategy devotes discussion to the PRC. The strategy is, after all, a document focused on the Asia-Pacific region and the PRC is a major power. At the same time, the strategy is not just about the PRC. The strategy also speaks to the larger interests the US has in the region and discusses how the current administration will pursue those interests. On the PRC, what stood out to me in the document was this statement: "Our objective is not to change the PRC but to shape the strategic environment in which it operates …" To me, this statement was a significant articulation of US policy on two accounts. First, it can read as a message of assurance to Beijing that the US has no desire or intentions to change its political system or attempt to "split and Westernize China" — as the Chinese Communist Party often asserts — or undermine the CCP as a matter of official policy. This is an important message given the rhetoric of the last US administration. But second, the statement and the strategy also make clear that a key approach the US will take in dealing with PRC policies that are deemed inimical to US, ally, and partner interests will be to create a diplomatic, economic and security and environment in the region that will either mitigate problematic PRC policies or behaviors or, alternately, encourage it to go in different more palatable directions. This can only be accomplished in concert with others; hence the strategy emphasizes working with many other actors in the region and beyond who share the same views.

Hwang It seems the Indo-Pacific strategy previously focused on the military, however, has expanded its boundary to diplomacy, economy, security, and others. For instance, it has suggested Indo-Pacific Economic Framework (IPEF) for the action plan. How feasible would this be?

Finkelstein I think it is very important that you are pointing out that the current strategy is not just about military affairs. Just to remind, in the previous administration it was the Pentagon that published an Asia-specific strategy: The Department of Defense Indo-Pacific Strategy Report (June 2019). Not surprisingly, the focus of that document was on the military and security dimensions of the region and how the Defense Department intended to deal with them. As I mentioned earlier, the current document was issued by the White House. Consequently, the range of issues covered is broader than just military affairs. Reading through the current document it is clear that the intention of the White House was to make this strategy for the Indo-Pacific be a "whole of government" strategy. This makes eminent sense given the myriad and diverse interests the US has in the region.

It is worth underscoring that the current Indo-Pacific strategy lists the need to "drive Indo-Pacific prosperity" as one of the five key objectives of US policy toward the region. The strategy makes the important assessment that, "The prosperity of everyday Americans is linked to the Indo-Pacific." As a result, there is a good deal of anticipation as we wait for the Indo-Pacific Economic Framework to be rolled out. In the meantime, there are also a lot of questions about the details of the IPEF. Before we can make any judgments about IPEF, we will need to have those details. I think it is fair to say that US officials are attuned to the perception that Washington needs to enhance the economic dimensions of its Indo-Pacific engagement on an official level. I say "on an official level" because there can be no doubt that American businesses are deeply invested in the region and have been for decades. So, let's wait and see what IPEF brings to the table.

Hwang Improving the trilateral cooperation between US-ROK-Japan was also suggested as an action plan in the Indo-Pacific strategy. Since Korea-Japan relations is not in the most comfortable flow, the Indo-Pacific strategy seems to be applied to drag Korea into what the US is drawing, whether it is the improvement of Korea-Japan relations or US-ROK-Japan trilateral cooperation.

Finkelstein It goes without saying that the Republic of Korea and Japan are two of the most critical actors in the region and have gravitas beyond the region. Both South Korea and Japan have highly developed economies, both are regional as well as international trade heavyweights, both are global leaders in cutting-edge technologies — which is the coin of the realm in the 21st century. Both have international soft power and cachet, both have vibrant democracies, both face pressing security challenges in the region, and both are much-valued treaty allies of the United States. Without strong trilateral ties between the ROK, Japan and the US it is difficult to imagine a future political, economic or security environment in Asia that will reflect the values that all three countries share or that assures their many common interests. So, it is not surprising to me that the US Indo-Pacific Strategy specifically mentions ROK-US-

Japan relations.

All three countries will at times have differences and disagreements. But the pressing need to strengthen trilateral ties, as well as ROK-Japan bilateral relations, could not be clearer. North Korea's launch of the Hwasong-17 ICBM on March 24 is but one example that makes this imperative crystal clear, in my view. The US can help with the former (trilateral relations). It is up to Seoul and Tokyo to deal with the latter. Finally, it is worth pointing out that the current crisis in Europe underscores what is possible when unity of effort among allies and partners is achieved, and what is at risk when it is not.

Hwang The US-ROK Summit last year has stressed Korea's international role. How far do you anticipate Korea's role to be in the frame of the Indo-Pacific strategy?

Finkelstein South Korea brings a lot to the table in terms of being able to buttress key aspects of the US' Indo-Pacific Strategy. For one thing, the ROK, along with the US and Japan, is an absolutely indispensable partner, a vital partner, in any collective attempts to work toward the complete and verifiable denuclearization of North Korea. And needless to say, the US-ROK military alliance remains a powerful deterrent force.

Next, Seoul's "New Southern Policy" (NSP) — with its "Three Pillars" of "People, Prosperity, and Peace" — and the "New Southern Policy-Plus" are very much simpatico with aspects of Washington's approach to the region. Like the US Indo-Pacific strategy, the NSP recognizes the immense importance of the member nations of the Association of Southeast Asian Nations, as well as India, to the future prosperity and security of the entire region.

Finally, the ROK has an important role to play in regional and global supply chain security, dealing with the increasingly pressing challenge of climate change, and certainly contributing to the international battle against COVID-19 and future pandemic preparedness. As important as anything else, however, it is the ROK's democratic values and its commitment to a regional and international order based on law that makes Seoul such a valued partner for many in the region and beyond.

Hwang Ukraine is not an ally of the US and is facing a great crisis. Taiwan is not an official ally of the US as well. How important and what role does Taiwan take in the Indo-Pacific strategy?

Finkelstein The US administration, and many of its allies and partners, are seeking an Asia-Pacific region in which coercion is rejected as a policy choice. In this regard, there is growing concern in Washington and abroad over Beijing's increasing diplomatic, economic, and informational pressure on Taiwan. This concern, for example, was evident in the May 2021 joint statement by our two presidents in which it was stated that "President Biden and President Moon emphasize the importance of preserving peace and stability in the Taiwan Strait."

A recent disconcerting development is the ramping up of PRC military pressure on Taiwan. That military pressure includes military aircraft flying dozens of sorties into the island's Air Defense Identification Zone, the People's Liberation Army joint exercises in the vicinity of the Taiwan Strait, and PRC naval activities to the east of the island. This increasing pressure is called out in the strategy. As a result, the document states that the US will continue "supporting Taiwan's self-defense capabilities" in a manner consistent with the various US government guidelines, policies, or laws that guide relations with both Beijing and Taipei, such as the Taiwan Relations Act, the Three Joint Communiques with Beijing, and the Six Assurances.

Notably, the strategy reaches out beyond regional actors, stating the willingness of the US to work nations outside the Asia-Pacific in creating an environment conducive to peace and stability across the Taiwan Strait. So, while it may be going too far to say that Taiwan has a "role" in the strategy, the strategy certainly sees a stable and peaceful cross-strait dynamic as something it aspires to underwrite.

Hwang You are currently serving as vice president and director of CNA's China and Indo-Pacific security affairs. What are the goals and the capacity of the Indo-Pacific strategy from a military perspective?

Finkelstein Another noteworthy feature of the Indo-Pacific strategy is that the need to "Bolster Indo-Pacific Security," which is the section which discusses military affairs, was the fourth of the five objectives in the document. In other words, this document is about much more than the military dimensions of US policy in the region. And if I were a betting man, I would wager that the authors of the strategy placed the discussion of military and security affairs toward the end of the document precisely to make that point.

Having said that, the section on security affairs provides a pretty good thumbnail sketch of some of the key approaches by which the military element of national power will be applied by the US. It highlights innovation in high-tech domains, the critical importance of allies and partners, and forward presence. Once again, we note that the document refers to allies and partners not just in the Asia-Pacific region, but also those from beyond the region as part of the political-military approach to the Indo-Pacific. This latter point underscores that many countries beyond Asia have rising equities in the peace and stability of the Indo-Pacific. One notes that in the recent past naval forces from the United Kingdom, France, Germany, and Canada have all made deployments to the region precisely because of their important national interests in this part of the world.

Also noteworthy is that the document states that, "Integrated deterrence will be the cornerstone" of the

US approach to security affairs in the Indo-Pacific — and beyond, actually. This is a security concept that is worth exploring in more depth. It is ubiquitous in US defense circles and speaks to tighter whole of government coordination, closer ally and partner unity of effort, operations in multiple battlespace domains, and across the spectrum of conflict.

Hwang Would you please explain what is the naval dimension in the Indo-Pacific strategy?

Finkelstein The United States armed forces is a joint force. Therefore, technically speaking, there are no separate US Navy, US Marine Corps, US Army, US Air Force, or US Space Force operational strategies for the Indo-Pacific. If readers are interested in how the US Navy in particular is planning to build and train the maritime forces that the commander in the Indo-Pacific, and other regional combatant commanders, will need to execute their geographically focused missions, I would refer them to the December 2020 tri-service maritime strategy entitled "Advantage at Sea: Prevailing with Integrated All-Domain Naval Power." This document was developed jointly by the US Navy, US Marine Corps, and US Coast Guard, and is publicly available.

Japan's Indo-Pacific, Vision, Region, or Strategy?

Apr 13, 2022

Tetsuo Kotani
Senior Fellow, Japan Institute of International Affairs

Seiko Mimaki
Associate Professor, Takasaki City University of Economics

As the recent US-China competition intensifies, the strategic significance of the Indo-Pacific region is also rising. In this situation, major countries are presenting new Indo-Pacific Strategies with the purpose of strengthening their respective political, economic, and military influence in the Indo-Pacific region. The US Biden administration has set its Indo-Pacific vision as its main diplomatic policy in order to maintain the US' influence within Asia and to check China's growing influence. The European Union also announced a Joint Communication on the "EU Strategy for Cooperation in the Indo-Pacific" in 2021. Japan already drew the blueprint of its own Indo-Pacific Strategy back in 2006 under Abe's first government, and showed its active willingness in the second. At the same time, Japan has shifted the term from "strategy" to "vision," and seems unwilling to step to the very front line of the Indo-Pacific Strategy while it targets China. Recently, the Indo-Pacific Strategy is frequently read either as a vision or a regional strategy. What is Japan's national strategy, particularly in regard to its Indo-Pacific Strategy? Also, what is its national strategy as the world goes through new geopolitical risks including the post-COVID era and the crisis in Ukraine? This week, the discourse invites three experts from Japan who are contributing significantly to answering these questions. We have Senior Fellow Tetsuo Kotani at the Japan Institute of International Affairs, and Associate Professor Seiko Mimaki at the Takasaki City University of Economics.

Hwang What is the Indo-Pacific Strategy from Japan's point of view?

Kotani First of all, I would like to stress that the US Biden administration's Indo-Pacific Strategy and Free and Open Indo-Pacific will remain as just regional strategies, not policies aimed at China. What both the US and Japan seek is to establish a desirable regional situation for ourselves, not to pressure or change China. While the Trump administration focused on weakening the system under the Chinese Communist Party through competing with China, the Biden administration is aiming to manage China through competition with the purpose of creating an ideal environment in the Indo-Pacific region. The US and Japan have come to a consensus on this approach. This approach includes strategies for expansion of regional economic cooperation and promotion of economic security. President Biden has emphasized the importance of universal values since the beginning for his administration, and his ideas are well reflected in the Indo-Pacific Strategy. However, when it comes to the overall Indo-Pacific area, the US weighs the balance of power over values. Therefore, I assume the US will steadily show how it strengthens cooperation with such states as Vietnam or Singapore that could not participate in the Summit for Democracy last year. Moreover, it will move on to intensifying the cooperation with ASEAN countries with the existing regional cooperation frames. These include the Quadrilateral Security Dialogue (Quad), the AUKUS pact, and others.

Hwang I would like to ask you about Japan's National Security Strategy.

Kotani So far, Japan is considering revising the current National Security Strategy (NSS) which was formulated in 2013 by the end of this year. As the current NSS does not contain Indo-Pacific Strategy or FOIP, these flows will be newly added in the revised one. Also, Japan's relations and positions with China and Russia will be altered. The existing one defines China and Russia as a significant partner in order to resolve the regional issues, nonetheless, they are likely to be changed into the competitor or threat rather than partners in the upcoming revision. Additionally, details about missile defense, striking capacities, expansion in deterrence will be added as well as the revision of regional frames and economic security.

Hwang The importance of the Taiwan Strait is gradually growing in the US' and Japan's Indo-Pacific Strategy.

Kotani The US and Japan are recognizing the significance of peace and stability of the Taiwan Strait in the strategic context of the Indo-Pacific. In this sense, US-Japan and US-Republic of Korea-Japan cooperation in the region are continuously underlined since last year. Not only the US,

Japan and Korea, but also Australia and other European countries agree with the importance of peace and stability on the Taiwan Strait. Its value will be progressively highlighted from the economic security perspective due to semiconductors – of which Taiwan is a leading producer -- as well as from the balance of power.

Hwang Continuing our discussion on the US' Indo-Pacific Strategy, democratic values are the most utilized approach in terms of implementation. Do you see it as effective?

Mimaki I guess the ideology diplomacy that the Biden's administration is pushing has some problems. The Biden administration seems to perceive the world as a competition between "democracy" and "authoritarianism." Such a perception tends to encourage division, not enhancing solidarity between democratic countries. The Summit for Democracy back in 2021 led by the US was a perfect example that explains such a tension. This summit was held online for two days from Dec. 9, and invited 100 countries and regional leaders. The population of participating countries and regions were a bit less than 60 percent of the entire world's total population, and represented about 70 percent of the world's GDP. On the other hand, details at the end were not sufficient, which was shown in the depression of the US' Asian policy.

Hwang How would the war in Ukraine influence the Indo-Pacific Strategy?

Mimaki On Feb. 24, the UN General Assembly held an Emergency Special Session for the first time in 40 years due to Russia's invasion of Ukraine in which 141 countries out of 193 voted in favor of the resolution. The countries in favor criticized Russia and demanded an immediate cessation of the invasion, and the resolution requiring Russia's immediate withdrawal was adopted. The UN Secretary General Antonio Guterres said, "The message of the General Assembly is loud and clear." However, I personally still have some doubts as to whether this is a sincere general assembly of international society. Going deeper, five countries opposed this resolution, and 35 countries abstained. The countries that voted against the resolution were Russia, Belarus, Syria, North Korea and Eritrea. Great powers in Asia including India and China abstained, along with Bangladesh, Laos, Pakistan and Vietnam. There were also some other countries from Africa and Latin America that abstained.

Hwang Although India is a core country in the Indo-Pacific, it is being quite passive with sanctions on Russia.

Mimaki On March 19, Japanese Prime Minister Fumio Kishida held a talk with Indian Prime Minister Modi regarding Russia's invasion of Ukraine. However, in the end their Joint Statement Partnership was no more than calling for an immediate cessation of violence and expressing concerns on the war in Ukraine and the ensuing humanitarian crisis. We could see this as India avoiding an explicit criticism of Russia. The Indian government has declared its position of continuously importing Russian oil under the excuse of skyrocketing crude oil prices. The amount Russia takes up of India's oil imports is only about 2 to 3 percent, though Russia is suggesting trade by providing massively cheap prices to India. Furthermore, as China is also making a similar move to India, we may have to keep our eyes on how China moves, considering the long-term influence of sanctions on Russia.

Hwang How is ASEAN doing as the major stage for competition in the Indo-Pacific Strategy?

Mimaki What mattered in the last Summit for Democracy were Southeast Asian countries. Among the 11 Southeast Asian countries, the only four that were invited were Indonesia, Malaysia, the Philippines and East Timor. Also, considering that China and ASEAN's relationship was promoted to a "comprehensive strategic partnership" from the simple "strategic partnership" at the ASEAN-China Special Summit before the Summit for Democracy was held, the US's selective approach was a contrast to China's comprehensive moves. In short, it can be said that the US created a division among Southeast Asian countries by distinguishing between those who were invited to the Summit for Democracy and the ones those were not.

Hwang What effort would be necessary for a successful Indo-Pacific Strategy?

Mimaki As a consequence of the war in Ukraine, more and more countries will split. Countries will flock to various central pillars -- the US, Russia and China. Based on these circumstances and trends, I personally think that the US must pursue cooperation with countries in Asia and other regions -- even though some of them clearly do not belong to the democratic countries. As the Biden administration's diplomacy has shown over the past year, a rigid diplomatic policy that excessively stressed democratic values resulted in countries that were not strictly classified as "democratic" in Asia and Latin America choosing to stand near Russia and China. From now on, the US must develop and take a more flexible diplomatic attitude. Korea and Japan should also recognize the importance of sharing values and sustain further cooperation.

Hwang Within the frame of the Indo-Pacific Strategy, what would be the specific areas where Korea and Japan can cooperate?

Kotani Japan is expecting the invigoration of the US-ROK-Japan trilateral cooperation framework and a joint preparation against North Korea's nuclear and missile enhancement. It is also expecting cooperation on the Indo-Pacific Strategy and FOIP; support for Taiwan and the regional economy; and cooperation in terms of Quad Plus from Korea's new government. I look forward to seeing the two countries' efforts toward making outcomes in the areas above.

Everything roots in something, the reason Australia actively steps into the Indo-Pacific Strategy

Jul 13, 2022

Nick Bisley
Dean and Head of the School of Humanities and Social Sciences, La Trobe University

Australia is a country that has multiple similarities with Korea. Both are considered middle powers, both are allies of the US and have China as the largest trading partner, and the foreign policies in both countries depend on the domestic governing power. Above all, looking back at our choices between the US and China, they were mostly based on "Anmi-kyeongjung," depending on the security of the US and the economy of China. Just like Korea-China relations, Australia-China relations also have hit their lowest during the last few years. Australia's relations with China began to become tense in 2018 when Australia ruled out the participation of Chinese telecommunications equipment company Huawei in the 5G network business in line with the request of the Donald Trump administration. In April 2020, Australian Prime Minister Scott Morrison called for a survey of the origin of COVID-19, targeting China, and the relationship became more frictional. In response, China imposed retaliatory high-rate tariffs on Australia. Unlike the former Prime Minister Morrison, who sided with the US, the relationship between the two countries has improved as Prime Minister Anthony Albanese took office.

Australia has been actively involved in various US diplomatic, security, and economic initiatives, including the QUAD, Indo-Pacific Strategy, IPEF, NATO-AP4, and others. Will Australia alter its diplomatic, economic, and security stance? In this regard, this week's interview invites professor Nick Bisley from Australia. He is the dean and head of the School of Humanities and Social Sciences and professor of international relations at La Trobe University, Australia. He has been a Senior Research Associate at the International Institute of Strategic Studies.

Hwang Why did Australia rejoin the Quad again in 2018 after pulling out in 2007?

Bisley Australia was initially reluctant to join the Quad when it was first established in 2007. The country enjoyed very positive relations with all the region's major powers and saw the initiative as risking positive ties with the PRC. A decade later and Australia perceives the region as much riskier and much more unstable. In particular, the government perceives that PRC's ambition, its increased military capabilities, and the broader uncertainty in the regional security environment warrant the kind of focused minilateral group that the Quad represents.

Equally, its relationship with the PRC took a significant downturn in 2017 and, until the recent election of the Albanese government, was in its worst state since the establishment of diplomatic relations with the PRC in the 1970s. As such, the side costs of embracing the Quad were lower than before. A shifting strategic environment and the changes in its bilateral relationship with Beijing changed

Australia's perspective and have made it an enthusiastic member of the Quad grouping.

Hwang Besides the China factor, what other reason is there for Australia to participate in The Quad?

Bisley While Australia has the luxury of distance from acute flashpoints in the region, one of its core interests is stable regional security and, ideally, a favorable strategic balance in Asia. And it is this interest that is most directly challenged by the return of great power rivalry and Sino-American strategic competition. As a middle-ranking power, it has very limited ability to influence or shape the regional security setting. However, as a member of a multistate initiative, it can help advance its interests in the region. Australia's enthusiastic embrace of the Quad also reflects a degree of skepticism of the existing multilateral security mechanisms, such as the ASEAN Regional Forum or other ASEAN-centered mechanisms, to do much to help stabilize the region. There is also an important bilateral dimension to Australia's interest in the Quad: Australia's relationship with India. Canberra has long wanted to improve its relations with India, both in security and economic terms. Yet over many decades, it has struggled to convert the desire for better ties into a substantively improved relationship with India. There are many reasons for this, relating to the history of colonialism, problems of capacity constraints in Canberra, and the fact that India matters more to Australia than the other way around. By regularly working with Indian counterparts through the Quad, Australia sees the opportunity to build a more robust foundation for relations with India through much more regular interaction on practical policy concerns.

Hwang For Australia, China is the largest exporter and the largest importer. Considering this, why is Australia still in a confrontational stance toward China? How threatening does Australia perceive China to be?

Bisley Since around 2016, Australian policy toward China has become dominated by security concerns. The efforts to balance economic interests with political and security concerns that had been the central focus of years past were set aside as perceptions of security risk outweighed all other matters. In part, these threats are related to the international environment, prompted by the PRC's growing military power, its assertive behavior in the East and the South China Sea and its growing influence in the South Pacific. But the area that really accentuated the perception of the threat that Beijing posed was domestic. In particular, it was the belief that China was a malign influence in Australian domestic affairs. This included allegations that China was trying to influence domestic politics, concerns about Chinese intelligence activity in Australia, including allegations that Chinese intelligence operations were of industrial proportions made by the head domestic security agency and the belief that PRC economic activity within the country presented unacceptable risks. This led to the banning of Huawei and ZTE from participating in the country's 5G telecommunication network development, the introduction of legislation intended to limit foreign influence in politics, and a number of investments from

PRC-based firms being blocked by the Foreign Investment Review Board. These concerns, while real, were blown out of proportion and led to the deterioration of the bilateral relationship as well as significant problems for Australians of Chinese heritage who were the victims of overheated and careless rhetoric from the government and commentators denouncing the "Chinese" threat to Australia. This combination of domestic and international concerns has led Australia to have one of the most pessimistic assessments of the PRC in the region.

Hwang How is the Ukraine war affecting Australian security?

Bisley The Australian government has been one of Ukraine's strongest and most vocal supporters, and its stance is bipartisan. The Russian invasion confirms the view in Canberra that world politics has entered a decisively more dangerous and unstable phase -- a mood it captured in its 2020 Strategic Policy Update that brought forward the timeline of strategic risk confronting the country. Canberra has committed to significantly increasing defense spending to prepare for this situation, and the Ukraine invasion reinforces the need to ensure this plan is sustained even in challenging economic circumstances.

Australia's pessimism relates not just to a less stable balance of power but that the liberal system of rules and norms that have been so beneficial to the country over many years is at risk. The "no limits" relationship announced by Russia and the PRC before the February invasion reflects not just a security pact but an authoritarian challenge to liberal democracy, which has immediate implications for Asia. It will also make the efforts by the newly elected Labor government to try to improve relations with China more difficult, given the PRC's support of Russia.

Hwang How different are Australian parties' China policies? How strong an influence does the domestic factor have on China policy?

Bisley In its structural dimensions, Australian foreign and defense policy is firmly bipartisan. In the most recent election, the Labor Party, which won a narrow victory against the ruling conservative Liberal Coalition government, essentially presented the same foreign and defense policy as the government. The policy included reiterating support for the US alliance, commitment to the AUKUS arrangements to acquire nuclear submarines, and retaining strategic skepticism of the PRC. While bipartisanship is about policy in its larger orientation, the Labor party has a somewhat less hawkish approach to the PRC. It has argued and, since coming to power in late May, has indicated that it believes the country can have a productive diplomatic and economic relationship with China while retaining concerns about aspects of China's policy. The Coalition government, since 2017, made clear that its security concerns would be the dominant factor shaping the bilateral relationship, even to the cost of the Australian economy. In contrast, the Labor party aims to have a more functional relationship and wants to put security concerns in proportion.

Hwang Australia and Korea have strategic similarities. Australia and Korea are both allies of the US and have considerable economic exchanges and cooperation with China. Under these strategic similarities, Australia is more engaged in The Quad despite China's warnings, while Korea is getting to step into US's plan against China. How do you see Korea's diplomacy?

Bisley While there are some similarities between Australia and Korea, Seoul has had to navigate a more complex strategic setting than Australia. Korea is much closer to the PRC, and its economy is much more integrated with China's than Australia's. In Australia, we import consumer goods from the PRC and primarily export commodities; iron ore accounts for around two-thirds of Australia's exports. FDI is not extensive and has been actively kept at bay by the government in recent years, so navigating the relationship with China is somewhat easier. Korea's caution around the PRC makes sense, given its circumstances. That said, as a democracy that is closely allied to the US and which has a stake in a stable Asian strategic balance, it is probably in Korea's interests to be looking at ways in which it can work, in coordination with others, to buttress the strategic balance and to help support liberal democratic values in a region in which authoritarian polities are growing in influence.

Up until now, Korea's relative moderation in its foreign policy has been somewhat out of step with other liberal democracies, and a reconsideration of this approach would be welcomed by many countries both within Asia and beyond.

Hwang President Yoon has announced a Korean version of the Indo-Pacific Strategy. What do you anticipate this Indo-Pacific Strategy to be?

Bisley The Indo-Pacific has emerged recently as a way of describing two things. First, it is intended to describe a region that has thicker security and economic connections between the states and peoples of the Western Pacific and the Indian Ocean Region. Second, it has been used by the US, its partners and allies to describe not just the geographic scope of the region but as an indirect way of describing a preferred manner in which the balance of power, as well as the rules, norms and values, operate in that region.

More specifically, it is about limiting China's ability to change the regional balance or its rules and values. So any Korean Indo-Pacific strategy would need to reflect this larger theater of operation and grapple with the question of limiting China's attempts to change the region. Given the complexity of Korea's geoeconomic circumstances as well as the design of its military, any Indo-Pacific strategy is likely to be cautious in the first instance and focus most immediately on diplomatic and institutional dimensions rather than on military and security components.

For example, while it may not join the Quad at first, it may look at engaging with a number of the proposed areas of Quad cooperation that are focused on non-traditional security concerns, such as the Quad program on global health security or climate change. It may also include some areas of military interaction, but I would not expect those to be high profile in the first instance.

Hwang How do you evaluate the feasibility of the IPEF?

Bisley The IPEF is a very important, if belated, component of US strategy. Given how important the PRC economy is to the region and, more importantly, how effectively China has been using its economic influence to shape its relations with many countries, the US really had to have a much more coherent economic dimension to its Indo-Pacific strategy.

The problem that the US faces is that its greatest tool in this regard is something that, for domestic reasons, it is unable to use. Trade policy in general and improved access to the US market is of huge importance to countries. Yet circumstances in the United States mean that trade agreements are virtually impossible. So the US has to get creative to try to bind the economic interests of regional countries to those of its own.

The framework that it has put together is both impressive and underwhelming. It is impressive in that it has a large number of adherents, and it covers a wide range of areas of significance and for which multilateral cooperation is important. But it is underwhelming in the sense that we don't really know how any of these mechanisms will actually work, and in this domain, precisely how the rules work and what exactly the incentives are matters entirely for how it will function. Also, given the diversity of economic interests in the region and the continued salience of the PRC, both its investment and markets, to many countries in the region, the US will find it difficult to advance its ends on this front significantly, at least under the current IPEF. There is a good chance that the framework will be a statement of good intent and not much more.

Hwang Perhaps Korea's early participation in The Quad is premature. Do you think Korea will be put in a position to join, regardless of whether Korea is willing to do so or not?

Bisley It would be useful for the Quad and indeed the region to widen participation in its operations. A grouping with more members will increase its legitimacy, enhance its effect on the regional order and bring more capacity that can be used to shape the regional order. But expansion brings with it challenges, and these should not be rushed by a political imperative, particularly that of the existing members seeking to bring others into the fold. Any move by Korea to join the Quad or to engage in its activities should be determined entirely by Korea, particularly given the domestic challenges that participation might bring.

Hwang How should diplomacy be between middle powers, such as Korea and Australia? Do you think middle powers have a certain level of autonomy and diplomatic space?

Bisley Because Asia is a region in which a few very major powers' interests clash, and because of the dominance of US-China rivalry in recent years, one can assume that only these great powers matter. Yet the recent past shows how middle-ranking powers have crucial roles to play, not only as the major power's junior partners but as players in their own right. More importantly, times of great power rivalries increase the relative value of middle powers because of the way competition plays out and the benefits their action can bring to powerful states. And if middle-ranking powers work in coordination with others, either in institutional settings or in more ad hoc forms, they can play an outsized role.

To capitalize on these opportunities requires shrewd statecraft and a willingness to take on risks and costs which previously may have been avoided. The challenge is that, since the late 1970s, Asia has been strategically stable and one in which risky and costly statecraft was unnecessary due to this stability. Adjusting to this new environment, while it provides middle powers with influence, can be challenging, given that history. But both Korea and Australia have shown that in the past, they have the capacity to rise to the occasion, and I am confident that this will occur again.

India is not the weakest link in the Quad

Aug 1, 2022

Dhruva Jaishankar

Executive Director, Observer Research Foundation America

India is expected to grow to have the world's greatest population, overtaking China. Its economy also has a huge role in the United States' Silicon Valley, as India produces numerous advanced IT human resources. And its low-key but powerful influence can also bee see in Indian diplomacy. India's biggest antagonist is China. The Indo-China border dispute is appalling. In 2018, there was a military confrontation for more than 70 days in the Doklam region of the Himalayas, in which both countries had casualties, but Indian Prime Minister Narendra Modi soon flew to China and had tea and a boat ride with Chinese President Xi Jinping at Donghu in Wuhan, Hubei Province.

How should we understand India's diplomatic thinking and actions? What is India's idea of crossing from Ukraine, Russia, China and the Indo-Pacific to the Quadrilateral Security Dialogue? To find the answers, this week's interview invites Dhruva Jaishankar. He is an executive director of the Observer Research Foundation America (ORF America), and is also a non-resident fellow with the Lowy Institute in Australia.

Hwang India abstained from voting on United Nations sanctions against Russia on the Ukraine war. What could be the reason?

Jaishankar India has several reasons for preserving a positive relationship with Russia, which largely explains its position on the Russia-Ukraine war. Most importantly, Russia is the largest foreign supplier of defense equipment for the Indian armed forces. Since 2020, India has faced a very large deployment by China on its disputed boundary and its military has been in a state of high readiness since. Russian cooperation is still required for spares and maintenance of existing equipment, including India's front-line combat aircraft. Russia also provides India with nuclear-propelled submarines on lease and has helped India in the development of its indigenous nuclear-powered ballistic missile submarine program. Beyond military considerations, India is very resource dependent, including for energy, fertilizers, food, and critical minerals. Russia has not always been a preferred source for India in these areas, but cutting it off economically through sanctions has tremendous consequences for the global market, and India is particularly vulnerable to volatile price fluctuations and scarcity. Just as Europe has exempted energy and fertilizers from some sanctions, India has been reluctant to sanction Russia on these grounds, even if over the longer term it is unlikely to be a major direct beneficiary. India-Russia trade has been pretty modest, at about $10 billion-$12 billion per year, and may only rise temporarily this year due to diverted energy flows. A third consideration is that there is some sympathy for Russia's great power ambitions: India would feel very uncomfortable if another major power – even a friendly one – were to exercise influence in its vicinity.

Hwang Do you think India had some sympathy for the background and policies of Russia's Ukraine war?

Jaishankar That said, India's position should not be misread as an endorsement of Russia's actions. India has called for an immediate end to violence, respect for territoriality and sovereignty, and an independent investigation into alleged war crimes in places like Bucha. Over the longer term, there is a broad assessment in New Delhi that Russia will be diminished by its actions, even it if does make some gains in the Donbas. In fact, since Feb. 24, India has stepped up its engagement with the US, the European Union, and US partners in the Indo-Pacific. This includes through the Quad, the establishment of an EU-India Trade and Technology Council, and the completion of an interim free trade agreement with Australia. Meanwhile, with Russia, there are deep concerns over Russia's ability to deliver existing military sales, due to supply chain disruptions (Russian hardware was reliant for example on semiconductors from Europe), risks of secondary sanctions, and attrition due to the ongoing war. Therefore, while voting at the UN, India's short-term considerations had to be balanced against long-term consequences.

Hwang In NATO's new strategic concept, China was described as a potential threat. What do you think its meaning was?

Jaishankar I previously worked in the Asia Program at the German Marshall Fund, and part of the purpose was to engage with European policymakers on strategic issues in Asia, chief among them being China's rise. Over the past decade and more, I've sensed that there is a growing recognition in Europe that China's rise is not just a commercial opportunity, but also brings with it certain political and sometimes security challenges. Efforts at dividing the EU through the "16+1" format is just one case in point, as well as opaque Chinese investments in central and eastern Europe, and cyberactivity. For Britain, the national security law in Hong Kong, which London saw as a violation of treaty commitments, was a turning point. For France, there is greater concern about Chinese aggression – beginning with assertive and militarized fishing activity – around French territories in the Pacific and Indian Oceans. Some of these changes are reflected in the NATO strategic concept.

Hwang Not all countries share this perception equally.

Jaishankar Yes. The countries of southern Europe, such as Spain and Italy, generally do not see China as much of a major challenge. Nor does Hungary. Others have shifted their positions, Lithuania and the Czech Republic most dramatically, and more recently even Poland due to China's support for Russia. The biggest question mark surrounds Germany, given its weight as a leader in Europe. While the German government has made some signals indicating a shift, they have not always been followed by actions and policies that might jeopardize the commercial relationship with China. That would be the space to watch.

Hwang Do you see if India will correspond to NATO's eastward policy?

Jaishankar India has not had a productive relationship with NATO, although it does have positive relations and burgeoning partnerships with almost all NATO members, barring perhaps Turkey. In my personal view, this has been short-sighted on India's part: Even if there were disagreements, as on Russia, it would have been worth engaging with NATO on areas of common concern. For example, NATO and India both had counterpiracy missions in the western Indian Ocean, both had direct stakes and interests in Afghanistan, and both have concerns about international cyberactivity. The outlines of a common agenda are readily apparent, and different assessments, as over Russia, could yet be shared and discussed. Indeed, it's ironic that China and Russia have more institutional engagement with NATO – such as through the NATO Defense College in Rome or through policy planning dialogues -- than does a democracy such as India.

That said, I think New Delhi largely welcomes the growing concern about China in Europe, even if it is reflected through NATO. This opens up room for greater partnership with India, whether on defense and strategic technologies, or in terms of investment and commercial activity. At the same time, there is a firm realization that NATO -- as an organization -- will have as its primarily mission the defense of Europe and perceive Russia as the primary challenge to European security. Russia's invasion of Ukraine has given NATO a renewed purpose, and its ability to address China, especially outside the European theater, will be limited by resources.

Hwang Between the Quad and the five major emerging economies of Brazil, Russia, India, China and South Africa (BRICS), where does India belong? Is India still pursuing non-aligned diplomacy?

Jaishankar Strangely enough, the term non-alignment is no longer in favor in India, at least under the current government. In fact, it is more commonly used by outsiders now, because of its association with past Indian political dispensations. I do not think BRICS and the Quad are remotely similar or equivalent. BRICS once served a specific purpose, which was after the global financial crisis, to advocate for new international institutions in which developing countries were better represented. Arguably, BRICS has outlived that purpose, and even Beijing and Moscow see less utility in it, outside of a venue for political grandstanding. Xi Jinping barely mentioned BRICS in his second inaugural speech as Party General Secretary, whereas it was repeatedly invoked in his first speech. So BRICS is the past.

The Quad, on the other hand, represents the future. India has much broader interests with Quad partners, from trade and technology to security and people-to-people links. There is also greater convergence in addressing India's overarching objective, which is responding to China's rise and assertiveness. So despite India continuing to remain a member of both coalitions, I sense the Quad growing in importance and BRICS diminishing. All of that can only be turned around if China were to adopt a very different approach to India, but that does not seem likely. That is not specific to India, but the self-perception of Chinese leadership under the Communist Party of China, and especially under Xi Jinping.

Hwang India is recognized as the weakest link in the Quad. What is your view on this?

Jaishankar I don't think that is a fair characterization, and is mostly a reflection of outmoded thinking by those out of government in the US, Japan, and Australia, and amplified by those in India who have deep reservations about India getting close to the United States. Even today, many in India's strategic establishment are deeply uncomfortable with a closer partnership with the US, both on the political left and right, and use many nonsensical arguments to try to undermine or diminish that partnership. One example is many using Aukus -- a trilateral security pact between Australia, the United

Kingdom -- to argue that the Quad is meaningless, when in fact a long-term defense technological partnership between the United States and Australia actually strengthens the Quad.

Hwang It is true that India is an outlier in that it is not a treaty ally of the US, unlike Japan and Australia.

Jaishankar Tokyo and Canberra have over seven decades of working with the US military, and India does not. But this is a very specific yardstick and some habits of cooperation are forming much faster than observers realize. Already, India participates in military exercises with the United States at a frequency and degree of sophistication that few non-allies do. And India now has agreements on classified information, logistics, and maritime domain awareness with Japan and Australia, as well as regular ground, air and naval exercises with both. Still, we may never get to the stage where India has joint basing, joint commands, or mutual defense treaties with any of the other Quad countries, and for that reason the comparisons with NATO are misleading and incorrect.

In terms of Quad participation today, India is actually leading several Quad working groups. These working groups now span a very large array of topics, from infrastructure and health to cybersecurity and humanitarian assistance. And more importantly, in each of these areas, the four countries have concrete projects working toward real outcomes. I would also add that for all the reservations about India's continued participation, New Delhi harbors similar concerns that future governments in the US, Japan and Australia may not share the enthusiasm of, say, Joe Biden, Shinzo Abe, or Scott Morrison for the Quad partnership.

Hwang South Korea is considering joining a Quad working group. What should the cooperation be like?

Jaishankar There is much that the Quad can do with other partners, especially South Korea. But it's unclear whether formal membership is the way forward, or even what that looks like, given that the group is informal and not treaty-based. There are still concerns that South Korea's inclusion will slow down progress given differences with Japan. Rebuilding that trust between Seoul and Tokyo is key. A second concern is South Korea's ability and willingness to play an "out of area" role. Could we see the South Korean military playing a more proactive role, in alignment with partners, in the western Indian Ocean or in the South Pacific? I do not know, but such demonstrations would reinforce to the other Quad countries the value of strategic engagement with Seoul.

Hwang How do you evaluate the conservative South Korean government's value diplomacy?

Jaishankar Overall, a more activist South Korea on the international stage ought to be welcomed. It is an example of a successful democracy, with globally competitive businesses and industry, that has transformed as a society from a developing to a highly-developed economy. Its success stands in stark contrast to North Korea. Successive generations of leaders in Seoul have pursued policies on trade, industry, agriculture, and social welfare that people in India would benefit from learning more about. But my superficial sense is that much more needs to be done for South Korea to project its power globally. That would require a better sense of security challenges in the broader Indo-Pacific and perhaps less of a focus on Korean Peninsula-specific issues.

Hwang How important is economic security considered in India's national security?

Jaishankar Economic security is a very high priority, and arguably always has been, given the number of Indians who have lived below the poverty line, often in precarious conditions. As mentioned, this partly informed India's approach to the Russia-Ukraine conflict. The challenge is that the terms and opportunities are shifting, sometimes quite rapidly. Today, securing energy and other resources is imperative, given that India is poor in natural resources. Access to labor markets is another consideration, although India often faces an uphill challenge given anti-immigration sentiments in many other countries. Finally, India has to shift from a world in which knowledge and technology were scarce and hard to access, to policies that enable the rapid absorption of readily available knowledge and technology. China has done this quite adeptly, but in India this is still a fitful exercise. Complex domestic politics make this an even more daunting challenge.

Hwang How do you view South Korea's dilemma between the US and China? Do you think it is inevitable, or is it perhaps a self-inflicted consequence?

Jaishankar I'm not in a position to judge South Korea's dilemma, but do try to appreciate the complexities of its relationship with China, both from a commercial perspective, but also Beijing's necessity for engagement with Pyongyang. That said, it's my view that we have already entered into a period of sustained, overarching great power competition between the US and China, akin to the Cold War, but with many important differences as well. The challenge is that today, economic and security issues cannot be kept distinct from each other. The future drivers of economic growth will involve a number of technologies -- from automation and artificial intelligence to quantum computing and new materials -- that have enormous national security implications and dual use applications. 5G is just the canary in the coal mine.

In this context, some difficult choices will have to be made by all countries – including the US and China, and of course India and South Korea. To what extent do you prioritize national security, industrial security, and national competitiveness over short-term commercial considerations and market access issues? In this respect, we have had three shocks: the US-China trade war, the coronavirus pandemic, and now the Russian invasion of Ukraine. All three have reinforced the views among national planners in many countries that a world of partial decoupling is inevitable. What remains an open question is how and when that decoupling will take place and to what degree. To this, there are no ready answers, and we are still in a period of experimentation and exploration.

Hwang Previously, India and South Asia were in the spotlight of South Korean diplomacy following the South Korean government's New Southern Policy. How do you expect South Korea-India relations to develop during the Yoon administration?

Jaishankar I think the Moon administration's New Southern Policy was well-intentioned, but the focus was more on Southeast Asia and less on India. There were also concerns that it was not accompanied by progressive policies, and that trade-offs were not always made. I would hope that the Yoon administration can pursue a similar approach with more resolve. One little-known but quite significant achievement has been the growth -- albeit from a low base -- in India-South Korea defense relations. Today there are successful examples of joint production of defense articles, and Seoul is emerging as an important partner in India's defense industrial ecosystem. Still, much more can be done, particularly in areas of high technology such as semiconductors, where South Korea is a global leader. Some of that will require India to become more competitive and attractive as a partner and investment destination.

Changes in European security environment: A temporary shake or an overall paradigm shift?

Jul 20, 2022

Liselotte Odgaard

Professor, Norwegian Institute for Defense Studies in Oslo

Lee Jaeseung

Professor and Jean Monnet Chair, College of International Studies at Korea University

The NATO summit at the end of June signaled a shift in global security. The summit identified Russia as a direct threat and China as a systemic challenge. The results of the NATO summit indicate where the United States' policy objectives stand. The US' new strategy in the Asia-Pacific region is the Indo-Pacific strategy, and its strategy in Europe is NATO's eastward expansion. The US is aiming to build a connection between the Indo-Pacific and NATO. We can see that the US extended from the Asia-Pacific to the Indo-Pacific through the Indian Ocean and reached the Atlantic Ocean in the end, while the Atlantic Ocean is stretching its arm to Asia, going through the Indian Ocean. The US is trying to make a tie between these two. It does not necessarily mean that the US' intention can be accomplished or is accomplished as it wishes. However, what matters is that the US intends to establish a new order on an absolute position that excludes China and Russia. It is now clear that China is the next target after it addresses the direct threat from Russia. No one knows when the Ukraine war will end. However, the US will certainly turn its eyes on China, when the situation in Ukraine settles down either into Donbas' "independence" (Russia's desire) or a "breakaway" (Ukraine's stance). In order to understand the current security situation from Europe to the Indo-Pacific, this week's discussion invites two experts from South Korea and abroad. Liselotte Odgaard is a professor at the Norwegian Institute for Defense Studies in Oslo and a nonresident senior fellow at Hudson Institute. Lee Jaeseung is a professor and Jean Monnet Chair at the College of International Studies, Korea University.

Hwang In February, witnessing Russia's invasion of Ukraine, Sweden and Finland abandoned their some seven-decades of neutrality and decided to join NATO. What was the background for the decision?

Odgaard Finland and Sweden are already well-integrated into NATO, and have expensive defense cooperation agreements with NATO member states. However, as nonmembers they do not have the same influence on NATO decisionmaking. In addition, they do not have the protection of the collective defense obligation of Article 5 in the NATO treaty. In view of Russia's confrontational approach to the post-Soviet sphere and its willingness to use hard power in this region, it makes sense that Finland and Sweden wish to join NATO to protect themselves against threats from Russia.

Lee The military threat from Russia was clearly and seriously recognized this time. Sweden and Finland agreed on the point that the post-World War II neutrality system cannot guarantee the safety of their countries anymore. As shown in Ukraine, NATO and its allies showed hesitation to intervene directly in the crises in the nonmember countries. These two countries needed a more stable collective defense structure to prevent possible military confrontations. In fact, these two countries were not unfamiliar with the NATO framework. Sweden and Finland joined the NATO Partnership for Peace in 1997, and began collaboration with NATO at that time. As member countries of the European Union, the two countries have also built a network between the EU's Common Security and Defense Policy and NATO. In the face of the growing military threat from Russia, Sweden and Finland could mobilize strong domestic consensus to defend core values such as democracy, freedom and the rule of law within the NATO architecture.

Hwang NATO Secretary General Jens Stoltenberg mentioned that "with 32 nations around the table, we will be even stronger." Do you agree with what he says? Who exactly is the opponent and what is the purpose of being strong?

Lee The cohesion of NATO and collective defense will increase. Russia was named as the most significant and direct threat to the allies. The term "threat" replaced the previous usage of partner, challenge, or competitor. The rise of China was also noted as a systematic challenge that threatens NATO's interests, security and values. Threats from China were perceived in a broad range of political, legal and economic arenas. Furthermore, there are growing numbers of global-level threats such as pandemics, climate change, cyber, and human security. NATO and its global allies need to be organized more systematically to deal with these challenges effectively. This announcement implies that NATO and its allies will be more active in building a new security and economic architecture in vying with Russia, China, and other authoritarian regimes. The consolidation of the NATO partnership involves both functional and structural reinforcement.

Odgaard I think NATO's ability to deter aggression from adversaries such as Russia depends on the ability of Europe and the US to stand together with solidarity in their willingness to defend each other. It would be significant for Finland and Sweden to be not just NATO partners anymore, but full member states and as such covered by Article 5.

Hwang Turkey announced that Sweden and Finland have pledged to address "Turkey's pending deportation or extradition requests of terror suspects" -- referring to Kurds, who Turkey considers a terrorist group -- in exchange for agreeing to Sweden and Finland's NATO membership. Shall we understand this as Sweden and Finland putting their national interests first?

Odgaard It remains to be seen how this is resolved in practice. Promising to address Turkey's pending requests in a rather watered-down statement leaves how the issue is handled from now rather open to interpretation.

Lee NATO membership has certainly been a priority for Sweden and Finland. The PKK (Kurdistan Workers' Party) issue is a sensitive one, but was expected to be handled with a political solution. A quid-pro-quo was made at the Madrid summit. Sweden and Finland agreed to Turkish demands by declaring the Kurdish PKK "a terrorist organization" and assured prompt and thorough measures to be introduced. In return, Turkey gave consent for NATO membership for the two countries. As long as the compromise does not hurt the fundamental principles of democracy or freedom of Sweden, Finland and NATO, the deal was indispensable. Turkey emerged as a key political player within NATO that could determine Swedish and Finnish membership by taking advantage of its minority agenda. The implementation of the compromise, however, needs to be observed, especially in terms of human rights and democratic norms.

Hwang In case Ukraine gives up its bid for NATO membership, do you see any possibility of negotiation in terms of neutrality, one of Russia's three demands?

Lee I would like to highlight that what we should pay attention to is not the form of neutrality itself, but the specific features of Ukrainian neutrality if it is introduced. The biggest question is the defense capability of Ukraine: whether neutrality is armed or disarmed. Armed neutrality would bring the issue of military support from outside, most notably from the US and NATO. Disarmed neutrality could risk becoming Russia's de facto satellite country unless Ukraine would equip itself with sufficient counterforces. As mentioned above, the age of neutrality is declining in Europe. The legitimacy of multilateral agreements is often questionable. The 1994 Budapest Memorandum that guaranteed the security of Ukraine was almost nullified in 2014 when Russia annexed Crimea. The neutrality solution requires strong commitments from all stakeholders, but the feasibility and credibility of the neutrality option do not look high in Ukraine at this moment. As a political agreement, however, a limited neutrality concept could be discussed in the peace talks. The diplomatic alliance of Ukraine will be another key issue to be addressed. Ukrainian membership in NATO does not seem probable, but Ukraine strongly wants to join the EU, and the EU may give it candidacy country status.

Odgaard It is too early to predict anything about Ukraine's future status in my opinion.

Hwang What is the European stance regarding an Indo-Pacific strategy?

Odgaard If we're talking about the US' Indo-Pacific strategy, it is a commitment from the US to maintain that China is threat number one, and the primary long-term focus for US deterrence. As a result, it is also important for Europe and the US to stand united around a more critical and defensive stance towards China and Russia. NATO's strategic concept is concerned about Chinese-Russian cooperation, and it is a good sign that Europe and the US are managing to maintain unity of purpose. However for Europe, Russia is threat number one. There is a recognition that the two countries' security threats to the West are linked. It is also intended to signal that the US and Europe will help each other out in both the Indo-Pacific and the European theater, and hence try to create strategic dilemmas for Russia and China by building strong deterrence forces in both Europe and the Indo-Pacific.

Lee The EU announced its strategy for the Indo-Pacific in 2021. While recognizing the growing political and economic importance of this region, the EU no longer wanted to remain as an outsider. Chinese naval expansion, as well as the aggressive Belt and Road Initiatives, also raised European awareness. The EU's Indo-Pacific strategy highlights governance by rule of law, free navigation and sustainability. Building multilateral governance in the region is still a key concern of the EU. It also went together with the EU's connectivity strategy toward the Asia-Pacific region. France, the Netherlands and Germany began to engage in a number of military exercises in the Indo-Pacific region in recent years. However, the EU has been cautious not to single out China as a rival, and has tried to avoid any nuances of a containment strategy in the document. Policy coordination with the US is necessary, but Europe may want to build its own path toward peace and prosperity in the Indo-Pacific region.

Hwang How do you evaluate South Korea's participation in the US' Indo-Pacific strategy?

Lee South Korea has maintained strategic ambiguity toward the US' Indo-Pacific strategy. While the South Korea-US alliance has always been the core of security policy, South Korea has also tried to maintain constructive relations with China in recent years, especially regarding economic issues and the North Korean agenda. As the Indo-Pacific strategy could be seen as anti-China, South Korea has been cautious not to provoke politically sensitive issues with China. The South Korean navy was hesitant to expand its operation area beyond the Korean Peninsula, especially in the East and South China Seas. However, the middle ground for strategic ambiguity is rapidly shrinking amid escalating Sino-US competition. South Korea-Japan relations are another key agenda item, as Japan has been playing a key role in the US' Indo-Pacific strategy. South Korea's Indo-Pacific strategy inevitably involves more engagement with Japan. The European engagement in the Indo-Pacific region may provide South Korea with a more positive platform on which a more multilateral approach and issue-specific participation would be enabled. The South Korean president's participation in the recent NATO summit, together with three other Asia-Pacific countries—Japan, Australia and New Zealand—also signal that South Korea is taking some steps closer to the US' Indo-Pacific strategy in the coming years.

Odgaard South Korea's participation is very significant. After feeling neglected by the US half a decade ago, the last showdown between North Korean leader Kim Jongun and former US President Donald Trump brought South

Korea back in focus. South Korea is now a key country in the eyes of both Europe and the US, and Indo-Pacific allies such as Japan and Australia. It is important that South Korea is integrated in the emerging security architecture of the Indo-Pacific, which is built on the US alliance system. South Korea is obviously important as a front-line state for North Korea and China, but it also has a lot to offer technologically and industrially. This is essential to its allies and partners in the West and the Indo-Pacific.

Hwang Is the Ukraine war a gain or loss for China?

Odgaard I don't think China is happy about Russia's invasion of Ukraine, because it will damage Russia's relative power. As Russia is a key strategic partner, the war will also damage China, mainly because China has been forced to clarify its priorities. Does it support noninterference and the classic concepts of sovereignty on which the UN system rests? Or does it show loyalty toward Russia? China has not been comfortable having to clarify its position, as demonstrated by its reserved attitude toward breaching Western sanctions in its dealings with Russia. Nevertheless, China has demonstrated that it remains committed to working with Russia as a close strategic partner. China is thinking it can do as it did during the last North Korean standoff, where it pretended to put pressure on North Korea, but breached sanctions in reality. Once it was clear that North Korea could not obtain an attractive deal from its point of view, China resumed its full support for North Korea. We are likely to see a similar pattern during the conflict with Ukraine.

Lee China would find both collateral benefits and collateral damages from the war in Ukraine. If Russia could have achieved its political goals, such as preventing the expansion of NATO and the control of the Donbas region without big opposition, China would have been motivated to expand its "sphere of influence" in East Asia, including Taiwan and the Korean Peninsula. These could have been collateral benefits. However, the open war by Russia brought strong resistance from Ukraine and Western countries, and a series of tough sanctions measures on Russia. China may assume those sanctions could be applied to it in the future in the case of confrontations with the US and European countries. China, in that sense, may worry about collateral damages from the war. In the short run, Sino-Russian ties would get strengthened both in the political and the economic domains. In case Russian power weakens after the war, China may secure its status in the Group of Two, a proposed informal special relationship between China and the US, and vie with the US.

Hwang Do you think that Taiwan could be the Ukraine of Asia?

Lee The geopolitical burden is huge for Taiwan. However, I do not think Taiwan will follow the Ukrainian path. Taiwan has steadily strengthened its partnership with the US. The industrial supply chain, especially in semiconductors, is another key connecting cord that motivates the US and its allies to keep Taiwan in a secure economic network. The strategic importance of Taiwan to the US is much higher than that of Ukraine. Taiwan has been very adamant about keeping its independence from mainland China. Taiwan's internal and external conditions are quite different from those of Ukraine. However, the path of the Russia-Ukraine war certainly affects Taiwan's fate. If Western allies -- NATO, the US and the EU -- were divided, and if Putin could achieve a favorable deal to control Ukraine from the peace talks, China will increase pressure on Taiwan, and vice versa.

Odgaard I don't think China has much appetite for an invasion of Taiwan when watching how Russia is faring in the Ukraine conflict. So for at least something like the next decade, I don't think an invasion is likely.

Hwang Do you think that a new Cold War has already started?

Odgaard I would not call it a Cold War because the geographical divisions we had then do not apply anymore. Decoupling can probably only go so far, and for now it is mainly rhetorical. The importance of the cyber and space domains also means that we cannot separate from each other, because of cyber, space, investments, and so on. China is a part of Europe and the US, just as we are a part of China and the Indo-Pacific. Conflicts and wars play out in different ways that are not always very visible physically, but the general public still very much feel the consequences of cyberattacks against civilian targets. There is also a merging of civilian and military spheres in the cyber and space domains that makes it difficult to distinguish between these two spheres. So a new Cold War is in many ways a strange description of the international system that we are living in now, which doesn't adequately describe its central dynamics.

Lee Yes. The new Cold War is becoming a new normal in international relations. The confrontation between the two blocs -- the US, Europe and Asia-Pacific allies on one side, and Russia and China on the other -- became clearly visible. Even before the Russia-Ukraine war, Sino-US competition signaled the advent of a new Cold War. The Russian invasion of Ukraine brought back two old ghosts from World War II: open war based on the use of force and the sphere of influence. The unstated optimism that actual military confrontation was improbable was broken, and global security had to deal with the bare nature of power politics. However, the world has already established a high density of economic interdependence vis-a-vis the old Cold War period. The cost of a new Cold War would be much higher than the one from half a century ago. The door to a new Cold War has been unlocked, but is not yet fully open. The task of peacebuilding in Ukraine in the coming months bears importance not just for stability in Europe, but also for the prevention of another Cold War in many other regions of the world.

Europe's security dilemma: Can it pave its own 3rd path?

Nov 30, 2022

Thomas Christiansen

Professor, Political Science and European Integration at Luiss University

The EU has a strong image of an exemplary student in many ways. As the EU expanded to Eastern and Central Europe after the end of the Cold War system, its political and economic influence further stretched to the international community. The EU is strengthening cooperative relations with other regions through common foreign and security policies and has pursued peace and prosperity in Europe by simultaneously providing mutual cooperation and development support to the regions outside of Europe. Europe's status could be maintained by sharing the political values underlying democracy, the rule of law, and respect for human rights, and the EU was considered as the answer in terms of its goal and methodology in building communities, as it has proved mutual consideration and cooperation are feasible within the EU.

Europe seems to have learned from history that only coexistence in the international community deserves to enjoy its own peace and prosperity. However, along with these advantages and competitiveness, there are also many weaknesses and problems. The geopolitical dilemma seen in the Ukraine War is that Europe could not overcome the realism, and the policy distance between it and China and Russia basically shows a gap in understanding between civilizations.

Whether Brexit is a step forward or a step backward in European history will be judged by history in the future. In the various features of the non-polar, unipolar, bipolar, and multipolar international order, we are watching Europe's choice of whether Europe will remain a protective shield for the US due to its decision-making disorders, whether it can operate as a single pole by paving a third path in a multipolar system, no matter France and Germany come up front and lead.

This week's interview invited Professor Thomas Christiansen, a leading expert in this field, to answer these various questions. He is a professor of political science and European integration at Luiss University, Rome, as well as executive editor of the Journal of European Integration. He previously held positions in several universities including Maastricht University, and Aberystwyth University.

Hwang What political, economic, and security impact is the Russian-Ukraine war bringing on Europe?

Christiansen The war obviously creates huge challenges for Europe, as it does for the wider world: rising living costs, increases in military spending, the energy crisis, a looming economic recession, another refugee and humanitarian crisis and new divisions in domestic politics. The confrontation with Russia has also reminded Europeans of their dependence on the United States for military security. But in the longer term, one can also see positive developments, namely a renewed purpose in the EU to cooperate on security, diversify global supply chains and strengthen cooperation with countries in the neighborhood. The new EU membership applications of Ukraine, Georgia, and Moldova demonstrate the continuing attraction of the European Union for countries that have been under attack by Russia, and confirm that the EU continues to be a political model with a future perspective, despite a decade of continuous crises. And the new "European Political Community", which held its first summit meeting in Prague in October 2022, brings together all European states except Russia and Belarus. It provides an inclusive framework for cooperation among EU members, candidate countries and non-members.

Hwang Do you think the EU's hard-line policies against Russia can be continued? It seems members' positions are different from one another.

Christiansen I am not sure I would call EU policy on Russia "hard-line." In the face of Russia's attack on a sovereign state in the EU's immediate neighborhood, the interruption of gas deliveries for the purpose of blackmail, a sustained campaign of political disinformation, repeated threats of a nuclear attack, and general disregard for international law, one might consider the EU's response rather measured. Russia likely blew up the Nordstream gas pipelines in the Baltic Sea, conducted cyber-attacks against political institutions in EU countries, and has been proven to be behind the shooting down of Flight MH17, the Malaysian airliner, in July 2014 which killed almost 300 people, among them many EU citizens and the murderous attacks on Russian dissidents in European countries -- most famously the assassination attempt in Salisbury in March 2018. While Russia's invasion of Ukraine now received -- quite rightfully -- all the attention, Europe has been under attack by Russia

There continues to be hesitation to provide Ukraine with the heavy armor that it has been requesting, and more broadly a sense that diplomatic channels with Russia need to remain open. Of course, there are differences between the member states, with frontline states such as Poland, Finland and the Baltic States being more fully committed to the support of Ukraine, whereas the French and German governments have been more ambivalent in this regard, and kept open the possibility of an eventual negotiated settlement. But only Hungary, where Prime Minister Viktor Orban is openly supportive of Vladimir Putin, has departed from the EU's common position on the war.

Hwang EU-China relations seem to be deteriorating rapidly. Do you think Europe considers China a larger threat than Russia? If so, is this because of the third factor, the United States?

Christiansen EU relations with China are deeply affected by the war in Ukraine, and it is becoming more common now to see both Russia and China -- authoritarian regimes with aggressive foreign policies -- in the same light.

While China is not actively supporting Russia in the conduct of the war, it is nevertheless seen to be on the side of Russia in this conflict. However, despite some rhetoric, there is no alliance between Russia and China. Indeed, there are fundamental differences between the two powers: China is not seen as a direct threat to Europe in the sense of a territorial attack that we have seen from Russia, and both business and political elites are aware of the significance that China has for Europe in terms of trade and investment. I would say European policymakers are becoming more cautious about a deeper engagement with China, and are working to avoid a greater dependency on China in critical sectors, but at the same time, there is a recognition that the economic costs of a genuine de-coupling would be very high, and should be avoided. As far as pressure from the United States is concerned, Europe is rather resisting that and searching for a "third way" of dealing with China, beyond the antagonism of the US and the specter of greater dependency in the future.

Hwang What is the international order that the EU is thinking of? Does the unipolarity, bipolarity, multipolarity, or non-polarity fit in here?

Christiansen I believe Europeans are generally aware that the global order is changing, and that their influence on its future shape is limited. To the extent to which the EU has a strategy, it is to support multilateral solutions to global issues, to maintain the role of international institutions and to prevent a complete descent into global power politics. The EU is not about protecting national sovereignty, but indeed about overcoming its limitations, and that means that it seeks to strengthen the rule of law internationally and address common challenges such as the climate crisis, the global pandemic and the threats to world trade -- all issues that threaten global security and prosperity more than anything. And these challenges can only be addressed jointly, by countries and organizations working together rather than against one another.

Hwang Do you think we are entering the New Cold War?

Christiansen History does not repeat itself, but the danger that the deterioration in relations between the US and China could resemble the Cold War between the Soviet Union and the West is clearly there. The "old" Cold War divided the world along multiple lines -- militarily, economically, ideologically, and culturally. Today's situation is more complex: There is an increasing strategic rivalry between the US and China (albeit still very uneven considering the size of the US military), while the two powers' economies are deeply integrated with one another. The question for the coming decade is: Will these economic ties (and the high cost of severing these) ensure that the US (and their allies) continue to cooperate with China, or will the strategic rivalry ultimately lead to economic de-coupling and a Cold War-style division of the world into separate economic zones?

Hwang Since Brexit, do you see the UK's withdrawal has weakened the EU's role and capacity? Or did it make the EU's direction and integration seem more obvious?

Christiansen There have been no winners from Brexit: the EU has lost an important member state, with a global reach, and the UK lost easy access to its largest export market. Politically the hard choices imposed by Brexit have deeply divided the UK, created political chaos and weakened its international standing. As a result, more and more people in Britain now regret the manner in which the UK left the EU -- according to the latest surveys, 60 percent of the population consider Brexit a mistake. But we will have to see if and when that translates into a different approach by the government.

For the EU, the Brexit experience has been sobering, but indeed also unifying: governments and institutions were remarkably united in the negotiation of the UK's withdrawal, and the "domino effect" that some have expected -- one country after the other seeking to leave the EU -- did clearly not happen. As a matter of fact, the opposite has occurred: Under the impression of the damage that leaving the EU can do to a country's economy and political culture, people across the remaining member states now see greater value in EU membership than before. It is as if what was invisible and taken for granted before -- the many benefits of EU membership -- have now become more transparent to the wider public.

Hwang The EU's advantage must be its diversity, but I assume it can also be a disadvantage.

Christiansen 'Unity in Diversity' is indeed the EU's motto, and it does practice that on a daily basis. But there are of course many areas in which common rules and uniform practices are needed, and that does create tensions on occasion. Member States often suffer from a kind of political schizophrenia: They do want the EU because the benefits of working together -- efficiency gains, greater security, access to a large market -- are clear, yet at the same time they frequently try to avoid the kind of commitments and limitations to the freedom of maneuver that comes with it. "Having your cake and eating it" -- as the British call it. Having said that, cooperation is the rule in an integrated Europe, even if occasional disagreements catch the headlines more than the daily routine of joint decision-making through the EU institutions.

Hwang What are the challenging factors that both the EU and Korea are facing today?

Christiansen Despite all the differences between a European regional organization and a state in East Asia, and the great distance between them, the EU and Korea have surprisingly many things in common with one another: Both are middle powers in a world that is moving toward great power rivalry, both rely heavily on exports in their economic models, and as a result, both have also been among the staunchest supporters of trade liberalization globally and regionally. As strategic partners, they cooperate frequently on a variety of policy issues, and the Free Trade Agreement signed in 2011 was the first in a new era of comprehensive trade deals.

Given these similar backgrounds, the EU and Korea also face similar challenges, namely the threat of a global recession and the decline of global trade in an era of rising protectionism and economic statecraft. Both depend on the United States for the provision of military security in the face of aggressive neighbors, but both also have concerns about Washington's role in their security: Can we (in Korea and/or Europe) continue to rely on the US for our protection? Can we avoid being dragged into the looming conflict between the US and China, given how costly that can become for Europe in particular?

Hwang What should be the direction for the further development of EU-Korea relations?

Christiansen The EU and Korea need to further strengthen their bilateral cooperation, in particular to expand that to questions of security and military defense. The EU has recently approved the setting up of a military training mission for Ukrainian soldiers, and that might be something for Korea to consider joining as well, given its superior experience in military preparedness. More important still is economic cooperation and the search for diversification of supply chains -- areas where both sides can gain a lot from sharing information and working together.

Hwang The German Chancellor has recently visited China, and this trip seems quite divergent from other European positions including that of the EU or NATO. How can we interpret this visit?

Christiansen The visit itself attracted a lot of attention, and meeting with Xi Jinping is certainly a noteworthy event, especially against the background of China's Zero COVID policy. But it is also not that unusual, as the meetings of Xi with President Biden and President Marcon during the 2022 G20 Summit have shown. What was more disconcerting was the presence of a large delegation of representatives of German industry, and the continuing attempts to deepen economic ties with China, even though the official line is now diversified. Permitting the Chinese to part-purchase facilities in Hamburg harbor also added to this negative image.

In line with many other European states -- but against the wishes of the United States -- there has been close cooperation across the range of issues identified in the context of the strategic partnership (even though that has now been suspended), and indeed in that regard, there is a fundamental difference to the attitude of the United States, namely that Europe seeks to continue a policy of active engagement with China, whereas the US agenda has a much more antagonistic stance toward

China. The future will tell which of these assessments will be more accurate but in the meanwhile occasional tension is definitely to be expected. Ultimately, past experience is hopefully still a good idea.

Mapping out Korea's diplomacy through Canada

May 5, 2022

Colin Robertson
Vice President and Fellow, Canadian Global Affairs Institute

Just as how Korea is referred to as the East's Land of the Morning Calm, Canada is the West's. Despite its vast territory, Canada has often flown under the radar on the global stage because of its small population and proximity to the world's largest economy, the US. From Korea's standpoint, news from the four major powers -- the US, China, Japan, and Russia -- have mostly dominated the headlines here. What we do hear occasionally about Canada, such as the young prime minister coming to power or Canada being the active model country in international development and public diplomacy, gives the image that Canada is a wealthy advanced country.

Meanwhile, Chinese Huawei founder Ren Zhengfei's daughter, Meng Wanzhou, was arrested in Canada in December 2018. At the request of the US, Canada arrested Meng, who is also Huawei's deputy chair, and China later detained Canadians on spying charges. China's tit-for-tat move was in response to Canadian Prime Minister Justin Trudeau's open criticism in 2020 of China's "Wolf Warrior Diplomacy." He took aim at Beijing's human rights suppression in Hong Kong and Xinjiang Uyghur Autonomous Region at the 50th anniversary of China-Canada diplomatic relations.

But when we realistically consider that China is the second-largest trading partner to Canada while Canada is not a major country to China, does Canada have the actual power to counteract China? Is it possible for Canada to stand up alone and play its own diplomacy without leaning on the US?

Canada's middle power diplomacy is a significant learning lesson to Korea which has emerged as a new middle power itself, and is seeking to reestablish relations with China as the Korean government changes hands.

In this regard, this week I invited former Canadian diplomat Colin Robertson, currently vice president and fellow at the Canadian Global Affairs Institute. He is an executive fellow at the University of Calgary's School of Public Policy and a distinguished senior fellow at the Norman Paterson School of International Affairs at Carleton University.

Hwang What drives Canadian foreign policy?

Robertson With a relatively small market (38 million) Canada must trade to generate our prosperity. Trade requires peace and stability. For a middle power like Canada to have impact, a rules-based order is essential. We are, by nature and habit, multilateralists. We enjoy membership in just about every multilateral organization going, notably the G-7 and the G-20; NATO; and the North American Aerospace Defense Command; the United Nations and its alphabet soup of agencies; the Commonwealth and la Francophonie; the World Trade

Organization; the Asia-Pacific Economic Cooperation; the Canada-USA-Mexico Agreement; Comprehensive Economic and Trade Agreement; the Comprehensive and Progressive Trans-Pacific Partnership among others.

Hwang Does Canadian foreign policy have a theme?

Robertson Canadian foreign policy aims active and constructive internationalist engagement, especially in multilateral fora. At our best, we are a quietly competent helpful fixer. At our worst, we are a tiresome, sanctimonious preacher. Canadians were engineers to the American architects during the post-World War II reconstruction, admitted to the G-7 (1976) and then a godfather to the G-20. In helping to create the rules-based order, Canada introduced the principle of "functionalism." This is the abiding legacy of Louis St. Laurent, Lester Pearson and others -- internationalists by conviction, they were realists by experience. Canada was not a great world power, but in certain sectors -- food and energy -- we had vital interests and capacity. This merited a place at the table. With competence, investment and artful diplomacy we earned our seat in the UN's functional agencies and, albeit temporarily, joined the great powers on the Security Council.

Hwang Today, Canada's international status is quite impressive. Canada belongs to almost every multilateral club, be it economic, security, or with a general or specific purpose in creation.

Robertson Yes. On balance this is a good thing, but prioritization of attention and resources is overdue. We pride ourselves on our multilateralism but the defeat (2020) in our quest for a temporary seat on the UN Security Council (we lost to Norway and Ireland) should serve as a wake-up call that proclaiming "Canada is back" does not make it so. It means investments in collective security and defense as well as development assistance and the kind of helpful fixing that we are doing with the Lima Group in Venezuela and through the Ottawa Group in working to reform the World Trade Organization and in using our convening power as we did by hosting a discussion on Korea during the Trump administration.

Hwang What is the core national interest from Canada's perspective?

Robertson Like most nations Canadians strive for prosperity but because we are a pluralistic society -- 1 in 5 Canadians was born outside of Canada -- we must also strive for national unity. Our diversity as a people and as a place to live obliges us to practice tolerance, accommodation and compromise. We try to govern by consent. Managing this diverse, often fissiparous, federation is no easy task. It depends on mutual accommodation, first with our climate and geography and then between political parties, between different interests, between the regions, between rural and urban, between English Canada and French Canada, with the Indigenous peoples and with newcomers. We depend on immigration who bring new skills and ideas with them. The challenge is to weave these many constantly evolving threads into a kilt for every place and every season.

Hwang Canada's national characteristic is like having no shape in the shape, but also having shape in no shape.

Robertson We don't have a lot of history in comparison to Europe or Asia. Some would argue that this is a good thing. Canada continues to be a country "in development" and an experiment in pluralism. The humorist Will Ferguson remarked that the great themes of Canadian history were keeping the Americans out, the French in and the natives out of sight. We've managed the Americans and the French fact. Today there is realization and recognition on reconciliation with our Indigenous peoples.

To say governing Canada requires the capacity to listen and the capacity to balance would be an understatement. The poet F. R. Scott sarcastically described the modus operandi of our longest serving prime minister, Mackenzie King, a pudgy bachelor who engaged in seances so he could speak to his dead mother:

We had no shape / Because he never took sides; / And no sides / Because he never allowed them to take shape ... / Do nothing by halves / Which can be done by quarters.

While it was not meant as a compliment, Scott unwittingly captured the Canadian formula of accommodation.

Hwang How can Canada be a meaningful partner in the Indo-Pacific?

Robertson For now, our Indo-Pacific policy focuses rather more on promoting trade and investment than on effective geopolitics. Canada needs to invest more in to support security presence -- more naval and air presence -- and by joining the East Asia Summit and AUKUS and looking for a meaningful role in the Quad. We need to take more advantage and increase business utilization of our freer trade agreements i.e. CPTPP, Canada-Korea FTA while continuing our efforts to liberalize trade with ASEAN, India and Indonesia. Ministerial visits need to be regular and results oriented.

Hwang Standing in between the US and China, what would be a better choice? The strategic ambiguity? Or the strategic clarity?

Robertson While strategic ambiguity has its advantages for some nations and in some circumstances, in the confrontation between China and the USA, Canada must side with the USA. There is no question that for Canada it will always be the United States and then the rest. for Canada it is "America First" -- in trade, security and people-to-people relations.

Pre-pandemic, more than 400,000 people cross in both directions over the border daily. We trade nearly $2 million a minute with the US. The US takes 74 percent of Canada's exports (we provide about 18 percent of US imports) and provides 64 percent of our imports. Americans hold nearly half the stock of foreign investment in Canada.

Hwang There must be both pros and cons for depending on the US.

Robertson This dependence on the US comes at a price, especially for our oil and gas which are both sold at a discounted price. We need to diversify our trade and increase the number of Canadian companies that export. We need to make better use of the people-to-people relationships. Our active, global immigration adds about 1 percent to our population each year and this adds to our people-to-people ties.

The renegotiation of the NAFTA (1994) and implementation (2020) of the Canada-US-Mexico agreement restores investor confidence and enables the potential for an enhanced North American manufacturing platform with continental supply chains, especially post-COVID and the requirement for security of supply and redundancy in sourcing. While life with Uncle Sam can be frustrating, we cannot change our geography, nor would we want to. Canada's influence in the world is determined in large part by the perception that preferred place. The US looks to us to help interpret the rest of the world and the rest of the world looks to

Canada to interpret the USA.

Hwang What is the lesson that Canada has learned from what happened to Meng Wanzhou and the two Michaels (Michael Spavor and Michael Kovrig)?

Robertson Canadians have had another reminder that authoritarian regimes, this case the leadership of the Chinese Communist Party, cannot be trusted. As a first step we need to put teeth -- real sanctions -- on states like China that use hostage-taking.

Hwang What kind of world do you think is coming after the war in Ukraine?

Robertson Sadly, a world that is messier and meaner. It will be increasingly divided into three shifting blocs. The liberal democracies -- EU, G-7, NATO, Korea, Australia, New Zealand, Taiwan -- are small but their economic weight is significant. But they also face internal divisions as the age-old divide between right and left is replaced by the starker division between populists and nationalists on one side and liberals and globalists on the other. The liberal democracies are pitted against the authoritarians -- China, Russia, North Korea, Belarus, Hungary, Serbia, Myanmar -- and sundry others in Latin America, Africa and Asia. A Xi Jinping-led China offers an alternative authoritarian system based on state enterprise and near-total surveillance aligned to a system of what the Chinese call "social credit" designed to keep the population in check. Both Xi and Putin are also convinced that the West is both decadent and in decline. And, as Putin told the Financial Times, liberalism has "become obsolete." The rest include India, Brazil, South Africa, Turkey, Indonesia, Saudi Arabia and most of Africa, Latin America and Asia. Like the G-7 and the Non-Aligned Movement before them they will pursue their own interests.

Hwang What do you think the roles of the international regimes are?

Robertson The multilateral institutions will fall into further disrepute. The UN Security Council is dysfunctional. The UN General Assembly and WTO are essentially just talking shops. Most multilateral organizations need reform e.g. WTO, WHO, IMF, World Bank at a time when we need them more than ever to deal with the big multilateral issues around climate, pandemics and inequality and nuclear proliferation.

Hwang How do you evaluate Korea's diplomacy? What direction should Korea head toward?

Robertson Like Canada, Korea is a middle power. While the approach depends on the government of the day it seems to me that Korea has embraced the middle power concept, defined to suit Korean needs. While Korean policy is focused by necessity on North Korea, its external policy over the years is illustrated through, for example, "trustpolitik," the Global Public Diplomacy Network, and the grouping of Mexico, Indonesia, South

Korea, Turkey and Australia as a forum for middle powers to convene on global issues, and more recently in the New Southern Policy Plus.

Hwang In case the middle power countries group themselves, how large would their influence be in the international society?

Robertson Not as much as we would hope but in the absence of American leadership the liberal democracies will have to try to hold things together, although the Franco-German Alliance for Multilateralism did not meet the test in its first incarnation. While it is fine to talk about a D-10, the lesson of the Trump presidency is that without American leadership the rules-based multilateral system flounders.

Hwang Korea will soon have a new government. Do you have any suggestions on where Korea-Canada relations should walk on, and where both can cooperate together?

Robertson Canada and Korea are joined by ties of trade, history and a shared commitment to internationalism and a rules-based order. Over 500 Canadians gave their lives during that Korean conflict and Canada continues to contribute to the UN mission that continues to this day. Sadly, Korea remains divided and South Koreans live daily with the uncertainties created by Kim Ilsung, Kim Jongil and now Kim Jongun. This underlines the importance of our security relationship. Meanwhile, the Canada-Korea FTA (2014) provides a framework and platform, but the meat of these deals comes from deepening our business-to-business ties and developing partnerships in sectors including medical devices, smart cars and e-commerce as well as in the practical application of artificial intelligence and robotics, all areas in which Canada has interest and growing competence.

Hwang What can Canada and Korea do as middle powers?

Robertson To capture our relative potential as middle powers, Korea is sometimes described as a tiger while Canada is presented as a "cool moose." We also are both stuck between much bigger neighbors that are variously described as dragon (China), bear (Russia) or eagle (USA). We are not without capacity, ranking as we do in any top 20 ranking of GDP and, perhaps more importantly, in the top 20 of the UN Human Development Index. As middle powers we need to defend those concepts that reflect our values and advance our interests. These include: first, free trade and market economies while recognizing that rising tides don't lift all boats; second, managed migration that relies first on the neighboring nations, with financial and technical support from the wider community; third, peace operations that rely on armed forces from neighboring nations; fourth, sustainable development preserving the global commons, mitigating climate change and addressing pandemics.

Strategic perspective over the Afghanistan crisis

Sept 8, 2021

Hwang Jaeho

Professor, Division of International Studies at Hankuk University of Foreign Studies

The chaotic scenes of Afghanistan women desperately crying out in fear, cheers from Taliban, Kabul airport covered with bloody terror, and President Joe Biden's frustrated looks. ... With the recent withdrawal of Afghanistan, there has been growing controversy over the credibility and morality of US leadership; over whether "America is Back," "America can be Back," or even "America is Willing to be Back'. Criticisms of the Biden administration's irresponsibility and non-strategy are pouring in from all over the world, as we witness the current situation in Afghanistan. However, to be exact, the Afghanistan crisis is not a failure of the US, but rather a failure of the "failed state" Afghanistan itself. It is just that the US withdrawal process was not as smooth as it had to be.

Donald Trump's diplomacy was rough, Biden's diplomacy is sophisticated, but the ultimate priority for both is America First. It is more profitable and a natural decision to break up with

Afghanistan for the sake of US interests.

The importance of energy security in this region has already been devalued as shale gas came to the surface. Though the US has spent $2 trillion over the past two decades, supporting the incompetent regime was like pouring water into a broken bucket, as seen in Afghan President's shameless escape.

Biden bears the burden of winning over some of the 46.9 percent of Americans who supported Trump in the last Presidential election ahead of the upcoming midterm elections. In this sense, as Biden has to be conscious of the isolationist voters, it is inevitable for US foreign policy to become more introverted.

The withdrawal from Afghanistan is ultimately the Biden administration's new strategic choice and concentration. It aims to gather up the existing but scattered capabilities, minimize the consumption of its capabilities, and share the burden with its partners and allies.

The US will minimize its unnecessary use of national power from now on. However, it might be a risky misinterpretation to say that the US leadership is over as well. In case the Biden administration succeeds in its choice and concentration during his four years, it will be "one step backward, but two steps forwards" for the future US. Then Biden's era will be evaluated as the period of the successful transition for the US diplomacy.

On the other hand, the US' failure means China's fortune. In other words, the failure of the US is an opportunity for China. From China's point of view, the Taliban's unexpectedly prompt return is because the previous Afghan government was the transplant regime of the US. The forced transplantation of the Western system in the Islamic "Tribal State" is like water and oil. The previous Afghan government was based on its people's desperation and disappointment, rather than a warm welcome.

As the Chinese Foreign Minister Wang Yi has already declared a desire for constructive cooperation with Afghanistan back in 2017, China is likely to step in as a constructive interventionist soon. Afghanistan is geopolitically useful for China and is the essential transiting area for China's Belt and Road Initiative to extend westward. Furthermore, as Xinjiang shares a border with Afghanistan, China will see cooperation from Afghanistan as important for its crackdown on Uighurs. Moreover, there is the issue of energy supply and demand.

In addition to these practical interests, China also sees psychological and strategic interests. As China regards itself as the global power, there is no reason for China not to intervene in Afghanistan as the most powerful neighboring country. China is confident that it will not get bogged down in Afghanistan, unlike the Soviet Union and the US. Since China is still standing on the principle of non-intervention in internal affairs, there are probably not many factors that conflict with the Taliban government.

China believes the pressure on China will increase after the US's withdrawal from Afghanistan. As seen by the recent establishment of the "Mission Center for China" in the CIA, the US has shifted its strategic pivot from counterterrorism to containing China. The effectiveness of the inland bases in Central Asia has limits in pressuring China. As the Indo-Pacific region is the main battlefield, the main frontline of the US is still East Asia.

Since the withdrawal from Afghanistan, some in Korea worry that South Korea cannot be an exception, but it seems to be a bit excessive. Korea is useful in restraining China from the very first line of the Indo-Pacific, and in this sense, a US withdrawal from Korea would run counter to the "America first" principle. The US is reaffirming its commitment to an ironclad alliance with Korea, since it has upgraded the alliance with Korea to the global level last May. Within the overall calculation, the US's withdrawal from Korea will be infeasible, therefore, we may delete the nightmare of Afghanistan from our thoughts.

Eurasia's vulnerable geopolitical points: Ukraine, Kazakhstan, and North Korea

Feb 9, 2022

Hong Wansuk

Professor, Department of Russian Studies at Hankuk University of Foreign Studies

Stanislav Pritchin

Senior Research Fellow, Institute of World Economy and International Relations at the Russian Academy of Sciences

Li Kaisheng

Director, Research Division of International Relations theories at Shanghai Academy of Social Science

For the last two years, people the world over have lived with the invisible fear of the COVID-19 pandemic. We are now used to applying sanitizer to our hands and repeatedly lifting up our masks to keep them above our noses. Now the world is somewhat getting used to the pandemic situation. With the number of omicron cases in South Korea going into the tens of thousands a day, and while people are now screened with quarantine passes on their way into restaurants and malls without concern, the traditional security fears that had been forgotten have suddenly returned to the forefront of our minds.

Two countries in Eurasia have been subject to boisterous military moves and reports of casualties in the international news since the beginning of this year. The Russian-led Collective Security Treaty Organization deployed troops to Kazakhstan in the name of an anti-terrorist operation. Following what happened in Kazakhstan, Russian troops have been busy at the border between Russia and Ukraine, preparing to invade when the time comes. The US and some countries from the West were preparing for military intervention, but are in standby mode under the "Olympic Truce" for the Beijing Winter Olympics. North Korea has also raised tension by launching missiles seven times leading up to the Olympic opening ceremony. During the first month of this year, security flames successively sparked from the far east of Eurasia, crossed the middle of the continent and reached westward.

These discussions invited three experts of the respective countries to foresee if the recent fires would spread all over or if they can be extinguished. Discussing the tension in Ukraine is Dean Hong Wansuk from Hankuk University of Foreign Studies, who is an expert in Russian diplomacy and security. For Kazakhstan, we were joined by Dr. Stanislav Pritchin, senior research fellow of the Institute of World Economy and International Relations of the Russian Academy of Sciences, and Dr. Li Kaisheng, director of the research division of International Relations theories of Institute of International Relations at Shanghai Academy of Social Science, contributed to the discussion on the rising tension coming from North Korea.

Hwang How do you assess the recent tension in Ukraine?

Hong The US is still the representative power in the West. In these circumstances, embracing Ukraine basically means restraining Russia's imperial revival and guaranteeing NATO's power expansion. Moreover, it allows a smoother approach to the Caspian coastal area, which is a massive repository of energy resources. On the other hand, from Russia's perspective, preventing Ukraine's further pro-Westernization, having it stay neutral and attracting it to the Slavic community is a defense against NATO's stretch toward the east. At the same time, it is a stepping stone for Russia in extending its influence over Central and Eastern Europe, as well as anq essential precondition for hegemonic domination over the Black Sea and CIS (Commonwealth of Independent States) region. In short, Ukraine is the cornerstone of the Kremlin's efforts to restore a great and strong Russia. This explains why Ukraine is the substantial battlefield between the US and Russia in terms of seizing the hegemony in Eurasia.

Hwang What would the intervention in Ukraine present to Russia? Would it be a gain or loss?

Hong The reason Russia struck Ukraine as the lever must be seen in a multilayered and complex way. The strike itself is not the main purpose. It seems Russia has achieved its own strategic goals in certain areas and various levels through forming a strength-to-strength confrontation with NATO by setting Ukraine as the partition line. In terms of issues such as raising the Russian people's overall pride, distracting its people from the domestic exhaustion that comes from a prolonged Putin administration with external affairs, roping the US into diplomatic talks and occupying the high ground in negotiations, showing off Russia's geopolitical presence as the great and strong power -- which has been overshadowed by China -- cleaving Europe, examining

Russian military readiness posture in case war breaks out and strengthening its operation capacity, and containing Ukraine from making rash decisions, we can evaluate that Kremlin's move to raise the tension in Ukraine succeeded in accomplishing at least half of its strategic goals. The fact is that the other half is the core. That would be Russia's leverage to demand a security guarantee at either official talks or under-the–table negotiations in the near future.

Hwang If the US does not accept Russia's demands, would Russia invade Ukraine?

Hong If Russia's troops enter the sovereign state of Ukraine, Putin will lose his justification, since he has criticized the US in international society for unilaterally and militarily abusing its power.

It will eventually stigmatize Russia for being not only the invading country, but also one that points out others' shady practices when it has done the same. Then the Kremlin's authority and international status will be diminished. Moreover, the concern in losing the Slavic community's human and material sources, and destroying historical heritage would make Russia hesitate before taking military action against Ukrainian territory.

Though Russia does not really show it, the West's highly intensified sanctions have also been quite influential in preventing Russia from making armed provocations toward Ukraine. Above all, Russia's fear in overusing its power without sufficient economic backup -- in other words "overstretching" -- is the main reason for Russia's hesitation. This arouses trauma from the collapse of the Soviet Union, which Putin defined as a geopolitical disaster. Considering these perspectives, Russia has too much to lose by invading Ukraine, including strategic aspects.

Even if Russia finally decides to take military action, the possibility of striking Ukraine first and directly is very low under various circumstances. To Russia, Ukraine is the "core interest," the geopolitical vital point, which is never a matter that can be given up or negotiated over. Therefore, Russia's actual invasion will only be possible when Ukraine's admission to NATO is almost at the final stage.

Hwang At what level or circumstance do you expect the Ukraine tension to settle down?

Hong I guess we can specify three scenarios. The first is when both the US and Russia cannot find a satisfying point. Especially if the US rejects Russia's red line, which is on Ukraine and Georgia to joining NATO. If the US pushes ahead with their admission, then direct armed conflict between the US and Russia will be inevitable.

The second scenario is the status quo. If the US and Russia go through negotiations behind the curtains and find some negotiation point which is neither's maximum but an acceptable point, in other words, meeting the equilibrium at Pareto optimum in terms of exchanging security interests, the status quo scenario is feasible.

The third is breaking the status quo by promoting US-Russia relations, if the US largely accommodates Russia's demand, in contrast its diplomatic rhetoric. Going a bit deeper, in such a case as the US admits Ukraine's Crimea as Russian "territory" and lifts the sanctions on Russia, we might see the flare of new diastrophism of the international order in the 21st century.

Hwang If the tension in Ukraine resolves as Russia desires in some aspects, how do you see Russia's next moves?

Hong At the security guarantee negotiation table, I assume the legal document that contains two agendas is necessary. First, the promise that Ukraine would not further proceed joining NATO, which is Russia's Maginot Line, and second, that NATO would not further deploy troops and military equipment in Ukraine territory. In this case, Ukraine would endure as the buffer zone between "East" and "West." Also, continuously maintaining Donbass as a "disputed area" is critical, just in case the US changes its promise, because a country with a disputed area cannot be accepted as a member of NATO, according to its admission requirement.

Hwang Both Ukraine and Kazakhstan are geographically distant from Korea. Nevertheless, do you see any strategic implication that Korea should keep in mind in terms of security?

Hong The geopolitical implications that Korea must glean from the Ukraine of 2021 can be explained at various levels, however, I would like to emphasize "self-strength." Although we are watching a national crisis of Ukraine, what we only see are the strategies and confrontations between the US and Russia, not Ukraine.

In this context, what I would like to require of Korea with urgency is first, the sustainable strengthening of national defense power, and second, the transfer of wartime operational control authority as soon as possible in order to lower its dependency on its alliance. A balance of power without one's own strength heads toward subordination to foreign influence in the end. Korea's geopolitical fate is to struggle for survival in the tight crack among the world-ranking strong countries, such as the US, China, Russia and Japan. This is the reason Korea must constantly advance its economy, modernize its military and globalize its culture.

Hwang What are the reasons for the recent unrest taking place in Kazakhstan?

Pritchin From the economic point of view, Kazakhstan seems to be the leader in the region of the post-Soviet space by many indicators, such as investment and resources. However, it should be noted that there is a significant gap in the distribution of income between regions and different social strata. Naturally, there were serious protests and clashes taking place from year to year. In addition, Kazakhstan is experiencing rapid population growth, especially in rural areas in the southern part of the republic. The state is not able to provide normal education, health care and jobs to the people in these areas.

Hwang Would there be any possibility of a "Color Revolution"?

Pritchin The term "Color Revolution" is hardly applicable to Kazakhstan events for a whole range of reasons. Color Revolution is an attempt to change the governing elite of the country through a coup supported from the outside. Such revolutions include the Rose Revolution in Georgia in 2003, the Orange Revolution in Ukraine in 2004, and the Tulip Revolution in Kyrgyzstan in 2005. The events in Kazakhstan, as I mentioned in the question, are primarily due to internal reasons, none of the external players was the initiator or operator of destabilization with the aim of changing power.

Hwang Do you think Russia is able to control both situations in Kazakhstan and Ukraine at the same time?

Pritchin In the case of Ukraine, I see it is a tension or the buildup of armed groups along the border against the background of Russian-American negotiations on deterrence measures in Europe. Russia is not interested in escalating the conflict with Ukraine. Firstly, it would cause a diversion of resources without the possibility of winning something from this conflict. Secondly, it is an automatic deterioration of already difficult relations with Western countries. That is why Russia is committed to the implementation of the Minsk agreements in the Normandy format. Note that it is Ukraine that is not interested in returning Donetsk and Lugansk to its responsibility, because it will immediately lose the instrument of involving the West against Russia and will be forced to restore the infrastructure destroyed during the conflict. Meanwhile, Kazakhstan's situation is not man-made and no one expected it to come. Russia contributed to the stabilization of the situation in the republic with limited resources with the support of CSTO partners, and it did not become something overly costly for Moscow.

Hwang What would be Russia's reason for being "assertive" wiht the former Soviet Union countries?

Pritchin I would not call Russian policy in the post-Soviet space assertive. It is quite predictable. Due to the fact that the former republics of the USSR are neighbors of Russia, respectively, they are part of a common regional security system. In the case of a change in foreign policy priorities from a constructive point, neighbors' approach to creating threats, such as the cases of Georgia and Ukraine seeking to join NATO, which is initially viewed by Moscow as a hostile organization, problems in relations begin. In other cases, we see constructive cooperation, integration and joint responses to security challenges.

Hwang The world is concerned about worsened relations between the US and Russia. I would like to hear how you see the situation.

Pritchin Russian-American relations are overshadowed by the unilateral withdrawal of the US from a whole range of important regional security and stability agreements, which were reached after months of difficult negotiations. In such circumstances, it is difficult to expect a noticeable improvement in relations between Moscow and Washington. We can only count on the formation of a conditional nonaggression format that would allow us to insure the current level of relations from further decline.

Hwang When we look from a geographical point of view, both Kazakhstan and Ukraine are quite distant from Korea. Even so, what strategic implications could Korea learn from the recent happenings in terms of Korea's security?

Pritchin A comparison of the model of foreign and domestic policy of Ukraine and Kazakhstan provides an excellent demonstration of how to build relations with a large and powerful neighbor. Kazakhstan pursues a fairly free, multivector policy, but gives priority to constructive and mutually beneficial cooperation with Russia and China, with which it has a long border and a high level of interdependence in security and economic issues. On the other hand, instead of pragmatic cooperation with Russia, Kyiv has taken a course toward nationalism and the displacement of all (things) Russian in domestic politics, integration into NATO in foreign (politics), and curtailing all economic and political projects with Russia. Thereby, it became a source of threats for Moscow rather than a partner.

Hwang On Jan. 30, North Korea tested an intermediate-range ballistic missile. It was the seventh launch in a month. Do you think North Korea's intention is to sway South Korea's upcoming presidential election or to pressure the US? In case of neither, what could be North Korea's real message hidden in the provocation?

Li There could be a few purposes in North Korea's recent moves. First, North Korea seems to test, update and develop its missile system to prove its national defense capacity and to strengthen it. Second, North Korea is seriously unsatisfied with the Moon administration for just cautiously reading the US' intentions until today and only paying lip service to North Korea. Third, since Biden was inaugurated, the fact that North Korea's position in the US foreign agenda is largely downgraded is never a positive signal to North Korea.

Hwang What is China's stance on North Korea's recent moves? Does China see any necessity for additional sanctions?

Li From China's perspective, North Korea's nuclear and missile tests are a problem for sure. However, the US and Korea's sanctions or the international sanctions from the UN are also causing complexity. China believes that practical measures are needed for the US to solve the North Korean issue. The US is a way stronger actor as well as the core actor in resolving the current North Korean issue, therefore, it should do its best and duty in implementation rather than requiring additional reckless sanctions.

Hwang What do you expect as to North Korea's further actions?

Li The Olympics is the festival for peace. Last December, the UN General Assembly adopted the Olympic Truce for the Winter Olympics in Beijing unanimously and 173 countries co-sponsored. Therefore, North Korea does not seem to initiate force during this period. This does not necessarily mean that the possibility for North Korea to violate UN sanction clauses is completely out of the question. However, in any circumstances, we should take diplomatic measures that positively respond rather than unquestioningly criticizing North Korea's "provocation." We should not miss the timing to solve the problem.

Hwang Regarding North Korea's intermediate-range ballistic missile tests, South Korea had some degree of justification for deploying additional Terminal High Altitude Area Defense anti-missile systems. South Korea considers THAAD as a measure to respond to North Korea's threats.

Li The deployment of THAAD might be able to plant some psychological comfort to the South Korean people, nevertheless, it will not be able to practically root out the threat from North Korea's missiles. In fact, the main role of THAAD is simply tightening the military ties between the US (which deploys THAAD) and Korea. In case an extra THAAD (battery) is deployed, it will cause not only the concern from North Korea, but also doubts from China. In particular, considering that North Korea is out of the top priority in the US foreign agenda, the reason the US wants an additional THAAD deployment is not to target North Korea but as the strategic and security frame to fully compete with China. Regarding the issue, China's opposition is largely a normal response.

Hwang Can the Korean Peninsula issue be the turning point for the US and China to cooperate? Or would it be one that worsens the competition?

Li I see that it depends on the US' attitude. If the US adheres to diplomatic solutions and simultaneously makes a flexible and practical approach with negotiation to North Korea's nuclear problem, the Korean Peninsula can be the common field for cooperation between the US and China. On the other hand, if the US does not attempt to change its policies and nothing changes in the peninsula, it will only aggravate US-China relations, which are already vulnerable.

Hwang South Korea and China have maintained cooperative relations when it comes to the North Korea issue so far. Regarding the North Korea issue, what kind of stance from South Korea would bring problems in its relations with China?

Li I guess there could be trouble in the South Korea-China relations if South Korea implements the following two approaches regarding the North Korean issue. First is imposing additional sanctions or excessively intensive policies toward North Korea. As China has emphasized policies to solve the problems through dialogue, Beijing would not support any kind of assertive or forceful policies, and South Korea is not an exception. Secondly, Korea is strengthening its cooperation with the US, using North Korea as an excuse. These steps are influential in the US-China relations, which go beyond the North

Korea issue, and especially will weaken China's strategic trust toward Korea and sway the foundation of the two countries' relations.

3 Issues facing Pakistan: Human Security, National Security, China-Pakistan Economic Corridor

Oct 15, 2022

Ghazala Yasmin Jalil

Research Fellow, Arms Control and Disarmament Center at the Institute of Strategic Studies in Islamabad

Kim Hor Toh

Chief Architect in Pakistan for Temasek Holdings

A third of Pakistan was completely waterlogged due to a record flood in August. More than 33 million Pakistanis are estimated to have suffered from this unprecedented flooding. Pakistan's Climate Change Minister Sherry Rehman stressed that the entire country is "all one big ocean, there is no dry land to pump the water out" and called it a "crisis of unimaginable proportions."

This year, we have more severe damage in Pakistan caused after the global warming, and many other factors including inefficient early warning systems, poor disaster management, political instability, and sprawling natural development may have added to its devastation. Meanwhile, waterborne infectious diseases such as cholera also increased, worsening human security.

This year Pakistan's GDP growth rate, which was expected to be 5%, has dropped to 2% due to the flood and the amount of economic damage is expected to reach $12.5 billion, putting human security into a more difficult condition. At the same time, its nuclear possession and the maintenance of traditional conventional forces have made Pakistan's finances more difficult, while being absolutely necessary for national security. In the absence of any particular incentives in foreign trade and investment, the China-Pakistan Economic Corridor provides momentum for an important national economy, but also causes problems.

Two experts were invited to talk about Pakistan's domestic and international security environment and situation -- Ghazala Yasmin Jalil is a Research Fellow at the Arms Control and Disarmament Center at the Institute of Strategic Studies in Islamabad, Pakistan. Kim Hor Toh is currently on assignment as Chief Architect in Pakistan for Temasek Holdings' wholly-owned portfolio company that is "building cities and shaping lives".

Hwang Pakistan was recently hit by extensive floods. What is the impact of the devastating floods on the people, the economy and politically?

Jalil The devastating floods have left a third of Pakistan underwater. Pakistan's Climate Minister Sherry Rehman said that according to a conservative estimate, more than 1,300 people have died and more than 1.75 million homes were destroyed. Approximately 33 million people were affected by the destruction brought upon by the floods. There are 637,000 people living in camps, 3.6 million acres of crops have been destroyed or damaged and 750,000 livestock have been killed. Economically

Pakistan is already facing record high inflation of 24.9 percent. According to one estimate, it will take Pakistan $10 billion to rebuild and rehabilitate. Other sources estimate the damage from the floods to be as high as $28 billion. The floods have exacerbated the economic crisis in the country due to huge loss of crops, infrastructure and other livelihood opportunities. The damage to food supplies means that Pakistan will have to import a lot of food in the coming months which will put pressure on the country's foreign exchange reserves and widen the balance of payment gap. The floods have also put further strain on a country that is already in political turmoil.

Toh The devastating floods certainly has brought to sharp focus how disastrous climate change can be. Pakistan is a developing country that emits less than 1% of the world's greenhouse gases but is ranked the 5th most vulnerable country to climate change on the Global Climate Risk Index. UN Secretary General Antonio Guterres described the massive climate induced flood as a "monsoon on steroids" with melting glaciers. Rising temperatures have been blamed for both phenomena. During July and August of this year, Pakistan saw nearly 187 percent more rain than the national average.

Hwang Where does national security sit in this current context for Pakistan, which is a developing country?

Jalil The National Security Policy (NSP) made public in January 2022 puts economic security at the forefront of its national security vision. Launching the document, the prime minister at the time, Mr. Imran Khan said that a country without a stable economy cannot be considered secure. This is so true and it is what lies at the heart of the document. The NSP distinguishes traditional security defined as defense, sovereignty, and diplomacy, from non-traditional security. The latter takes a more holistic approach and includes human security and the well-being of its citizens. In line with the vision of NSP, the Arms Control and Disarmament Center, at the Institute of Strategic Studies in Islamabad, where I hail from, has increasingly focused on research on peaceful uses of nuclear technologies, space technologies, emerging technologies and their potential to contribute to the socio-economic development of the country.

Hwang In the current post-flood crisis, the NSP seems more relevant than ever.

Jalil Yes, it endorses human security which essentially means food, health, physical, education and security for all, as well as overall economic security. For a country that is struggling to provide all these elements of human security, the floods have presented an unprecedented challenge. At the moment, the extent of the catastrophe caused by the floods is so huge, it is beyond the Pakistani state apparatus' means to provide for the victims of the flood and to ensure human security for all. At the moment, their only hope lies in the international assistance that is coming in. However, it is coming too slowly and much more is needed. Many victims of the floods may not make it through the next few weeks.

Hwang Are nuclear weapons necessary for Pakistan's national security?

Jalil Nuclear weapons are imperative for Pakistan's national security. While there are a lot of fault lines and disputes within Pakistan, this is one issue where there is national consensus. Pakistan's nuclear program is security driven and India specific. When India conducted its first nuclear test by diverting peaceful nuclear assistance in 1974, there was no condemnation from the international community and no any security assurances were offered to Pakistan. Following the self-help principle coined by Kenneth Waltz, Pakistan pursued a weapons program of its own. When India tested and became a nuclear weapons state in 1998, there was immense pressure on Pakistan not to follow suit. However, Pakistan also tested and declared itself a nuclear weapon state. Pakistan was cognizant of that fact that it was responsible for its own security. Pakistan, thus, was a reluctant nuclear state.

Toh It is estimated that annual aggregate expenditure on nuclear weapons globally is more than $105 billion. Pakistan is also a country that possesses nuclear weapons. This makes clear the enormity of the burden placed on Pakistan's society simply by the continued possession of these weapons. If these financial resources were directed domestically to health, social welfare and education programs or to development aid for Afghanistan refugees, the positive impact on people's lives and dignity would be incalculable. As such, I hope that efforts will be made to re-kindle the Lahore Declaration for the sake of the "safety, security, dignity and prosperity" of the people of Pakistan as articulated in Pakistan's National Security Policy. Another step Pakistan could take is to declare a "No First Use Policy" for its nuclear weapons. Adoption of a policy of No First Use can significantly enhance the regional security climate. To cite an example, when China and India engaged in border clashes in June 2020 that resulted in dozens of casualties, their standing commitments to No First Use helped contain tensions and acted as a brake on escalation.

Hwang Will Pakistan put human security first and foremost amid the challenging national security situation, particularly with India, Afghanistan and terrorist groups?

Toh I believe now is the critical moment for Pakistan to put human security first and foremost in its national agenda. This is the time for Pakistan to re-think on how it can build back better. There are many possibilities. For example, Daisaku Ikeda, a Japanese Buddhist philosopher, educator, author, and nuclear disarmament advocate, in his peace proposal titled "Value Creation for Global Change: Building Resilient and Sustainable Societies," proposed the establishment of a regional co-operative mechanism to reduce damage from extreme weather and disasters, strengthening resilience in regions such as Asia and Africa. He added that these could function alongside global measures developed under the UNFCCC. Pakistan too could initiate such regional co-operative mechanism in South Asia. Having said that, I'm not denying the need for national security either. My position is that the highest priority of the state must be the well-being and security of ordinary people.

Jalil The US withdrawal from Afghanistan has created a power vacuum and unrest in the country. This directly impacts Pakistan's security since the Pakistan-Afghan border is a porous one and any instability is likely to spill over into Pakistan. This brings yet one more challenge to a country that has more than its fair share of challenges already. Pakistan has for decades and continues to host 1.3 million refugees, mostly from Afghanistan. The instability in Afghanistan means the refugees cannot be repatriated back to their country. In fact, there are fears that more refugees may come to Pakistan. While Pakistan has helped the refugees for decades and would continue to do so, they are a drain on its economy and also impact its human security. Pakistan has always put human security first and will continue to do so. However, this does not mean that it will dismantle or give up its military capabilities or give up its nuclear weapons capabilities. Pakistan's military capabilities make its borders secure so that it can focus on economic prosperity and human security. There has to be the right balance of traditional and non-traditional security.

Hwang The China-Pakistan Economic Corridor (CPEC) aims to improve connectivity for China through Pakistan by stimulating Foreign Direct Investment with infrastructure projects. How is the current context (politically, economically and the devastating floods) for CPEC's future in Pakistan?

Toh There is a need now to re-consider more rigorously the impact of climate change, which will adversely affect the infrastructure developed by CPEC in Pakistan. My recommendation is to invest in resilient infrastructure that incorporate the latest strategies on nature-based solutions that are sustainable -- to mitigate and adapt to climate change. I welcome policy makers on CPEC and the government of Pakistan to explore this potential asset class which is aligned to climate finance/adaptation and can deliver superior economic value for Pakistan.

Jalil The CPEC is the flagship project of the Belt and Road Initiative and aims at building power, road, and rail networks within Pakistan. The severe flooding has affected and damaged various power projects, highway routes, and special economic zones. While some projects involving Chinese companies have suffered partial damage, several state-owned companies have had no casualties among their employees and the impact on their projects are controllable so far. They are working to minimize disruption while also offering support to those in need. They have organized construction personnel and promptly repaired damaged roads. The floods have given a set-back to the CPEC related projects but it has by no means sabotaged the projects. It will once again get back on track and bring prosperity to Pakistan and its people in the future.

Hwang How important is CPEC for Pakistan from a national security and human security perspective?

Jalil For Pakistan, CPEC is the centerpiece of the prosperity agenda with China. It was originally stipulated to bring $47 billion of investment in Pakistan but the estimate was later raised to $62 billion. Launched in 2015, the project has so far brought $25.4 billion worth of investment to Pakistan. Pakistan hopes the CPEC will uplift its economy to jumpstart domestic growth and alleviate poverty. The project is of great importance. Both China and Pakistan aim to make Gwadar port the economic hub for the region in future. It has great potential since it can reduce the distance for China to import oil and other raw material from the rest of the world. It can also serve as a shortcut for trade with Central Asian Republics. Even CPEC has the potential to be a game-changer for Pakistan since it will improve the infrastructure of the country. The power generation projects will help meet the electricity needs and industry and businesses will grow. This is not only creating thousands of jobs for the people of Pakistan but also helping them improve their living standards. CPEC is set to provide a boost to Pakistan's economy. Thus, by bringing prosperity to the country and the people, it will help advance the agenda of human security. Human security will improve in the country by bringing food and health security, energy security and economic prosperity.

Toh We need to ask what the purpose of the state's existence is -- however successful it may be in economic or military terms -- if it fails to make efforts to alleviate the suffering of its citizens and support their pursuit of a life with dignity. I believe that if national security and human security were to be viewed from this lens, CPEC can be an important platform to further improve the bilateral ties between China and Pakistan beyond being "iron brothers".

Hwang What could be the possible problems of CPEC or points to improve?

Jalil While CPEC is set to bring prosperity to Pakistan and its people, it also has its downside. The development gains are marred by environmental concerns regarding the project. The infrastructure-related development in some areas may increase deforestation and subsequent loss of biodiversity. Gilgit Baltistan which is part of the CPEC corridor remains particularly vulnerable since it is a habitat for diverse wildlife, glaciers, and forests. There is also increase in carbon emissions due to movement of heavy vehicular traffic. Many of the power projects under the CPEC are coal-based which will further increase the carbon emission. Thus, the ecological costs of the project must be mitigated. CPEC projects must be calibrated to protect the environment and ecosystems. Environment-friendly and -focused policies by Pakistan and China can transform CPEC into a development venture that can shape the human security landscape of Pakistan.

Toh Apart from building resilient infrastructure, there's also a broader view of resilience that has been articulated. CPEC has the potential to create enormous value and benefit Pakistan as a whole and the future. When I think about this challenge, I am also reminded of the words of the great twentieth-century historian Arnold J. Toynbee (1889-1975): "But we are not doomed to make history repeat itself; it is open to us, through our own efforts, to give history, in our own case, some new and unprecedented turn."

Today's Ukraine, tomorrow's Taiwan?

Mar 10, 2022

Kwei-Bo Huang

Professor, College of International Affairs at National Chengchi University

Jiann-fa Yan

Professor, Department of Business Administration at Chien-Hsin University of Science and Technology

While Ukraine fell into dire straits due to Russia's attack, on the other side of the world, the US and China are scrambling to make an elaborate effort in dealing with Taiwan. On March 1, the Joe Biden administration has sent US delegations including the retired Navy Adm. Michael Mullen and former Under Secretary of Defense Michele Flournoy to Taiwan. On the following day, former Secretary of State Mike Pompeo also visited Taiwan. Given that a number of high-level US delegations are visiting Taiwan, it might be a message warning against a "power vacuum" in standing against China.

In response, China announced that there will be no normalization in China-US ties without the "One China" principle. On Feb. 28, the date of the Commemoration of the 50th Anniversary of the Shanghai Communique, Chinese Foreign Minister Wang Yi stressed that the "One-China principle is the cornerstone of China-US relations" and that the US should stop "encouraging and supporting 'Taiwan independence' moves, stop attempting to use the Taiwan question to contain China, and stop saying or doing things that interfere in China's internal affairs." Wang made it clear that is the way to "maintain peace and stability across the Taiwan Strait and uphold the larger interests of China-US relations."

Would the reality of the US drawing a line in NATO's military intervention to Ukraine raise China's will in using military force? The overall international consensus is that the possibility of China using military forces against Taiwan would be extremely low. In the end, Taiwan's future is up to the change in US-China strategic competition, both in qualitative and quantitative perspectives. For Taiwan, would this US-China strategic competition become an opportunity or a crisis?

This week's discourse invited two Taiwanese experts to explore Taiwan's domestic and foreign circumstances and deeply analyze the related followings. Both experts are now in academia and have previously worked at the Kuomintang (KMT) and Democratic Progressive Party (DPP), and in the government. Professor Kwei-Bo Huang is currently the director of Center for Regional and Global Risk Assessment under the College of International Affairs at National Chengchi University, and has served as the KMT's deputy secretary-general supervising mainland and international affairs. Jiann-fa Yan is a professor of the Department of Business Administration at Chien-Hsin University of Science and Technology and was the director of mainland affairs at DPP. They both have served as the chairman of the Research and Planning Committee of Taiwan's Ministry of Foreign Affairs.

Hwang What is Taiwan's perspective on US-China relations?

Huang From a "blue perspective," it is more of a competition-cooperation than a confrontation game. Not only is it affected by respective governments' strategy and foreign policy, but it also hinges on a variety of regional and global issues in which both governments' key interests either overlap or collide.

Yan From a "green perspective," since late 1949, the Republic of China was tacitly permitted to resume its government in Taiwan, safeguarding the first island chain from China's invasion. The US has been a constructive factor for Taiwan's development, while China a threat for Taiwan. Clearly, Taiwan has to side with the US against China.

Hwang Do you see it as a new Cold War or a competition?

Huang A "new Cold War" is an exaggeration of what's going on in such bilateral relations. Beijing isn't ready for the so-called "G-2" position, and no military confrontation or proxy war has taken place between the two powers. It may be better to portray contemporary Washington-Beijing relations as a "US-led bloc" versus a semicoalition of Beijing and Moscow.

Yan China's rising has challenged the hegemony of the West led by the US. The confrontations between the two are not only on power sharing but also challenges systems and ideologies. The forthcoming confrontations are structural and inevitable.

Hwang What kind of strategic value does Taiwan have from the US' stance and how can the US apply it?

Yan From a geo-strategic view, Taiwan located in the center of the first island chain can be a buffer for the US in coping with China in terms of national security. In applying Taiwan's strategic value into practice, the US may enhance its relations with Taiwan in every sphere of life regardless of China's objection. The US has to make China accustomed to its will and the order abiding by universal truth. The US has to be determined in bringing China into an order accepted by more people instead of a small group of the power-holders.

Huang Taiwan is located in an important strategic position in the often-heard first island chain. The sea lanes and air routes over the Taiwan Strait and the east of the island of Taiwan are of strategic significance for the US armed forces operating between Northeast Asia and Southeast Asia. Taiwan is also a place to set up long-range radar stations that can monitor the People's Liberation Army's military activities from afar. In addition, the US' continued reassurance aimed at helping Taiwan maintain enough self-defense capabilities can generate a strategic value for the US' commitments to its allies and quasi-allies.

Hwang Under what circumstance would Taiwan no longer have its strategic value for the US?

Yan Once Taiwan drifts away from the good model for free economy and pluralistic democracy, or its modern architecture is under decay from within or under threat from without, it will become a burden for the US. Certainly, the sustainability of Taiwan in a physical sense is also very important in showing Taiwan's value for the US and the world. Nowadays, Taiwan has performed well, the US may have to take this opportunity to enhance its linkages with Taiwan to make it much better and more solid during the process of modernization as a young democracy.

Huang Taiwan will lose its strategic value for the US on one of the following three conditions. First, it decides to surrender to the Chinese communist regime. Second, it decides to stand neutral between Washington and Beijing and even move toward a position of de-militarization. Third, it suffers a very serious deadly natural disaster that ruins the strategically important parts of the island.

Hwang What options does Taiwan have in any case its security supporter, the US, decides not to protect Taiwan anymore?

Huang If so, Taiwan needs to map out a plan in advance that can ensure its peaceful co-existence with mainland China, probably followed by an incremental integration between the two sides of the Taiwan Strait. Neither maintaining Taiwan's defense capability to resist the offensive measures from mainland China nor making Taiwan a politically neutral entity would be literally impossible because no other countries are willing to sell advanced weapons to Taiwan and because the Beijing authorities have not given up the possibility of using force to achieve national reunification.

Yan Like all the other countries, the US seeks its own national interests. It is so real and practical. This scenario would presuppose some change of the international environment, such as the decline of the US national strength or its appearance of internal turmoil, making the Taiwan issue no more urgent. Or, at the same time, if Taiwan's domestic economy and politics are dominated by China. Besides, the other stakeholders in this region may also show the US their own interests and concerns if the US is to change its mind in supporting Taiwan.

Hwang Xi Jinping has made a historical decision in the sixth plenary session at China's 19th Central Committee of the Chinese Communist Party. What does Taiwan basically mean to either China or Xi?

Yan In the report of China's 19th Central Committee of the CCP, unifying Taiwan is one of the three major goals to accomplish the China Dream in 2050. As a matter of fact, it can be seen as a strategic rhetoric since the incumbent leaders may be removed from the political circle by 2050. The CCP knows that it will be a tough job to annex Taiwan because of the US factor. The timetable is unrealistic but needed politically. For China or Xi, the Taiwan issue may play as an instrument to fulfill the interests of the CCP or leaders.

Huang Taiwan is an integral part of Xi's scheme of the great rejuvenation of the Chinese people. Taking Taiwan back into the arms of China, being represented by the PRC, is both a long-educated goal of national reunification on mainland China and a crucial symbol of China countering back the Western hegemony and influence since the so-called "New China" being established by the Chinese Communist Party in 1949. If Taiwan is drifting away from "China," both historically and legally defined, Xi will encounter a series of challenges from within regarding his "Taiwan policy," which may affect his legitimacy for the continued leadership as the CPC general secretary and the PRC president. Opposing Taiwan independence and promoting reunification has remained as the two pillars for the Chinese communist regime's Taiwan policy.

Hwang Do you see Taiwan being able to endure the economic pressures from China? We see Taiwan standing on a dual track that distinguished politics and economy when it comes to the relationship with China. How has that gone?

Huang It will be an unrealistic or wishful thinking to separate Taiwan from mainland China economically. Therefore, for a smaller economy like Taiwan that is so close to mainland China, economic exchanges with mainland China represent both opportunities and challenges or pressures. Taiwan's trade dependence on the mainland and Hong Kong has reached a historical high, i.e., roughly 43 percent, in the second term of President Tsai Ing-wen. Some in Taiwan argue that it's the mainland who has been dependent on Taiwan due to the former's strong need for semiconductor products from Taiwan. Yet, in general, the center of economic gravity continues to be in favor of the mainland since the mid-2000s. That's why the Tsai administration has to distinguish political interactions -- denying the political foundation that paved a way for cross-strait dialogues while still asking for conversations with no preconditions -- from economic ones in the Taiwan Strait.

Yan The Taiwanese economy has relied on small and midsize enterprises. The nature of the SMEs is its diversity and flexibility. Since mid-1980s, due to the deteriorating economic environment and dramatic appreciation of the New Taiwan dollar, the SMEs were forced to move their businesses abroad. In a sense, businesses are very global; they are very sensitive toward the changing environment. Besides, the well-known reputation of Taiwan SMEs attracts many foreign conglomerates to build partnerships with them. The Taiwanese economy is highly dependent on Chinese market, but Taiwanese SMEs are not.

Hwang It seems the KMT is steadily diminishing in Taiwan's politics. The expectation for both the general and presidential elections is getting lower. Do you have any hidden cards or strategies that could turn the tides?

Huang The leadership of the KMT has been in a weak position in the upcoming local elections in November 2022. Two possible "game changers" may help the KMT in the said local elections. First, the KMT may turn the tables if the impacts of large-scale power outages, air pollution and inflation that has eaten up people's paychecks loom large. Second, if the KMT candidates in at least one of the four special municipalities -- in particular Taipei City -- can win an advantage over the ruling party's candidates, thus serving to boost the momentum in the KMT's campaigns in the other cities and counties.

Hwang The DPP is being more and more influential in Taiwan's politics. It seems KMT is no longer a competitive opponent. The international flow also seems quite favorable as well. Is Taiwan's independence the ultimate goal?

Yan Generally speaking, Taiwanese people are very practical, pragmatic, realistic, flexible, and durable; most of them are not ideology-oriented. Hence, independence is not a fatal or an urgent issue; survival and development are more important and significant. Once maintaining the status quo is much more supported by all the stakeholders in this region, most Taiwanese people will be patient and wait for the coming opportunity toward internationally recognized independence.

Hwang How are inter-Korean relations different from Taiwan-China relations?

Yan They are more different than similar: First, inter-Korean relations are "two different ideology-based countries under one roof of the Korean nationality." Taiwan-China relations are controversial and debatable among stakeholders in the region, shown on the spectrum of independence vis-a-vis unification; the CPP's cognitive picture of one China is different than that of the KMT while the KMT's scope of the ROC is different from that of the DPP. Besides, the PRC's claim of the one China principle is rhetorically similar to US' one China policy, but with different strategic implications; the US has never recognized that Taiwan is a part of China. The US position on cross-strait relations are much clearer than ever since China's rise.

Huang Despite the lower level of people-to-people and economic interactions and despite sporadic military skirmishes between the two Koreas, there are five top leaders' meetings on the Korean Peninsula, whereas there is only one between the two sides of the Taiwan Strait (in November 2015). Generally, the two Korean leaders call each other's official titles, occasionally with the use of the "peninsula flag." In the case of the Taiwan Strait, no official titles were used in the summit and no symbols of reunification were represented.

Hwang How do you evaluate the two Koreas' relations?

Huang The probability of armed conflicts between the two Koreas may be higher than that between the two sides of the Taiwan Strait. The reason is threefold. First, there is no natural division such as a strait between the two Koreas. Second, the decision-making of North Korea is more unpredictable. Third, the uncertainty of North Korean leaders about whether the US can assure the security of North Korea may lead to a higher level of military tension between the two Koreas, as well as between North Korea and the US. However, it appears less likely that the two Koreas are going into war in the short run.

Yan A peaceful reunification of the two Koreas will not be happily seen by China since a new Korea, likely to be an economic and military giant, will be a potential threat to itself; a divided Korea is of China's interests. For the US, a new Korea must be in line with democracy as the basic requirement. China will not sit idle seeing that scenario happen, especially if the future China after Xi Jinping still sticks its political doctrine to the one-party-rule politics. The prospects of inter-Korean relations are bleak with the widening cultural gaps between the two societies. It is not improbable to see that North Korea remains isolated and South Korea keeps on modernizing for decades on.

Hwang This year marks the 30th year from the time that Taiwan and Korea terminated diplomatic ties. What is Taiwan's perception of Korea?

Huang Generally speaking, Taiwan sees the Republic of Korea (ROK) as a rising middle power on the world stage. Some Taiwanese people still perceive South Korea as one of the four little dragons of East Asia, a phrase widely quoted in the 1980s and 1990s. Some know the ROK has been one of the G-20 member states and has participated in the Regional Comprehensive Economic Partnership (RCEP); besides, its former official was once secretary-general of the United Nations. Also, some Taiwanese people think South Koreans are patriotic, openly emotional, and less patient.

Yan The strong wave of Korean culture erupting in the early 2000s has challenged the Taiwanese image of Korean culture and people. That can be seen in the booming availability of Korean language courses in universities.

Hwang From Taiwan's view, what could be the advantages and disadvantages of Korea's diplomacy?

Yan As an economic and technological giant, if Korean people contribute more to this region than just to itself, namely more altruistic than egoistic, it could lead to a drastic change in outsiders' perspective of Korea. The development and performance of NGOs worldwide will be an indicator for us to gauge. Above all, people living in the Korean Peninsula have survived in face of hegemonic challenges from all sides. Korea can play a bigger role in this region as a rising power since the early 2000s.

Huang Korea's economic and political status has been higher than ever in the international community. In addition, Korea, who faces Washington-Beijing tensions -- can strike more or less of a balance between these two major powers. Korea has been leaning too much toward Beijing diplomatically. Yet, actually, Seoul-Beijing relations have been a bit volatile, or to put it another way -- have not been as stable as some imagine, with the change of the leadership in Seoul. The long-standing quarrels between Korea and Japan have complicated the former's diplomatic context in East Asia.

Hwang How big of a part does Korea play in Taiwan's diplomacy and to what level do you anticipate the Korea-Taiwan relations to develop in the future?

Yan In contrast to KMT-ruled Taiwan-Korea relations, a DPP-ruled Taiwan may get rid of the interwoven history and start a new beginning for future engagement. To be practical and realistic, in the regional diplomacy, what can be learned by Korea is the Japanese model instead of the Singaporean one. By doing so, we may anticipate a growing development of Koran-Taiwan relations.

Huang In the near future, Seoul-Taipei relations may remain lukewarm in the context of Cross-Taiwan Strait tensions, in part because Seoul has kept in line with its "one China" understanding and doesn't want to get involved in Taiwan's bid for the RCEP membership for the sake of stable Seoul-Beijing relations, and in part because there appears to be weaker economic trade between Korea and the ROC.

US-Mainland China-Taiwan Relations after Taiwan's Local Election

Dec 8, 2022

Tang Yong-hong

Professor, Graduate Institute for Taiwan Studies of Xiamen

Tsai Tung-Chieh

Professor, College of Law and Politics at the National Chung Hsing University

Taiwan's recent local elections have received unprecedented attention from the international community. The election took place amid higher tensions in the Taiwan Strait than ever, due to US House Speaker Nancy Pelosi's visit to Taiwan and Chinese President Xi Jinping's remarks on the use of force. The ruling Democratic Progressive Party (DPP) won only five out of the 21 local chief posts, while the opposition Taiwan People's Party (TPP) won 13, including the capital Taipei. It was the DPP's biggest defeat since the regime change in 2004, and President Tsai resigned as the chairwoman of the governing DPP to take responsibility for the defeat.

This result is expected to bring a significant impact on cross-strait relations and US-China relations in the future. After President Tsai was elected in 2016, she made Taiwan's independence a priority, and tensions between Taiwan and China began to rise accordingly. Since then, Taiwan has been implementing a 'pro-US anti-China' policy that strengthens relations with the US, Japan, and Europe and confronts China. With the recent election result, we are watching whether Tsai's stance toward the US and China will be adjusted and how it will affect the next Taiwanese presidential election, which will be held in January 2024. Also, one of the additional concerns is about how these will affect the surrounding relations.

Given the current situation, this week's interview invites experts from China and Taiwan, who specialize in cross-strait relations. Professor Tang Yong-hong is from China and is currently at the Graduate Institute for Taiwan Studies of Xiamen University, and Distinguished Professor Tsai Tung-Chieh from Taiwan where he is a Dean in the College of Law and Politics at National Chung Hsing University.

Hwang How do you assess the recent local election in Taiwan?

Tsai Technically, this election had something surprising and something that is not. Surprisingly, the ruling DPP's defeat was very natural. First of all, according to the pendular effect on democratic political parties' changes, the ruling party suffers similar fatigue at the end of its second term. Moreover, the pressure accumulated throughout society due to COVID-19 and improper management of several domestic events during the election caused a 'revenge rebound' in this election. Nevertheless, the fact that the DPP totally defeated in some main areas and barely won in some areas was an unimaginable result. Also, this election recorded the lowest turnout in Taiwan's local elections, and from here, we can have another analysis which breaks down our existing thought that the low turnout should be in favor of the DPP.

Tang As expected, the KMT (Kuomintang, also known as the Chinese Nationalist Party) won a great victory. The overall election situation for the DPP was not well prepared than in 2018, showing the DPP's sluggish power, which was mostly suspected through opening up imports of pork and poor quarantine. Additionally, candidates' requirements and qualifications did not meet party and social expectations. As a result of this election, Tsai's confidence and leadership authority in the party will fall, and it will certainly affect the DPP's 2024 presidential candidate. The current vice president Lai Ching-te is likely to be the 'presidential' candidate within the DPP in 2024. Just because the KMT won the local elections does not necessarily mean it will win the 2024 presidential election. However, Taiwan's politics will fall back into a stand-off.

Hwang How will this local election affect cross-strait relations?

Tsai In the short term, this election may not have much impact on cross-strait relations. First, cross-strait relations are difficult to be affected by the results of local elections because they span the upper political and central government classes. Second, although the DPP has critically lost in this election, the 'middle effect' of Taiwan's local elections is not clear, for the instance of the 2018 election, and there is no possibility of completely breaking ties with the presidential election that the chain impact seems to be quite limited. The DPP initially tried to put anti-China agenda forward in this election, however, belonging to a particular party was not very important as nearly half of Taiwan's local Congressmen were independent. Third and more importantly, although the DPP has lost critically, only few will think it can win in 2024, at least in the short term, and the key is the selection issue. The impact of the local elections on cross-strait relations will be even more limited as the party might not be able to win the presidential election.

Tang China wants stability, but not everything goes as it wishes. Anti-China forces in the US and Taiwan that support its independence are the key variables in cross-strait relations. In the post-Tsai Ing-wen era, based on the social atmosphere and political ecosystem of seeking for independence, the DPP's stance will probably create a vicious cycle of cross-strait relations, as it will intensify 'Taiwan's independence' by strengthening the existing 'Independence Card' and 'Sovereignty Card'. Ultimately, the cross-strait relations before 2024 will go through a severe wave height.

Hwang How would you view the perspective that the semiconductor industry is ensuring Taiwan's security?

Tsai The semiconductor industry is often called a 'silicon shield' when discussing Taiwan's security issues. This mainly comes from a position that Taiwan's position cannot be underestimated in advanced semiconductor manufacturing processes worldwide. That is why many major and international political commentators said that if Taiwan's conflict jeopardizes the semiconductor supply chain, it will have a 'destructive' blow to the global economy. In this case, Taiwan can either strengthen its manufacturing advantage or provide its security advantage. However, since international relations still put 'national interest first' as a key principle so far, talented states like the US have asked TSMC to build a factory by mixing both the hardline and appeasements. The other, which is relatively incapable of negotiating leverage, may seek the possibility of disconnecting from Taiwan in order to search for alternatives. Therefore, the security of semiconductors alone cannot be the basis and source of Taiwan's security stability.

Tang Basically it must be a self-righteous expression of people who have no idea about international strategy and security. No industry can guarantee the security of one country, even if it is essential to the world economy. Furthermore, if a certain industry in a particular economy is indispensable to the other economy, and the other economy cannot receive their products or services, the industrial superiority will be difficult to be sustained for a long time and could lead to a security disaster at their industrial locations. In fact, in the course of realizing strategic objectives, no industry is fatally essential, and it can be reversed and restarted.

Hwang What could be the outlook for US's China policy after its midterm elections?

Tang Over the past 40 years, China has constantly been rising, is overtaking the US, and objectively, international political and economic patterns and roles have gradually changed in accordance. Due to the unique differences between

China and the US in terms of strategy and competition over interest, and value standards, social systems, and ideology, the current US-China relationship is facing a double-structured contradiction that it is not only a battle with the development of socialism and capitalism but also a battle of strategic interests between the emerging and defending powers. However, based on the hegemonic culture that 'your strength will weaken my power', the US recognizes that the rise of China is generally disadvantageous to the US hegemony and national interests, that its previous engaging China policy for China's peaceful transition has failed, and that the double-structured contradictions between China and the US are more difficult to reconcile, therefore in the end, that it has to effectively restraint China's developing trend. Thus, the US has made it clear that China will be the number one strategic competitor, and the US strategy and policy toward China have fundamentally changed from an engaging and exchanging policy to a suppressing strategic competition to contain China. Moreover, in the light of American culture and perception, this strategic competition between China and the US is essentially a strategic confrontation, and the competition that the outcome of victory or defeat cannot be determined will never stop. There is a consensus across the US regardless of the party. In this sense, fundamentally, the outcome of the US midterm elections will not change America's strategy and policy toward China.

Tsai Although the US-Taiwan relationship heated up for the first time since 1979 following the explosion of the US-China trade war and the US chose 'competition, not cooperation' after 2018, bilateral interactions between the US and Taiwan have continued for the last few years, even after the inauguration of the Biden administration in 2020. The problem is that although the 'anti-China' is the current all-party agreement in the US, the administration must be prepared to be 'risk-averse', which is also why President Biden spoke to President Xi Jinping as soon as he took office. Also, the world is now in full swing, like the Ukraine war, amid the double pressure of COVID-19 and the economy. In other words, it is in a difficult situation that lacks the capacity for anti-China flow. Nevertheless, if the Republican Party won the midterm elections as expected, it would have put pressure on the White House, but with a 'small defeat', the Biden administration will slowly have room for improvement with Beijing.

Hwang How do you see China's Taiwan policy after its 20th National People's Congress?

Tang We can generally see China's Taiwan policy after the 20th Party Congress from the report of the 20th National Congress of the Chinese Communist Party (CPP). Compared to the 19th Party Congress, the 20th Party Congress reiterated the resolution of the Taiwan issue and the realization of the complete reunification, which is an inevitable demand for the great revival of the Chinese people and it officially includes a comprehensive strategy for solving the Taiwan problem in the new era. It maintained the policy of 'Peaceful reunification and One country·Two systems' and makes it clear that 'there is no promise of giving up the use of force'. Based on One China

Policy and '1992 Consensus', China continues appealing to promote cross-strait exchange and convergence development, and at the same time, clearly calls for the peaceful development of cross-strait relations, the process of reunification of the mainland through negotiations, the unity of Chinese compatriots from around the world, support the patriotic reunification capabilities in Taiwan, firmly support the 'anti-independence pro-reunification', and further emphasize the division of Taiwan's separatist activists and the interference of external forces. On top of China's will, the CPP's strategy for Taiwan was adjusted according to the changes in the international and domestic circumstances, the Taiwan situation, and the main tasks of the new era.

Tsai The impact of Beijing's Taiwan policy is still limited. The reasons are first because structurally, China's policy toward Taiwan is originally an outcome of trilateral relations between the US, China, and Taiwan. In other words, if there are limits in structural changes (In case the DPP and Biden are in power until at least 2024), the meaning of the policy will not change much. Second, if Taiwan's 2022 local election does not influence the 2024 presidential election, Beijing has no other option but to consider the situation and trends in Taiwan. Third, since the DPP took power in 2016, Beijing's Taiwan policy can be said to be so-called 'Harder to hard, softer to soft' and basically 'you do yours, I do mine.' Xi's policy toward Taiwan was probably already decided before the 20th National Congress. There are two principles we can see for now. First, the shortcut to Taiwan always goes through the US and the second one is that the will of the people matters much more than the attitude of the political party.

Hwang What are the prospects for China's US policy after the 20th National People's Congress?

Tang US-China relations are related to the future fate of the US and China and the stability of world peace. For this reason, President Xi Jinping proposed the three principles of US-China mutual respect, peaceful coexistence, and cooperation for a win-win, and President Biden has repeatedly stressed "five nos" (i.e., not seek a new Cold War; not seek to change China's system; the revitalization of its alliances is not against China; not support "Taiwan independence"; not look for conflict with China). The key point is that the US is rapidly pivoting to the rational China policy. China's policy toward the US is clear. China is determined to engage in multilateral coordination with the US's side. China's attitude to strengthening bilateral economic and trade cooperation is also clear. China welcomes US companies' further developments in China and will continue to provide a market-oriented, international, and legalized business environment. Economic trade between the US and China should be focused on addition rather than subtraction, they should hold hands without letting go, and not tear down or build walls. The two countries should talk together with paying attention to each other's interests, not confront and negotiate, and not threaten one another.

Tsai Currently, US-China relations may have entered another stage of qualitative change, that is, the key point of solving the Taiwan problem and the most important variable that determines the final state of 'China's rise'. In particular, Beijing has already been put in a position where it does not want to be the enemy of the US, as the US considers China the biggest threat to the US hegemony since the Trump era. Even if China has accumulated obvious results since its rise till now, the fact is that China has no choice but to face the existing hegemony. From this point of view, the heating up of the US-China competition not only jeopardizes China's core interests but also makes its policy toward the US the top priority for Chinese diplomacy in the short term. Accordingly, there are three things China can do. The first is to improve its ability to deter counterattacks through military modernization, the second is to build a potential supporting platform by continuously expanding 'networks', and the third is to maintain a communication channel with the US to achieve a response time that is necessary.

Hwang Do you see all these are related to security on the Korean Peninsula?

Tsai US-China-Taiwan exchanges are inseparable from the Korean Peninsula. First, the geopolitical positions of the two countries are not far away. Therefore, they are within the scope of leaking influence. Second, the US and China are currently competing and both Taiwan and Korea have to rely on the US to ensure national security. In an unexpected situation, the US has no choice but to capture the two. Third, in the case of Korea, the US-ROK alliance is to counter North Korea's threats and South Korea does not want to subjectively intervene in the Taiwan Strait issue. However, it is understood that the US will constantly drag South Korea down from trying to hold the alliance's 'wartime operational control'. Fourth, Beijing should also prepare for situations in which the US is in a panic or North Korea triggers trouble with support from China in case Taiwan and the Korean Peninsula are in a conflict or the situation flows favorably to China.

IV

Korea-China Relations and East Asia Cooperation

30 years of Korea-China diplomatic relations: More gains than losses

Aug 24, 2022

Kwon Byonghyon
Korea's Ambassador to China from 1998 to 2000

Wednesday marks the 30th anniversary of the establishment of diplomatic relations between Korea and China. Both Seoul and Beijing opened a new era by establishing a good, neighborly friendship based on the principle of reciprocal equality and peaceful coexistence and by signing a joint statement supporting "One China" and "Peaceful Unification of the Korean Peninsula" in Beijing. The establishment of Korea-China diplomatic relations was meaningful in terms of history and civilization, from the viewpoint that the two countries reconciled the hostilities of the past, and led the post-Cold War era in Northeast Asia. In the past 30 years, Korea-China relations have made great strides in many areas, from politics, economy and society to culture, diplomacy and security.

The establishment of Korea-China diplomatic ties was a significant turning point in Northeast Asia, and both countries have grown into key countries in the international community. China, along with the United States, has emerged as a major leader on the international stage. In recent years, a number of sensitive issues such as the US-China competition, Terminal

High Altitude Area Defense and economic security have laid bare the intrinsic instability that underlies Korea-China relations.

However, we cannot deny that we have witnessed more gains than losses in general. Today's discussion invites former Ambassador Kwon Byonghyon, who was in charge of negotiations on Korea-China diplomatic relations 30 years ago, and was there for the historical moment in Beijing when the agreement to open formal ties between Korea and China was signed. He helped facilitate normalization of ties and was also the ambassador to China from 1998 to 2000. He is currently the chairman of the Korea-China Culture & Youth Association and an NGO called Future Forest to help reduce desertification and sandstorms by planting trees in China.

Hwang How do you see the historical value of Korea-China diplomatic relations?

Kwon It would be really encouraging if we had this talk when the atmosphere between Korea and China was in a positive cycle. As the overall atmosphere is not reviving so well, it is quite regretful we are having this conversation amid the current flow. At the bilateral level between Korea and China, I believe the two countries' diplomatic relations are in a sense of restoration of history. In fact, it has been centuries since we were overwhelmed by Western civilization, but the influence of Eastern civilization was significant and has maintained the mainstream for the longest time in human history. However, during the 18th-19th century, as the Eastern civilization centered on China started to shift, it confronted a crisis. And when we talk about the Eastern civilization centered on China, there was Joseon (now Korea) in the closest distance. This is why a large number of scholars in China and Korean studies say that the Eastern civilization was not created by China alone, but it could be said that it was founded by Joseon and China together. But then, the Eastern civilization lost its status to the Western civilization even though it was the mainstream, because it was too conceited. This led China and Korea to suffer a lot throughout the history. In this respect, I believe that diplomatic relations between Korea and China have provided a great starting point in the sense of the restoration of history or the restoration to a certain level.

Hwang Are there any behind-the-scenes moments you can share from the forming of the agreement?

Kwon Actually the establishment of diplomatic relations between Korea and China was a top confidential issue at the time, and both countries had certain groups opposing this establishment. Kim Ilsung was still alive at the time, China was in no position to fully ignore what he claims. Back then Kim Ilsung used to visit China once a year by train and met all the people he wanted to meet, and the last time he met (former Chinese leader) Deng Xiaoping was in November 1991. As known, Kim Ilsung told Deng not to establish diplomatic relations between Korea at least in the near future, and in case Deng has to, Kim Ilsung requested him to do so after North Korea establishes diplomatic relations with the US, or as a cross deal between South Korea-China and the US-North Korea at least at the same time. However, in such a circumstance, diplomatic relations between Korea and China could be achieved despite the opinions of many opponents because Deng made the decision in the end. Compared to how it was in China, Korea had fewer opponents than China did, as Korea was promoting the Northern policy. However, until then, pro-Taiwanism had a great influence on Korean politics or the mainstream society. Also from the perspective of Taiwan, it has been giving a lot of funding and effort to Korea, as Korea was the most important diplomatic country to Taiwan at that time.

Hwang What did you do to succeed in establishing Korea-China diplomatic relations beyond the position of North Korea and Taiwan, and the influence of opposition within each country?

Kwon We had to step into the process with a very limited number of key members in strict confidence. In addition, in case the establishment happens to fail, it would bring a negative impact on the upcoming presidential election in Korea as well as on China in domestic. Therefore, this whole process was a highly concentrated effort. A lot of people who were involved in the process, including myself, dealt with this situation in very strict confidence and kept it secret even to our families. The first and second meetings were held at Diaoyutai State Guesthouse in Beijing, and the last one was in Korea. Negotiations for the two most important diplomatic issues, the joint statement of diplomatic relations between Korea and China and the memorandums of understanding, had gone on for the whole night and had to be confirmed. That is why Minister Lee Sangok, Chief Secretary Kim Chonghwi, and the head of the National Security Agency Investigation were entrusted by the president and had to handle all the decisions on the spot including checking whether they would sign or not that night, so no information, not even a bit, would leak out.

Hwang What is the most different thing about China today compared to when you visited back in 1992?

Kwon First of all, I would say the color of the city Beijing has changed the most. As I remember, the overall tone of Beijing in 1992 was rather gray or like ash. That was what I felt from the very first moment I got off the plane. I am not sure if it was because of sand dust and coal, but the whole city was gloomy and stuffy. However, every time I visited China, maybe dozens of times a year after the establishment of diplomatic relations between Korea and China, the gray background surrounding the city began to turn into something else little by little. Beijing was getting brighter, bigger and a bit more colorful. It was just like how the light gets brighter.

Hwang Was there any change in China's attitude toward Korea as its national power rapidly grew?

Kwon I just think China's attitude changed on a case by case basis, rather than (just) being domineering as it rose. When I first visited Beijing, it did not have much access from and to the outside world as a socialist country, so its attitude and feelings were quite tough, like the inter-

Korean relations. On the other hand, after the diplomatic relationship was established, exchanges between the two countries poured out like a flood of water from a dam that had been completely locked down. There was a great change -- just like the (idiom) that describes how the "blue seas turned into mulberry fields" -- before and after the diplomatic relations, and these exchanges were not limited to certain areas but were all over the fields.

Hwang What do you think China's reason was to determine the establishment of diplomatic relations with Korea?

Kwon Through the establishment, China also benefited tremendously, as Deng envisioned. Since Deng pushed for reform and opening up, there were certain expectations in the West, and the US responded to China's steps toward capitalism with its own vision. However, the 1989 Tiananmen Square protest completely destroyed all Western countries' hopes and visions toward China, and the Western powers, blaming China's communism, withdrew capital from China. Deng was pretty shocked and concerned at the moves, and I assume his master card at the time was the establishment of diplomatic relations with Korea. In other words, in order to promote economic growth and to reach a certain level of development into capitalism, China did not have the current status at the time, but it tried to overcome the crisis through diplomatic relations with Korea, which has already grown and settled down very rapidly in the international community.

Hwang You were one of those who helped make history on site. I wonder what that would feel like.

Kwon When the China department was newly established at the Ministry of Foreign Affairs in 1973 as a part of the Southeast Asia department, I refused to be the chief in the Southeast Asia department and chose to be the one in the China department. I already had a dream about China's further growth and the establishment of diplomatic relations between Korea and China since then. When I studied at the University of Pittsburgh in 1967, I came across a whole new world in one class, during which I remember being told: "It is true that the Cold War between the East and West exists now, but it is practically collapsing. The conflict between China and the Soviet Union is rather much more serious than the conflict between the US and China." From then on, I began to draw a big vision of relations with China. For this reason, I put more weight and focused on the China department than the Southeast Asia department. Also, President Park Chunghee also paid attention to relations with China after the June 23 Declaration in 1973, and the atmosphere for diplomatic relations between Korea and China was already sprouting, so there was no reason for me to be interested in other departments.

Hwang The establishment of diplomatic relations with China happened about 20 years after you dreamt about it. You must have spent a lot of time and concerned about it till then.

Kwon Indeed. Until the actual diplomatic relations were established, I personally was concerned and worried about whether this would be really possible. Fortunately, however, I think that Deng, this outstanding figure, knew how to use Korea as an international political element very well, that Korea played a decisive role in China's reform and opening up.

Hwang The culmination of Korea's Northern Policy was the establishment of diplomatic relations between Korea and China. However, is there any particular reason why diplomatic relations between Korea and Russia took place before between Korea and China?

Kwon I think there are differences in diplomatic relations between Korea and China and Korea and Russia. First of all, (former Soviet Union leader) Mikhail Gorbachev internationally chose to establish Korea-Russia diplomatic relations as Russia had no other special alternative after the collapse of the Soviet Union. However, if we look at Korea-China relations, North Korea's Kim Ilsung was alive at the time, and Kim Ilsung was in fact very influential in China. From China's view, North Korea became a more important country after the Sino-Soviet conflict and it ultimately was a strategic partner that China could not lose. In other words, I guess as long as North Korea was there, led by the absolute existence of Kim Ilsung, it was inevitable that establishing diplomatic relations between Korea and China was more difficult to achieve and followed after the one between Korea and Russia.

Hwang Even if Deng Xiaoping promoted Korea-China diplomatic relations with the strategy that you have previously mentioned, can we say that Korea-China diplomatic relations would not have been guaranteed if Korea did not implement the Northern policy?

Kwon Yes, I also think so. (Former) President Roh Taewoo played an essential role in actually establishing diplomatic relations between Korea and China. I guess Roh personally wanted to make his mark in history during his term, and he actively promoted diplomatic relations with China and Russia as a very important strategy to strengthen his political position in the democratization process since the three parties merged. In that sense, Roh provided thorough support and fully delegated his authority during the process of establishment of diplomatic relations between Korea and China. I do not think this diplomatic relationship between Korea and China would have been possible without Roh's will and faith.

Hwang Then what could be our choices in dealing with a stronger China?

Kwon Historically, China was an empire from its origin and was forming a great power in the international community. In fact, China's neighbors have never been on par with China, and China sees itself as the center of the world. Again, it is China's traditional perspective to see the rest as the periphery. After modern times, China went through a major crisis and started to fall, but it gained power again and now it is at the level of competing with the

US. I think Korea's role in China's rise was quite critical, and at the same time, China's influence was also great to Korea in reaching today's status. We should not deny these historical facts.

Hwang It seems the outcome would be great only when businesses, academia, and governments come all together in building policies toward China.

Kwon Based on my experiences from the time back in when I was in the field, the reports and meetings or opinions from scholars were greatly helpful in the real diplomacy and I also have applied their comments. I believe the diplomatic experience and expertise from the field and the theories and opinions of scholars need to be balanced. In other words, the macro perspective (like a telescope) that scholars look at the overall flow of diplomatic relations and the micro perspective (like a microscope) and efforts of experts working directly in the field should collaborate together.

Hwang You are currently running a private organization, the Future Forest. I heard the youth from both Korea and China plant trees in the desert in your program. Please share with us about the achievements of the activities.

Kwon I personally believed that I had diligently lived my days as a Korean citizen and as a diplomat in the mid-20th century, when the international political turbulence emerged. However, after I left office, I came to think that maybe we had taken the future assets of the finite planet ahead of time. Then I met the conclusion that I have wasted my life, thinking that I had exploited the assets of future generations, and I was ashamed of it. Starting from these concerns, I launched the Future Forest in 1999. I have continued this activity with future generations for more than 20 years to pay off our debts with actions to save the Earth, not just by words.

Seeking new Korea-China relations: Evaluating politics and diplomacy

Sept 21, 2022

Jeon Sungheung
Professor, Department of Political Science at Sogang University

Wu Xinbo
Dean, Institute of International Studies at Fudan University

Now is the time for Korea and China to look back on the past, face the present and talk about the future. Over the past 30 years, Korea-China relations have developed explosively. The establishment of Korea-China diplomatic relations was an important turning point in advancing the new era of prosperity in Northeast Asia. And now both Korea and China have grown into the core countries in the international community. China has grown into a major powerhouse in the international community, and Korea has become a globally charming country. Nevertheless, it is also true that there are some friction and conflicts due to the rapid growth and compressed development of the relationship. However, the two countries should endeavor to overcome the current growing pains and build a more mature partnership. Korea and China are neighbors that cannot move away from one another. This geographic condition makes us take an approach in a longer-term perspective, with a longer breath. Meeting the 30th anniversary of Korea-China diplomatic relations this year, we should take it as an opportunity to further strengthen the infrastructure of the relationship and establish a new type of Korea-China relationship that enables strategic communication.

The third series for the New Korea-China relationship this week will be covering politics and diplomacy, following society and culture, and economy and trade over the past two weeks. For this week's discussion, we have invited two experts from the field. Professor Jeon Sungheung at the Department of Political Science, Sogang University, who was a visiting professor at Renmin University's College of International Relations in China, and professor Wu Xinbo at Fudan University in China, who also serves as the dean of the Institute of International Studies and a policy adviser to the Chinese Foreign Ministry, contributed to today's discussion.

Hwang What are the overall emotions and evaluations of the entire diplomatic relations between Korea and China?

Wu Thirty years ago, I think it was in mid-August when I was just settling down in my position and heard that China and South Korea are going to establish diplomatic relations. At the time, I only felt that China is attempting to have another neighboring country as its diplomatic state. However, over the next 30 years, relations between the two countries have made such great progress. It's actually a result that I personally could not expect.

Jeon The meaning of the 30th anniversary of diplomatic relations between Korea and China can be found in the maturity of the bilateral relationship as the number 30 proves it has been a long period of time. Thirty years have passed and it indicates that Korea-China relations have now reached a major turning point, as if moving from one generation to another. Therefore, regardless of the specific situation, it can be said that the relationship between the two countries is at the starting point of seeking new changes from a temporal point of view.

Hwang What particular meaning does the 30th anniversary of the diplomatic ties between Korea and China have?

Jeon Since the establishment of diplomatic relations, the two countries have achieved remarkable quantitative development across almost all areas. Statistics in respective fields, such as economic trade and human exchanges, support these achievements. On the other hand, as time goes by, conflicts and contradictions between the two countries are increasing at the same time. In particular, the current Korea-China relationship comes from Korea's Terminal High Altitude Area Defense (THAAD) deployment, which served as a turning point in bilateral relations, and China's response to Korea's decision. This atmosphere has continued and now is firmly fixed as the basic framework of bilateral relations. Nevertheless, the important fact is that Korea and China have made fundamental progress in relations over a 30-year period compared to their previous relations before the establishment of diplomatic ties. The fact that Korea and China have together climbed the steps from hostile relations to friendships, from renouncement to exchange of relations, and from disconnection to connection is a highly significant diplomatic asset for both countries.

Hwang Then how would you evaluate Korea-China relations in the political and diplomatic aspects?

Wu Politically, the status of bilateral relations has continuously improved, from partnership to comprehensive partnership, and ultimately to the strategic cooperative partnership. Moreover, the two countries have also maintained close high-level exchanges, and such closeness and frequency of exchanges are quite rare in China's relations with neighboring countries. Additionally, in terms of diplomatic perspective, the two countries have conducted effective coordination and cooperation in maintaining peace and stability on the Korean Peninsula, promoting cooperation in the Asia-Pacific region, and enhancing global governance. These achievements in the last 30 years of diplomatic relations between Korea and China are mainly due to the fact that the two countries have taken a pragmatic and positive attitude in dealing with bilateral relations based on their respective national interests.

Jeon If we may divide the assessment of Korea-China relations into four areas of economic trade, social culture, and diplomacy and security, the current diplomatic and security fields will be pointed out as the most insufficient part of bilateral relations. This does not necessarily mean that there have been no results, but it is because the actual diplomatic relations between the two countries in the current situation after THAAD are showing enough difficulties to overshadow the existing achievements. First of all, the deepening conflict and competition between the US and China, in terms of their international moves, is exerting considerable binding force on China's foreign policy. Second, as the North Korean nuclear threat accelerates and inter-Korean relations are strained for a long time, Korea's choices and diplomatic and security position toward US-China relations are limited. Third, in the case of China, the tone of the conservative hard-line policy has been strengthened since Xi Jinping took power, which eventually reduced China's own unique flexibility and let China to continue offensive behaviors. Lastly, Korea is also showing a pattern of heading toward dichotomous extremes in both politics and policymaking, centering on ideology and camps.

Hwang Please tell us more about China's rapid development in economy and constructive attitude toward peace and security on the Korean Peninsula.

Wu I believe these have been a great driving force in the development of bilateral relations. Korea considers its relations with China as one of the most important diplomatic issues, therefore, Korea has continued to strengthen ties between Korea and China by actively developing economic and trade cooperation with China, and by promoting human and cultural exchanges. Of course, it is also true that conflicts and friction exist between the two countries due to differences in the social system and security interests. Korea's THAAD deployment has brought a significant impact on Korea-China relations, which should be applied as a lesson to recover the relationship.

Hwang What achievements did Korea and China make in resolving the North Korean nuclear issue?

Jeon The term "strategic cooperative partnership" that defines Korea and China's relationship does not exactly refer to the current state, but just represents the current status of the bilateral relationship that desires or aims to be a "strategic cooperation partnership." In reality, the current situation between Korea and China is more of an "asymmetry in strategy." Korea and China are under a strange structure in which the two countries' respective ultimate enemies are the ally and quasi-ally to the opponent. China recognizes the US, Korea's target country to strengthen its alliance in response to North Korea's security threats, as its biggest security threat. North Korea, the root of South Korea's security threats, is a buffer zone that China should protect against the US pressure on China. In this double-layered asymmetry, if the latter factor defines China's diplomatic choices and actions toward Korea, then the former can be said to be a factor that determines China's attitude and manner toward Korea.

Hwang How do you see the new outlook of the two countries' relations in the next 30 years?

Wu The development of Korea-China relations over the next 30 years will greatly change the international environment. China will become the world's largest economy, meaning that there is more room for development in Korea-China economic relations and that there will be a high interdependence between the two economies as well. As

China's international status and influence will greatly increase accordingly, Korea should pay more attention to its relations with China while it maintains its alliance with the US. Meanwhile, there is a possibility that the Korean Peninsula will be unified. In case the Korean Peninsula is unified, political, economic, and security influence will be raised, which will increase the economic and political importance of the Korean Peninsula to China in the end. In addition, the trend of economic integration in East Asia will rise further, and the characteristics of regional economic communities will become more prominent. Looking ahead to this future, the two countries should plan the development of Korea-China relations in the framework of national and regional interests and sharing a common destiny.

Hwang Do you have suggestions for the future development of the Korea-China relationship?

Jeon I would like to emphasize two things for the "new Korea-China relationship." First, we need to draw a big picture to establish the new bilateral relationship in preparation for the next 30 years, as many changes and dynamics must happen that we cannot imagine for now. It is desirable to seek a future-oriented "symbiotic relationship," not just a "strategic dimensional" one based on interests, but one that goes beyond the general meaning of peaceful coexistence. Also, in case we face a situation in which each other's positions and interests conflict in reality, probably mutual conflict and friction may become inevitable. If there is one principle that we should keep and apply at that moment, it must be the fact that the situation should not get broader and worsen more than necessary. After the THAAD deployment, the public sentiment between the two countries deteriorated significantly in terms of private sentiment in addition to relations between Korea and China. Along with the recent impact of COVID-19, it is necessary to improve the situation in which the government and the private sector lack communication and dialogue efforts between the two countries.

Wu On top of all, we must respect each other's core interests and concerns and work on enhancing mutual political trust. China's core interest stays in maintaining the stability of its political system, protecting its sovereignty and territorial integrity, and ensuring sustainable economic development, while Korea's core interests are peace and stability on the Korean Peninsula, inter-Korean unification, and sustainable economic development as well. Additionally, among China's multiple core interests and concerns, political security is the one that cannot be challenged against the Chinese Communist Party's position and the country's basic system. In this sense, emphasizing the "One China" policy and the fact that Taiwan is part of China, and the government of the People's Republic of China is China's only legitimate government is the main principle that other countries should respect when they are interacting with China. If this principle is broken, the relationship between the countries will be in great trouble.

Hwang Would there be any concrete and specific plans for further cooperation in order to avoid trouble?

Wu First, we can think of expanding and deepening the economic integration and cooperation through bilateral and regional cooperation channels. By around 2030, China is expected to be the world's largest economy. Whether Korea can sustain and promote its economic and trade relations with China or not, and whether Korea can play its utmost priority in China's market or not will be critically important for Korea's future economy and its sustainable growth. Secondly, social and cultural ties must be strengthened. Cultivating rational and mature mutual recognition is essential and friendship between countries starts from the friendship between people. Since Korea and China are physically close neighbors that cannot move from one another, the social elites should get proactive when people from two countries start to have hostile or negative sentiments toward the other. Lastly, we must endeavor for the substantialization of the strategic cooperative partnership, strengthening the peace and stability of the Korean Peninsula, promoting cooperative coordination in Northeast Asia and even in East Asia, and co-enhance global governance to a certain level. Korea and China's active cooperation in regional and international affairs is not only a matter of respective countries' national interest but is also a way to contribute to the international community.

Hwang How would you assess the Yoon Sukyeol government's policy toward China?

Jeon I do not think we can clearly say that we have raised or suggested a Chinese policy that is conceptually definable.

In addition, although we cannot seriously "evaluate" given that it has not been long since the current government came to the power, we can set several keywords related to the principles that the current government has emphasized in relation to China's policy. They include "different, but harmonizing," "mutual respect," "reciprocal cooperation," and so on. I see that Korea's logic that requires China to respect Korea's sovereign decision for its own security, just as China demands other countries to respect its so-called "core interests," is reflected at the bottom of these wordings. However, as Korea's related policies are to secure its own security and as China is being wary and suspicious, Korea should be able to persuade China in terms of theory and action, that Korea is not joining the anti-China at the front on the US side.

Wu The Yoon Sukyeol administration has announced that it will conduct "value diplomacy" from the very beginning of his office, and is devising ideas to turn Korea's eyes toward Europe for economic and trade relations and to become a global pivotal state. It makes sense when we think that the new government comes to power with this kind of grand aspiration. However, if Korea plays value diplomacy, it will face the political realities of Asia. We must inherit the wisdom of Asia and observe the situations that flow in the US and Europe more closely. If Korea decouples from the Chinese economy and strengthens its ties to the European economy, the result will be simply like pouring water into a bamboo basket (meaning for nothing). If Korea fails to handle its relationship with China well, it will not only confront difficulties in becoming the global pivotal state but will also lose its status in East Asia and just become US' diplomatic tool. This is why the two countries will have to maintain developed relations.

Hwang Are there any words you would like to add?

Jeon There are a few direct contradictions and conflicts between Korea and China, but mostly due to the indirect forms of collateral effects resulting from the relations with third countries. With this in mind, I think it is more important than anything else to always look at bilateral relationships in a large and wide range and lead this bilateral relationship from a long-term perspective.

Seeking new Korea-China relations: Evaluating economy and trade

Sept 14, 2022

Yang Pyoungseob

Senior Research Fellow, Korea Institute for International Economic Policy

Tu Xinquan

Professor, University of International Business and Economics

Now is the time for Korea and China to look back on the past, face the present and talk about the future. Over the past 30 years, Korea-China relations have developed explosively. This week, as we continue the series on the New Korea-China relations, the second topic covers economy and trade, following the social and cultural dimensions. This week's discussion invites two experts from home and abroad. Senior research fellow Yang Pyoungseob at Korea Institute for International Economic Policy, who served as the director of its Beijing office, and professor Tu Xinquan at the University of International Business and Economics, who also is the dean of the China Institute for WTO Studies at the same university, have joined for the discussion.

Hwang What are the achievements of economic cooperation in the 30 years of diplomatic relations between Korea and China?

Yang For the last 30 years after the establishment of diplomatic relations between Korea and China in 1992, trade and investment between the two countries have grown dramatically through the process of coordination and expansion. In 2021, Korea-China trade rocketed 47 times (14.2 percent per year on average) compared to the period when diplomatic relations were just established, and at the end of 2021, the balance of direct investment between the two countries grew 472 times (23.7 percent per year on average) to $100.9 billion. The overall volume has expanded by establishing a complementary cooperative relationship in the manufacturing sector and by meeting the demands that the stages of mutual economic development require at the same time. Korea-China cooperation has grown both quantitatively and qualitatively by establishing complementary global production networks in major industries such as electronic devices, automobiles and petrochemicals. Then the economic cooperation has gone deeper from the vertical division of labor to the horizontal division of labor, and from interindustrial cooperation to within-industrial cooperation, as the two countries' industrial developments reached a similar level. The two countries also have an institutional basis for further economic cooperation. In December 2015, the Korea-China FTA Product Agreement was put into effect in order to enhance the strategic cooperative partnership, and the second stage, service/investment negotiations, is currently underway.

Tu The strategic cooperative partnership between Korea and China is taking place not only in the economy and trade, but also in various fields such as politics, humanities, science and technology. However, economic and trade cooperation is indeed a bright spot for bilateral relations, and trade between Korea and China is a crucial factor in the development of the two countries' economies. Since the two countries established diplomatic ties 30 years ago, their trade volume has increased more than 50 times. China has become Korea's largest trading partner for the last 18 consecutive years. In 2021, the trade volume between Korea and China exceeded $360 billion, equivalent to the total trade volume between Korea and the US, Korea and Japan, and Korea and Europe. This record is similar to that of China and Japan also. In the first half of this year, trade between China and Korea was $184.25 billion, which was about a 9.4 percent increase from the same period of last year. Korea is expected to become China's second-biggest trading partner this year. Against the backdrop of the vulnerable recovery of the global economy, Korea-China trade maintained rapid growth. This fully shows that the economies of the two countries are highly complementary and fully shows the resilience and potential of bilateral economic and trade cooperation.

Hwang Would you explain the development process and flows of Korea-China economic relations?

Yang The process of economic cooperation development between Korea and China can be divided into 1) the stage of establishing the foundation for economic cooperation

(1992-2001), 2) the stage of rapid growth based on a complementary cooperating system (2001-2014), which is the period from joining the WTO till the Korea-China FTA was enacted, and 3) the stage of maturity of economic cooperation from 2015 to the present. In particular, conflicts between South Korea and China over the deployment of THAAD (the US' Terminal High Altitude Area Defense anti-missile system) have continued since 2016, and economic cooperation between the two countries has been partially affected by the competition between the US and China since 2018. In addition, negative factors are reflected all over economic cooperation between Korea and China, for instance, the suspension of operations and human exchanges due to COVID-19 after 2020 and soaring global resources and energy prices after Russia's invasion of Ukraine in 2022.

Hwang From an economic point of view, what could be the nature of Korea-China economic and trade cooperation?

Tu It is the result of mutual benefit and win-win, not relying on either side. Although the industrial structure of the two countries, the factor endowment and the contents of cooperation and competition between the two countries have changed, cooperation between Korea and China still follows the principle of comparative advantage.

Hwang What could be the main problem of the bilateral economic relations between Korea and China?

Tu The reality that both sides must gradually accept and adapt to is the fact that the relative gap in volume between China and Korea will continue to widen and the industrial development gap will steadily narrow down. Indeed, the pace of China's economic development and industrial advancement exceeded our expectations. This is the fruit of our efforts in addition to a lot of internal and external favorable factors. China's economic volume has reached the second largest in the world, and the gap with Korea has widened from 1.4 times to nine times, compared to the early days of diplomatic relations. However, China's development has not reached very high levels and there is still room for sustainable expansion. We must therefore accept the growing gap in economic scale between China and Korea.

Yang There is a growing possibility that the scalability of the Korea-China trade will be limited. China's strategy to strengthen the domestic supply chain, the semiconductor-biased export structure, and the gap between China's import structure and Korea's export structure is likely to limit Korea's export expansion to China. These changes are leading to the trade deficit with China. In the case of 2021, it turns into a deficit if we exclude semiconductors (HS 8542), and in 2022, the overall trade with China was a deficit even when we include semiconductors. In specific, Korea reached a trade deficit with China (minus $1.68 billion) in the second quarter of 2022. The pressure on restructuring Korean companies in China is also escalating. The effect of inducing imports and exports by investment is decreasing due to sluggish local sales of Korean companies, those are invested in China. The share of Korean products in the Chinese import market fell from 10.4 percent in 2015 to 7.7 percent in the first half of 2022, as the competitiveness of Korean products in the Chinese import market, excluding semiconductors, declined.

Hwang From the perspective of the industrial structure, both Korea and China value the development of the manufacturing industry. Is Korea's competitiveness with China declining in bilateral trade?

Yang As China's role shifts from Korea's export market to intermediate goods suppliers, China's influence in Korea's supply chain and economic security is increasing. Korea's dependence on China for imports of intermediate goods (parts and materials) is also continuously rising. In Korea's imports, there are 1,275 items that record more than 90 percent of dependence on China, and 1,850 items with more than 80 percent (out of 12,586 items based on 10 HS units). Under this structure, the possibility of supply chain disruption (petrochemicals, steel, building materials, fertilizer, etc.) due to accidental supply chain interruption (wiring harness, urea water crisis) and policy change (China's 3060 strategy) is emerging.

Tu Once again, China relied on huge resource mobilization capabilities and the benefits of domestic market size to achieve sustained development in some industries and even caught up with Korea. A representative example is the new energy automobile. Regarding the area, China barely relies on the export market and bases on the pure domestic market, which in the end fostered enormous emerging industries and gradually gained international competitiveness. From China's point of view, just because its national power is getting stronger day by day, it cannot treat other countries with arrogance and abuse its power like how the US does. For Korea, it is meaningless to compare the absolute scale with China. On the other hand, it should pay attention to the opportunities that China's economic development has brought to Korea and form a complementary industrial partnership with China.

Hwang Is the competitiveness of Korean investment in China also declining?

Yang Actually we are going through the second phase of restructuring. According to the analysis of the Export-Import Bank of Korea, the sales ratio of Korean companies in China plunged from 7.3 times in 2013 to 2.7 times in 2020, the operating profit ratio from 4.9 percent to 2.2 percent. Also the sales and market share of Korean-brand automobiles in China decreased quite steeply. After the global financial crisis, the first restructuring (escape from China) was carried out mainly by labor-intensive small and medium-sized enterprises. Now, on the other hand, the second restructuring (business adjustment) is going on mostly in large companies such as the ones in automobiles, mobile phones, home appliances and steel since 2018.

Hwang What is the most significant risk that Korea and China are facing?

Tu It is a political factor in economic and trade relations. We know that there are differences in political systems between China and Korea. But the thing is Korea should not feel superior to China because of the difference in political systems, just as there should be no sense of superiority because China is larger than Korea. The political system is an independent choice between the two countries based on their respective history and culture, therefore, no one should interfere or evaluate one another. Both countries have suffered economic and trade friction due to differences in certain security areas, and in this regard, Korea and China should actively seek to establish more stable, transparent and enforceable mechanisms. They must also effectively control security interference or diplomatic differences involving in economic and trade cooperation. The Chinese government has always opposed politicizing the trade issue, and Korea did not want to be on either side under US pressure. In this sense, the two countries need to continuously strengthen their awareness of the separation of economic commerce and politics at various levels, including bilateral, regional and multilateral levels. Moreover, practical measures should be taken to maintain the stability of bilateral economic and trade relations.

Yang As the asymmetry of Korea-China economic power grows, the issue of mutual trust and respect is raised and various threats to Korea-China economic relations are rising in the process of reorganizing the global economic order (New Cold War, protectionism and blockization, reorganization of supply chain, the US-China decoupling and other unexpected variables). It is necessary to establish a direction for bilateral and regional economic cooperation that can wisely overcome these situations.

Hwang What should be the further direction of bilateral cooperation between Korea and China?

Yang First, in terms of the private-led Korea-China economic cooperation, it must be strengthened to enable the sustainable growth of mutual investment companies. When it comes to the fields of semiconductors, batteries and new energy automobiles, the companies should be able to make decisions through autonomous strategic judgments. Second, a practical use of the Korea-China FTA agreement should also be enhanced as a bilateral cooperation platform in responding to the US-China conflict. It is necessary to elevate the agreement to a comprehensive cooperation platform that encompasses cooperation in the field of new business and in stabilizing the supply chain. Third approach is the cooperation in supply chain stabilization, which responds to supply chain disruptions and cooperates in establishing stable supply chains. It will expand policy and information exchange cooperation for intermediate goods that are highly dependent on imports from China, and materials and parts (semiconductors, batteries, rare earths, etc.) that are involved in the US-China competition.

Tu In detail, first of all, both sides must continue to deepen their specific cooperation on trade and investment and strive to leverage more trade areas and potential. One way is to actively organize various economic and trade-promoting activities to establish more trade platforms for companies in both countries. We will support the two-way investment of strong and reputable companies in both countries and provide a fair and nondiscriminatory business environment for partner companies to invest and start their own businesses. Second, both sides should work together to accelerate industrial docking and cooperation and to promote trade and investment cooperation in various fields through industrial cooperation. We must foster new growth points for economic and trade cooperation between the two countries in this post-COVID-19 era. Third, both sides should continue to strengthen communication and coordination in regional and multilateral frameworks, secure the multilateral trading system and jointly promote the establishment of an open global economy.

Hwang Do you have any additional comments on Indo-Pacific Strategy, including IPEF?

Yang The regional cooperation which can minimize the impact of strategic competition in the Indo-Pacific region is necessary. It must seek cooperation in the Indo-Pacific area based on the principle of preventing supply chain disconnection and the open and inclusive cooperation. The Korea-China-Japan cooperation platform should also be promoted, with joint efforts to enact East Asian rules through the Korea-China-Japan FTA, while gradually raising its level of the open platform and moving toward advanced-country cooperation platforms including such as securing the supply chain, environment, digital, labor and competition policies.

Seeking new Korea-China relations: Evaluating society and culture

Sept 8, 2022

Dong Xiangrong

Senior Research Fellow, National Institute of International Strategy at Chinese Academy of Social Sciences

Min Kwisik

Professor, Graduate School of International Studies at Hanyang University

Now is the time for Korea and China to look back on the past, face the present and talk about the future. Over the past 30 years, Korea-China relations have developed to the point that we may call it explosive in respective fields. The establishment of Korea-China diplomatic relations was an important turning point in advancing the new era of prosperity in Northeast Asia. And now both Korea and China have grown into the core countries in the international community. China, along with the United States, has grown into a major powerhouse in the international community, and Korea has become a globally charming country. Nevertheless, it is also true that there are some friction and conflicts due to the rapid growth and compressed development of the relationship. However, the two countries should endeavor to overcome the current growing pains and build a more mature partnership. Korea and China are neighbors that cannot move away from one another. This geographic condition makes us take an approach in a longer-term perspective, with a longer breath. Meeting the 30th anniversary of Korea-China diplomatic relations this year, we should take it as an opportunity to further strengthen the infrastructure of the relationship and establish a new type of Korea-China relationship that enables strategic communication.

In this regard, we prepared a series on seeking new Korea-China relations for three weeks including today, from the perspectives of social culture, economic trade and diplomatic and security. This week's interview invites two representative experts on social culture, the first theme of our series. First, we have Dong Xiangrong, the senior research fellow at the National Institute of International Strategy, Chinese Academy of Social Sciences, and professor Min Kwisik from the Graduate School of International Studies in Hanyang University who also serves as the director of the Institute of Chinese Studies.

Hwang What is the scale of interpersonal communication between the two countries? Please analyze it from the perspective of quantity and quality.

Dong In terms of numbers, the number of people-to-people exchange is particularly valuable considering that South Korea has a population of only 52 million and the two countries are not connected by land, only by sea and air routes. However, as neighboring countries, although there have been over 100 million exchanges between China and South Korea in the past 30 years, the percentage of people who have visited each other's country is not high. It is estimated that no more than 3 percent of China's 1.4 billion population have visited South Korea, while a large proportion of South Korean visitors are business travelers who frequently travel between China and South Korea.

What is the percentage of South Koreans who have direct experience of China? 30 percent? "Seeing is believing." I hope more South Korean people come to China to experience the profound Chinese culture.

Min The people exchanges between Korea and China have grown rapidly. The peak was in 2016, with 8.26 million Chinese visitors to Korea and 4.76 million Koreans visiting China, exceeding 13 million in total. Since then, the number has decreased sharply due to the Terminal High Altitude Area Defense (THAAD) anti-missile system and COVID-19, however, it will recover to a considerable level after a while. The number of long-term residents from each country is the criteria to identify the qualitative exchanges. Today we have 1 Chinese for every 50 Koreans living in Korea, and 1 Korean for every 80 Chinese in China, which shows that the two countries are deeply linked and engaged to each other.

Hwang What is the situation for South Koreans in China?

Dong According to statistics from South Korea's Foreign Ministry, there were 256,875 South Koreans in China in 2021. The total number of South Koreans in China has stabilized at 250,000 in the past decade, and the number of South Korean students in China has fallen by nearly half compared with the number five years ago. Currently, the number of Chinese in South Korea is about 800,000, and there are about 60,000 Chinese students in South Korea. Sizable Korean-populated areas have been formed in Wangjing in Beijing, Chengyang in Qingdao, Gubei in

Shanghai, and these places have become attractive sites for Chinese people to experience Korean culture.

Hwang How would you describe the current circumstances of Chinese people in Korea and what challenges are there?

Min The long-stay Chinese in Korea are actually the major resource that supports the basic areas of the Korean economy, but the evaluation on these people is quite low. Technically they are the reliable speakers in terms of delivering Korean images to China. In this sense, it is problematic to portray Chinatown in a negative angle in films. In particular, the attitude toward Korean countrypeople living as second-class citizens in both China and Korea should be changed. Prior to improving the immigration policy, social and legal support for ethnic Koreans in China should be strengthened.

Hwang What are the achievements of the Korean Wave in China?

Min The Korean Wave first started with dramas and expanded into music, films and culture. But the thing is that Hallyu fans are limited to only certain generations. We must understand that the Korean Wave can only be maintained when it is supported by steady economic growth and democratic politics. Since the true Korean Wave can bear fruit by having people relish 'Korea' itself beyond just a few cultural genres, a comprehensive perspective and approach are essential to enhance Korea's soft power.

Dong The Korean Wave is an important channel for Chinese people to learn about South Korea. It has prevailed in China since the 1990s. In the beginning, some TV drama series with the theme of family life attracted a large number of middle-aged and elderly women viewers. The common identity in a Confucian cultural sphere made Chinese audiences regard South Korean culture as "an old friend." South Korean romance dramas have captivated many young Chinese. It is jokingly said that the popularity of the Korean Wave has greatly increased women's requirements for their partners, which indirectly had an impact on the decline of their desire for marriage. In recent years, Chinese teenagers have become enamored with K-pop and other popular culture. Regardless of China's security concerns, the deployment of the US THAAD system greatly dampened the enthusiasm for the Korean Wave fans in China. The Korean Wave's fever has been reduced. Even so, the Chinese public's appreciation for Korean pop culture is still palpable. I personally run a social media blog with more than 80,000 followers in China. I once asked which South Korean movie was their favorite and received thousands of comments. It had far more clout than similar questions related to other countries.

Hwang What are the achievements of Korean-language promotion in China?

Dong From a worldwide perspective, the place where Korean education has developed most rapidly in terms of either speed or scale over the past 30 years in the world is China. Before the establishment of diplomatic ties between China and South Korea, only five universities in China had a Korean language major, such as Peking University and Yanbian University. Since the establishment of diplomatic ties, there has been a boost in the number of universities offering Korean language as a major. At present, more than 200 universities in China offer Korean language as a major, which is unimaginable in any other country. The demand for Korean language talents from Korean enterprises in China, Chinese enterprises in Korea, universities, academic institutions and foreign affairs agencies in governments at all levels has promoted the widespread development of Korean language education in China. In recent years, as the expansion of market demand has dropped, the number of students majoring in Korean language has also declined. Nevertheless, some Chinese learn Korean simply to better understand Korean culture and listen to Korean songs.

Hwang Is there any particular stories on achievements or challenges of the Chinese language fever in Korea?

Min As can be seen from the fact that many private Chinese academies closed down, the current Chinese fever has cooled considerably. It may be in a sense of growing pain, however, actually not many people necessarily need to learn Chinese. With the advent of interpretation apps, those who are willing to travel or appreciate Chinese culture can easily and technically find the solution. In addition, as China's cultural capacity grows, the number of people who naturally learn Chinese will increase. Therefore, what we should do now is make more efforts to raise the level of graduates from related departments which are specializing in Chinese.

Hwang What is the scale of Koreans among international students in China?

Dong Before the pandemic, China was the top destination for overseas study in Asia. The biggest group of international students in China is South Korean students. According to statistics from China's Ministry of Education, there were 492,200 international students in China in 2018, 50,600 students of whom were from South Korea. After the outbreak of the pandemic, the number of international students in China dropped. Statistics from South Korea's Foreign Ministry show that 34,000 South Korean students studied in China in 2021. The number is significantly lower than the number of Chinese students in South Korea. When it comes to Korean students studying in China, it reminds me of Choe Chiwon from the Silla Dynasty (57 BC-AD 935), who came to study in the Tang Dynasty (AD 618-907) and spread Chinese culture far and wide. The large group of overseas students has made an important contribution to enhancing exchanges between China and South Korea. Many of them have become leading figures in South Korea.

Hwang How many Chinese students are in Korea? What kind of achievements have they made or what are the challenges are they facing?

Min Last year, about 67,000 students out of 152,000 international students were Chinese students and that makes up 44.2 percent. Although the ratio has decreased compared to 10 years ago, since the number of international students has been increasing slightly, we can say the number of Chinese students was not largely affected by the THAAD issue. However, the fact that Chinese students mostly choose to study liberal arts in Korea might mean that our level of science and engineering should grow further. On the other hand, the percentage of students who came to Korea because they liked Korea, but return to their country as an anti-Korean after studying here is recording a pretty high rate. This is a problematic phenomenon. Only when the academic management of international students become more active and cautious, Korea's competitiveness of studying in Korea will be maintained.

Hwang What is the situation of Korea-related majors at Chinese universities?

Dong There are roughly over 100 research institutions related to the Korean Peninsula in China. Korean institutions such as the Korea Foundation for Advanced Studies, the Academy of Korean Studies, and the Korea Foundation have provided various support to Chinese Korean Peninsula research institutes. In the past 30 years, Chinese scholars have applied for more than 300 projects related to the Korean Peninsula supported by the National Social Science Fund of China, which has greatly promoted Chinese scholars' all-round research on the Korean Peninsula in terms of politics, economy, society, history and culture.

Hwang There are a few Korean universities that have China studies departments. What are the current situations there and what challenges are they facing?

Min First of all, many of the Chinese departments in local universities have closed down, and overall admissions are falling. This is due to the result that reflects people's perception toward China, however, the abolishment of the department mustn't be a hasty decision. Chinese studies that aims to teach its social science should be remained, even if the department changes into East Asian studies. Looking at these changes from a distance, we need human resources who major in Chinese-related studies and have capacities that exceed what a university can teach them. Considering China's growth, its size and importance, we cannot say that the current number of majors in Chinese studies is excessive.

Hwang What is the status of media and public opinion exchanges between the two countries?

Min The media is usually a window to understand other countries, but the two countries' media have failed their roles in the sense of making the other countries understand objectively. This is due to the sensational reporting based on the commercial nature of media. In addition, the emergence of online media outlets is mostly focused on making certain targets unappealing, rather than extending the positive aspect of exchanging information. In particular, as the government cannot control such information, conflicts between the two countries' private sectors are amplified. In the end, when it comes to the solution, we have no other choice but to count on improvement in civic awareness although it must take some time.

Dong The mainstream media of China and South Korea have correspondents stationed in each other's countries. They send back a large amount of information to the people of the two countries for reference. A relatively stable exchange mechanism has been established between major media of the two countries, such as the China-ROK Media High-level Dialogue. The main problem is that the image of each other's country in mainstream media is not symmetrical. The coverage of China in South Korean media is generally negative. It has to do with South Korea's news predilection for grabbing attention and focusing on negative events. The coverage of South Korea in mainstream Chinese media is generally positive. However, a new phenomenon has emerged in recent years with social media flourishing. In pursuit of clout, some bloggers not only tend to report negative news about other countries, but also would like to hype up negative news about their country debated in other countries. Some harsh, extreme views end up rapidly spreading on the internet, which exerts a negative impact on China and South Korea's public opinion field and heavily affects people's mutual understanding between the two countries.

Hwang What are the social and cultural conflicts between Korea and China?

Dong China and South Korea are culturally homologous, geographically similar and historically intertwined. It is regrettable that the historical experience, which should have increased mutual recognition, has triggered conflicts in today's international political context. The social and cultural contradictions between China and South Korea mainly focus on two areas. The first is about the perception and collective memory of the past, including the nature of the relationship between the two countries in history, the Korean War and other issues. The second is the attribution of traditional culture. Basic principles need to be noted here, that is, the concept of the modern nation-state should not be used to analyze international relations in ancient times, nor can the concept of intellectual property in the contemporary world be used to define the ownership of ancient cultural products.

Min The core causes of the conflict between Korea and China are the issues that are highly abstract, such as the matters of historical and cultural sovereignty. As these matters are directly connected to the national identity, it is terribly difficult to make any kind of concessions or resolutions. This is why these problems usually stay under the ground but detonate once conflict arises. The basis of this sentiment comes from the reality that that historical superiority and inferiority are contradictory to the current national income level. Each has this psychological aspect to compensate their inferiority with a sense of superiority, therefore, even a small conflict tends to be greatly amplified.

Hwang What is the reason for the spread of anti-Korea sentiment?

Min As Korea and China built a functionalist approach that emphasizes reciprocal economic necessity, their emotional trust is relatively weak compared to the volume of trade. The root of the public's anti-Chinese sentiment is quite specific, for instance the fine dust problem. This anti-Chinese sentiment has been strengthened as it has caused inconveniences for people in life and such feelings tend to accumulate. Moreover, fear of China's rise has prompted resistance against the Chinese political system, and the continued ideological offensive by the conservatives has also played a major role. On top of that, the individualistic characteristics of the young generation might have overlapped, so the anti-Chinese sentiment spread to a degree that far exceeded economic benefits.

Dong Personally, I do not agree with the term "anti-Korean sentiment in China." It is not so much opposing Korea as disliking Korea, which is a negative perception and sentiment toward Korea. Two time points were vital in the spread of the sentiment of disliking Korea. The first was the deployment of THAAD, which made many Chinese people very disappointed in South Korea. Therefore, the sentiment of disliking South Korea rose in China. During the Moon Jaein administration, after China and South Korea reached a basic consensus on the THAAD issue and properly handled it, bilateral relations saw a turnaround at a critical phase. In fact, negative sentiment toward South Korea in the Chinese public has eased somewhat in recent years. However, it is a pity that the Beijing Winter Olympics this year has brought about some controversies on hanbok, referee's decisions, etc. South Korea's arguments were shocks to the Chinese people. From the Chinese public's perspective, as one of the 56 ethnic groups in China, there is no reason why the Korean minority should not be allowed to sing and dance in their traditional costume at the Winter Olympics. Besides, any dispute over a referee's decision in sports should be settled through established procedures, and an important basis for participating in sports competition is to accept the referee's decision. And, it was rare to see responsible Korean politicians, scholars and sports figures make a rational and objective analysis on these issues. Some of them would rather add to the disputes than calm them.

Hwang What is the best way to carry out social and cultural exchanges between the two countries for the next five years? What advice do you have for the two governments?

Dong We need to let history be history, and let culture be culture and sport be sport. The stable development of the relationship between China and South Korea should not be interfered or even hijacked by other factors. History, culture and sports should become an important bond for enhancing bilateral relations. Politicians and the people of both countries need to realize that developing bilateral relations is in the fundamental interests of the two countries and their peoples. The social and cultural exchanges between the two countries are not too much, but too little and too inadequate. The people of the two countries do not know each other well enough. Anyone who hypes up the so-called dispute between China and South Korea to pursue their own selfish interests will eventually be abandoned by history. As the theme song of the 1988 Seoul Olympics goes, "Hand in hand, we can start to understand, breaking down the walls that come between us for all time."

Min First of all, we must acknowledge the serious emotional conflict between the peoples from the respective countries and share the necessity for countermeasures. Since the two countries' national sentiments are sensitive to political and diplomatic issues, the most important thing is to reduce strategic conflicts and to increase political trust. China should be aware that its soft power has greatly weakened and readjust its public diplomacy toward neighboring countries. South Korean officials should reduce unnecessary misstatements that provoke China. Lastly, it is necessary to jointly start global citizenship education activities to get rid of excessive nationalist sentiment and to operate them as a 1.5 track that involves private organizations.

Seeking new Korea-China relations: Evaluating defense and military

Sept 28, 2022

Yoo Dongwon

Professor, Korean National Defense University

Chen Yue

Associate Research Fellow, War Studies Institute at the Academy of Military Sciences, PLA

Now is the time for Korea and China to look back on the past, face the present and talk about the future. Over the past 30 years, Korea-China relations have developed explosively. The establishment of Korea-China diplomatic relations was an important turning point in advancing the new era of prosperity in Northeast Asia. And now both Korea and China have grown into the core countries in the international community. China has grown into a major powerhouse in the international community, and Korea has become a globally charming country. Nevertheless, it is also true that there is some friction and conflicts due to the rapid growth and compressed development of the relationship. However, the two countries should endeavor to overcome the current growing pains and build a more mature partnership. Korea and China are neighbors that cannot move away from one another. This geographic condition makes us take an approach in a longer-term perspective, with a longer breath. In honor of the 30th anniversary of Korea-China diplomatic relations this year, we should further strengthen the infrastructure of the relationship and establish a new type of Korea-China relationship that enables strategic communication.

This week the series will be covering defense & military, following discussions on society & culture, economy & trade, and politics & diplomacy over the past three weeks. For this week's conversation, we have invited two experts from the field. Professor Yoo Dongwon from Korean National Defense University (KNDU), who served the director of US-China Research Center at KNDU, and Col. Chen Yue, associate research fellow at the War Studies Institute at The People's Liberation Army's Academy of Military Sciences and an expert on the Korean Peninsula, contributed to today's discussion.

Hwang Looking back at the last 30 years of history, how was the military relationship between Korea and China?

Yoo For the past 30 years, military relations between Korea and China have developed under the influence of political, diplomatic, and economic conditions both at home and abroad. Around 1993-94, a military attache to each embassy was established, and in 1992 and 1994, the Korean Chairman of the Joint Chiefs of Staff visited China to hold the first meeting between the military leaders of the two countries. In 1995, a working-level defense policy talk was first held to coordinate and cooperate in military exchanges between the two countries. Since 1999, Korea and China's Minister of National Defense held mutual visits, and in 2002, the Foreign Policy and Security (2+2) Dialogue between Korea-China began, followed by the mutual exchange visits between cadets and naval fleets. Later in 2003, another mutual visit of the Minister of Defense was held, and the Korea-China Defense Dialogue became more active along with regularization of defense policy meetings in the director levels and military exchange programs beginning in 2004. The navies of the two countries conducted joint search and rescue drills also, which was basically a preliminary form of joint military drills. Additionally, in 2008, Korea and China installed an air-sea direct line and conducted another joint search and rescue drill.

Chen Since the establishment of diplomatic relations, Korea and China have strengthened cooperation under the spirit of 'mutual respect, equal and mutual benefit, peace and coexistence, and good-neighborliness.' We are deepening mutual political trust, amalgamating our interests, and maintaining unprecedented level of consultation and cooperation in international and regional affairs. Ever since the establishment of diplomatic relations, high-ranking military personnel from the two countries have visited each other quite frequently, and the number of delegations visiting each other annually is more than 20 on average. These factors have supported the development of bilateral relations across a wide-range and in multidimensional areas.

Hwang There must have been damage to Korea-China military relations because of the THAAD issue.

Yoo The military relations between Korea and China were halted for a while in the wake of North Korea's attack on the Cheonan corvette in 2010 and another one toward Yeonpyeong Island. Bilateral military relations were restarted through the talks between Korea-China Ministers of Defense in May 2011. Later on, the relations were severed following Korea's decision to deploy THAAD in July 2016. In October 2017, the Moon Jaein government tried to improve relations with China by mentioning '3NO (no additional THAAD deployments, no joining of a broader U.S. missile defense system, and no Korea-US-Japan military alliance)', however, relations have been minimized due to COVID-19. Until now, defense strategy dialogues, the Foreign Policy and Security (2+2) Dialogue, and most of the defense academic exchanges in search and rescue training have been suspended.

Hwang How would you assess the current military relations?

Chen The militaries of two countries established a close functional department exchange system, defense strategy dialogue, working-level meetings in defense policy, and regular exchanges systems and have signed a Memorandum of Understanding for defense exchange and cooperation. Also, since 2014, remains of Chinese soldiers have been returned to China nine separate times. In addition, the Minister of Defense's direct lines to the army, navy, and air force were opened, which led to several mutual visits of deck planes. Now, the Ministers of Defense have direct lines to each side's army, navy, and air force, as well as lines to Korea's Master Control and Report Center and to China's Northern theater commands.

Yoo In general, we see military relations develop from military exchange, military cooperation, and to military alliance in an order, and the current Korea-China military relations could be said to be at the rudimentary military cooperation stage. Compared to other developments in economies or social and political areas, the process is going quite slow. In particular, the level of institutionalization is still low, despite the fact that the agreement on establishing military trust building measures (a hotline, search and rescue training, etc.) was signed recently, the internalized stage is insufficient.

Hwang What could be the reason that the military area is developing slower than any other part of Korea-China relations?

Yoo The reason for the conflicts in Korea-China military relations is not because of direct bilateral friction, but rather due to the impact of external factors such as North Korea and the Korea-US alliance, and lack of empathy in terms of strategic issues. In specific, it is largely influenced by North Korea's nuclear weapons, US-China relations, Korea-US and US-Japan alliance. In this sense, these issues constrain Korea-China military relations, and conflicts caused by external factors have accordingly become more complicated to resolve.

Hwang What do you think the future direction of military cooperation between Korea and China is?

Chen High-level military communication between the two armies should be sustained. Based on the principle of mutual respect and equality, we must work to exclude any interference from third-parties, resolve misunderstandings and deepen mutual trust through building close strategic communication. Moreover, high-level strategic communication between the two armies should be strengthened along with promoting high-level exchanges and dialogue mechanisms.

We can also think of adding Northeast Asia and the Asia-Pacific region's security issues in the bilateral strategic dialogue agendas to protect peace and stability, establishing a system between the two armies to notify and immediately communicate about serious situations, so that we can avoid strategic misjudgments and resolve various constraints. The development of military relations between the two countries should be promoted in all directions to become the joint pillar for peace and stability on the Korean Peninsula, regional cooperation, and further resolutions of global problems. Exchange and cooperation in bilateral, regional, and even global affairs should be further intensified, and the contents and measures of cooperation should be expanded. The Korea-China armies should continuously endeavor to broaden common interest and sustain cooperation in all dimensions by holding discussions on establishing a permanent cooperative system in areas such as disaster relief, maritime relief, public health, peacekeeping, navigation protection, and others.

Yoo For international cooperation, Korea and China should not be too immersed in either the international structure or the US-China competition, but should secure their respective security interests from a more flexible and open perspective. Under the current international structure, security and military interests between Korea and China overlap with each other, therefore, exclusive and independent claims of rights may eventually deteriorate the relations and might be misunderstood as interference in the domestic affairs of one another. This is why military and security issues must be pursued in a low key manner and carefully with responsibility.

Hwang What do you mean by excluding third-party interference?

Chen First of all, all the local issues and sensitive problems should be appropriately dealt with. As the THAAD issue has emerged as the most serious challenge since the establishment of diplomatic relations, joint efforts are required to manage it well. Recently, Korea and China's ministers of foreign affairs held a meeting and the two sides agreed to value each other's security concerns and make efforts for leniency so as not to interfere with bilateral relations. Both countries should not provoke each other and strictly follow the consensus so that these problems do not come up to the surface again. Another notable thing is that the cooperation paradigm of the Korea-US military alliance stays under the intention to expand the siege and territory. Korea and the US are allies, and Korea and China are inseparable neighbors and close cooperative partners at the same time. The Korea-US alliance should not undermine regional peace and stability, nor should damage China's strategic security interests. China consistently respects Korea's grave concerns. Therefore, the Korean and Chinese militaries should also continue to implement the agreement between the two leaders, remember the initial commitment from back when we were establishing diplomatic relations, maintain an appropriate position on issues related to the other's core interests, and further develop Korea-China relations with good military connections.

Hwang What are the major challenges to Korea-China military relations?

Yoo Military relations between Korea and China in the future are still dependent on variables such as changes in international relations, strategic competition between the US and China, the domestic politics of the two countries, and North Korea. The US-China strategic competition at the global and regional level is likely to pose various risks to the development of military relations between Korea and China as well as Korea's foreign policy. It presents new tasks for Korea's foreign affairs and security, as the prolonged Russia-Ukraine war increases the possibility of negative effects on the international political and economic order, along with the Korea-China relations. Changes in the global strategic environment will provide an opportunity and a great challenge for Korea-China military relations.

Hwang What should we do if we seek to specify cooperation between the two armies?

Chen The two armies should further strengthen exchanges between functional departments and related fields, resume maritime rescue, and expand practical cooperation in non-traditional security areas including maritime rescue, counterterrorism, sanitation, and others. It is necessary to also tighten up the communication exchanges between young officers, and to expand inter-visit of young officers by arranging short-term education, exchange learning, and student exchanges at military schools in various forms to develop more 'China Experts' and "Korea Experts'. Additionally we can think of increasing the number of mutual visits between ships and scale of direct naval and air phone line connections.

Yoo I guess we need to develop theories and logic development on "peace and cooperation" rather than "confrontation and war" at the global and regional level, and especially in terms of the Russian-Ukraine war, we must take a sober analysis at the academic level. In the end, exchanges between scholars are essential for the development of theories and logic related to "peace and cooperation." Efforts to expand communication with experts and strategists between Korea and China and to regularize or institutionalize low-level exchanges are highly suggested.

Hwang Do you have any other comments you would like to add?

Yoo The Korea-China military relationship has not fully recovered yet, but there are channels going on for dialogue and communication between the two countries' defense ministries and between the militaries. Also, the fact that the Korean and Chinese navies conducted three search and rescue drills as a coalition is meaningful in the aspect that it was a trial to realize the agreement into an action. If military relations between the two countries further develop in the future, it will basically provide an opportunity to promote military cooperation in non-traditional security areas such as PKO, disaster relief, anti-piracy, and so on.

Chen Both Korea and China have great influence in Northeast Asia and they play an important role in Asia-Pacific, Northeast Asia and the Korean Peninsula. Therefore, the Korea-China relationship is one of the most important bilateral relations in the Asia-Pacific region. There is no reason for the two countries to fail in establishing a firm bilateral relations, no reason not to consider each other's core security concerns, and no reason to alienate and even confront each other due to third-party factors. Korea and China should also take joint measures to cooperate in security challenges without missing historical opportunities.

What can South Korea and China work on together?

Apr 28, 2022

Lu Chao

Professor, Liaoning Academy of Social Sciences in Shenyang

Cha Du Hyeogn

Principal Fellow, Asan Institute for Policy Studies

The inauguration of South Korea's new government in May will be an opportunity to assess the current state of South Korea-China relations and seek further development in the future. President-elect Yoon Sukyeol presented his plans to turn South Korea into a global pivotal state during his election campaign. He has also declared that strengthening the US-South Korea alliance and South Korea-China relations are simultaneously achievable goals.

Since South Korea and China established diplomatic ties, all South Korean administrations have sought balanced development of relations with both the US and China. All have confronted barriers. Given that South Korea and China's interests are mostly heading in different directions, the outlook for their relationship is not very positive, even after the new administration's inauguration. Both countries need to reestablish their perspectives toward each other and see the relationship as it is, not as a measure to influence US-China relations or inter-Korean relations.

Back in the time of the Terminal High Altitude Area Defense anti-ballistic missile system's deployment in 2016, we saw how sensitivity on security issues overwhelmed South Korea and China's economic mutual dependence. Based on that experience, South Korea and China should respect each other's security concerns. At the same time, they should firm up their respective understanding of each other's positions on security to avoid creating tension. Therefore, South Korea and China should frankly admit that they are quite different in various aspects. Even if they do not agree, they should accept each other's policies as a reality. Work to find an optimum meeting point is critical and necessary.

This week's discourse invites two experts from South Korea and China to discuss South Korea-China cooperation, particularly on the North Korea issue. The two experts have contributed significantly to studies on North Korea. We have Lu Chao, a professor at Liaoning Academy of Social Sciences in Shenyang, and Cha Du Hyeogn, a principal fellow of the Asan Institute for Policy Studies in Seoul.

Hwang As Korea has a new conservative government (President-elect Yoon Sukyeol and the People Power Party) coming in, China seems to be concerned.

Cha I would like to ask if cooperation between the South Korean and Chinese governments was really successful during the last five years of the incumbent Moon Jaein administration. Of course, Moon could not neglect the US' interests while focusing on his policies toward North Korea. At the same time, he had to keep in mind that renouncing the US-South Korea alliance was not an option. These overall circumstances must be the same for the incoming Yoon Sukyeol administration, but I expect him to implement policies that aim to balance the US and China. From this perspective, the Yoon administration will revise all foreign policies from the previous administration and seek a new approach. But I would still like to say that the Yoon administration's approach will not be based on strategic ambiguity, which causes confusion for the other side.

Lu On March 25, President-elect Yoon Sukyeol and Chinese President Xi Jinping had a phone call. Considering the fact that President Xi normally does not have phone calls with newly-elected South Korean president-elects, the recent case proves how both China and South Korea are aware of the significance of two countries' strategic communication. In particular, President Xi said, "Facts have proven that the development of China-South Korea relations conforms to the fundamental interests of the two countries and their people, and promotes regional peace and development." This shows his view that both China and South Korea have a responsibility to keep the regional peace and promote world prosperity while the current international society is facing several challenges. Yoon also added that strengthening Korea-China cooperation will contribute to development of bilateral relations and interests for people from two countries, as well as the peace and stability of Northeast Asia. As seen, the phone call between Yoon and Xi is meaningful in the sense that it established the foundation for the development of healthy bilateral relations. The two countries made a consensus on that maintaining and improving two countries' relations is in the fundamental interests of both.

Hwang Please tell us about the new South Korean government and China's further policies toward North Korea.

Lu Basically, China is encouraging North Korea to proceed with reciprocal peace talks with the US, and insists on strengthening communication and cooperation with North Korea as well as parallelizing strategic communication with South Korea at the same time. Additionally, the North Korean nuclear issue is closely related to the security environment for the countries in the region, which make China's principle clear that the process for peace negotiation must be open and transparent. While inter-Korean relations are intensifying again, I think China and South Korea should be standing on the same side to keep the peace regime stable when it comes to peninsular issues. The two countries should calm the situation with a sincere approach and put more efforts into reopening talks based on mutual trust.

Cha First of all, while the Moon administration's policy toward North Korea was basically focusing on peace first and denuclearization later, the incoming Yoon administration is expected to take a "denuclearization first" approach, considering North Korea's highly escalated nuclear capability over the last 10 years. It is just that the new government is also aware of that denuclearization in a package is very difficult, since the previous conservative Lee Myungbak and Park Geunhye governments' "denuclearization first" approaches also could not make practical outcomes. Under the conditions, the upcoming government is likely to reflect how it went so far and stress some precedent actions for denuclearization first. In other words, as we are not able to clearly apprehend how far North Korea has elevated its nuclear capability, a report from North Korea will be required. Then a cross-check on North Korea's report must be held, which will be the base for freezing its nuclear programs. These steps have to be fulfilled to partially lift sanctions on North Korea. Additionally, from South Korea's perspective, it is within North Korea's missile range, including its intercontinental ballistic missiles. As a result, Korea's stance can be strengthened to require actions to restrain North Korean missiles from carrying nuclear warheads.

Hwang Regarding the nuclear issue, what specific actions can we take?

Lu Though the Korean Peninsula seems to face a significantly difficult problem, it surely has a hope and all the related countries must endeavor for a breakthrough. Under the current circumstance, we should think of what would happen if the aim of denuclearization of the Korean Peninsula is dropped. Moreover, denuclearization of the Korean Peninsula is not only for South Korea, but is also a part of international nuclear nonproliferation. Given these points, China will firmly stand on supporting the denuclearization of the Korean Peninsula. If North Korea keeps its promise on halting its nuclear development, Korea and China should work on mitigating sanctions on North Korea by pushing for international agreement. This will eventually assist a smooth process for denuclearization. Regarding the transition of an Armistice

Agreement to a Peace Treaty, China is a country that is influential in establishing a long-term peace regime in the Korean Peninsula and actualize the denuclearized Korean Peninsula. In this sense and for the regional security and stability, we oppose North Korea's military provocation, particularly the nuclear development, and I would like to suggest South Korea to minimize any type of provoking attitudes toward North Korea also.

Cha North Korea's denuclearization has to be the goal in common, and not just rhetoric. China has rhetorically supported denuclearization of the Korean Peninsula several times, however, from now on, Korea and China should have a common goal in the smooth dissolution of North Korea's nuclear capability. North Korea has particularly announced its development of ultra-modern tactical nuclear weapons at its Eighth Congress of the Korean Workers' Party in 2021, which was targeting South Korea. Moreover, now its capability is going beyond the Korean Peninsula and has expanded to the US mainland. This means North Korea has surpassed the "self-defense nuclear deterrence" that it has constantly insisted on. Some might argue that China is an exempt from North Korea's threats because of the special characteristic of their relations. Nonetheless, due to the characteristics this specific weapon has, no one can tell for sure that it will be exclusively used on a particular country. Regarding China's suggestions on freeze-for-freeze and dual track approaches, I am not quite sure on the dual track. However, we might need to reconsider whether freeze-for-freeze is actually an equivalent measure.

Hwang Besides denuclearization, what can South Korea and China work on together?

Cha Until today, both conservative and progressive governments made mistakes based on the idea that economic leverage can control North Korea's actions. However, for the last five years, North Korea has continuously said that allowing South Korea to use its economic leverage is directly connected to its weak point. It does not necessarily fit into North Korea's own ideas and desires on economic development. Let's remember that North Korean leader Kim Jongun ordered the removal of South Korean facilities during his visit to Geumgang Mountain in 2019, and that North Korean workers in economics emphasized their own approach to economic construction reflect all these realities. From this point of view, the new government is recommended to establish inter-Korean economic cooperation plans that can contain aspects favorable to South Korea while also reflecting North Korea's ideas and wishes. South Korea is a government leading aid for North Korea. There are also various ways to cooperate, like getting actively involved at the people or municipal level.

Lu Peace on the Korean Peninsula might come sooner if inter-Korean cooperation is achieved with China as the pivot in areas that do not violate sanctions. For instance, this can include sports, cultural exchange and economics which can settle a peaceful and stable atmosphere among China and the two Koreas. Furthermore, we can think of South Korea-China cooperation to solve North Korea's food security issues, as well as to improve the North Korean people's daily lives. Today, North Korea is suffering from food insecurity, as all its external trading channels are blocked due to economic sanctions from most of the international community including the US. Again, strengthening cooperation between South Korea and China to relieve North Korea's food security issue is essential. At the same time, the way they support North Korea should also be acceptable from its point of view. This is where we need more discussions. Lastly, South Korea and China can think of strengthening inter-Korean cooperation or connecting the China-Mongolia-Russia economic corridor. This would build the Eurasian network by utilizing China's Eastern railway and its connected networks. Establishment of all these networks will enable China, South Korea and North Korea's northeast Asian distribution point.

Hwang Regarding foreign relations, both Koreas have alliances or relations similar to an alliance. How can Korea and China approach issues that are sensitive to their alliances?

Cha Both South Korea and China have to acknowledge the historical values that the US-South Korea alliance and China-North Korea relations have. When it comes to policies toward North Korea, South Korea and China should limit excessive expectations toward each other in order to successfully achieve cooperation. Traditionally South Korea wanted China to be a mediator to invigorate inter-Korean relations and to exert pressure on North Korea to change. Meanwhile, China wanted to balance against the US-South Korea alliance by promoting South Korea-China relations. However, the problem is maximum feasibility. If South Korea and China are stuck in wishful thinking about the roles that the other side can play, mutual distrust will deepen every time they don't get what they want. In order to reduce such mistakes and errors, South Korea and China must acknowledge the opposing values that cannot be given up at this present point. South Korea should accept the fact that it is impossible for China to get very close to South Korea, if it comes at a risk for North Korea's regime and system. On the other hand, China should also admit that weakening the US-ROK alliance is realistically difficult. A new setting of cooperation should come to the table, which is marked by the minimal expectations of one another.

Lu When we talk about North Korea's nuclear issue, US President Biden is continuing the "strategic patience" that former President Obama has emphasized. However, he is not making any practical effort to persuade North Korea to abandon its nuclear weapons. North Korea has also not received any sign or message for a talk from the US. Accordingly, Kim Jongun laid down his will to continue negotiations with the US. As a result, from the beginning of this year, North Korea has launched several missiles and shown a firm attitude toward the US. This explains why the Biden administration had no other option but to resume unconditional peace talks with North Korea. President Biden is continuing to make efforts to attract more countries into its alliance amid the US-China strategic competition. As the incoming Yoon administration is highlighting the US' focus on strengthening the US-South

Korea alliance, South Korea is anticipated to conduct independent diplomacy. This diplomacy will not choose to bandwagon on either side of the US-China competition, as it is a global pivotal state.

Hwang We are greeting the 30th anniversary of South Korea-China diplomatic relations.

Lu First of all, South Korea and China should emphasize the fact that a strategic partnership in all dimensions fits with both countries' common interest. Even after the inauguration of the Yoon administration, the overall direction of South Korea-China relations must be consistent. However, the tension and conflict between North and South Korea is not an evitable issue, and we have to keep in mind that the problem can worsen anytime. Despite this current flow of events, China is South Korea's largest trading partner and also one of the most important countries in maintaining peace and stability on the Korean Peninsula. Therefore, we should be aware that generally, China-South Korea relations must not waver depending on any political changes. We should understand that China is striving to improve and develop China-South Korea relations once President-elect Yoon is inaugurated. China is anticipating a visit from President-elect Yoon at an appropriate time. In addition, given that 2022 marks the 30th anniversary of diplomatic ties between South Korea and China, we must actively work on cooperation in the private and public sectors, based on China-South Korea cultural exchanges.

Cha South Korea and China have already been together for the last 30 years since the establishment of diplomatic relations. The spectrum of further cooperation is expected to expand sustainably. Nevertheless, South Korea-China relations still have gaps to be filled in compared to 60 years of North Korea-China relations, or the 70-year US-South Korea alliance. This explains why we must perceive the existing confrontations between South Korea and China as growing pains to strengthen bilateral trust. For now, South Korea and China must recognize that both sides have to be patient and get to know each other more.

Hwang Do you have any additional comments to add?

Lu When we are setting a specific path, inter-Korean talks must be held before the US-North Korea dialogue takes place. When it comes to core talks on nuclear and security, the US, North Korea and South Korea are all seeking denuclearization of the Korean Peninsula. However, they are currently in conflict due to their own separate interests. South Korea should cooperate with its strategic partner China on various levels and channels to solve all these issues -- not only with the US and North Korea.

Cha South Korea and China must have strategic transparency toward each other. For both countries to have rational expectations of each other, honesty must come first. Moving on from strategic ambiguity, South Korea and China should clarify their respective strategic stances and establish which values South Korea respects. This strategic transparency may bring temporarily conflicts between the two countries, but will ultimately build trust and enhance their relationship.

Trilateral cooperation, now is the time to buckle down

Nov 17, 2022

Ou Boqian
Secretary General, Trilateral Cooperation Secretariat

It is true that Korea, China, and Japan have had ups and downs and sometimes conflicts throughout their long history. However, the risks of the traditional and non-traditional security areas faced by the three countries in the rapidly changing international order are essentially the same to the security and development of each country. In order to solve these challenges, common consensus and cooperation from the three countries are required. Vision and philosophy based on the keynote of 'Korea-China-Japan three in one' are what we need, not the exclusion. This was confirmed once again by President Yoon Sukyeol, Chinese Premier Li Keqiang, and Japanese Prime Minister Kishida Fumio's emphasis on practical cooperation during the trilateral summit between the three countries at the ASEAN+3 summit in Phnom Penh, Cambodia.

The basic infrastructure of trilateral cooperation is strong in economic and human relations, and the three countries are willing to cooperate in various ways for peace and development of the region. In 2019, the leaders of the three countries announced Trilateral Cooperation Vision for the next decade in Chengdu, China, as a three-nation cooperation vision for the next decade, and since the establishment of the Trilateral Cooperation Secretariat (TCS) in 2011, the three countries have been seeking, proposing, and promoting practical cooperation as best they can.

This week's interview features Trilateral Cooperation Secretariat Secretary General Ou Boqian to learn more about the future of trilateral cooperation, from someone who is always thinking about the topic.

The ambassador was appointed the secretary general at the 6th Consultative Board of the TCS in September 2021. She joined the Ministry of Foreign Affairs of China (MOFA) in 1989 and has served at multiple diplomatic offices in various regions and countries since then. Most recently, she served as the Ambassador to Grenada from 2013 to 2017 before working as the Vice President of the Chinese People's Institute of Foreign Affairs from 2017 to 2021.

Hwang What is the current status and level of trilateral cooperation between the TCS members, Korea, China, and Japan?

Ou Looking at developments that happened within the 6th Consultative Board's term, trilateral cooperation has seen continuous efforts made by the three countries in the fields of non-traditional security and political affairs. The 13th Top Regulators' Meeting was held in November 2021, during which ministries shared updates on status and progress regarding nuclear safety activities in each country. In July 2022, the Trilateral Ministerial Meeting on Disaster Management was held, in which the three governments introduced key disaster prevention policies and experiences in response to increasingly more frequent and intense natural disasters. Various other intergovernmental dialogues also continued at the working level. In addition, outside of official government channels, Track 1.5 and Track 2 dialogue also kept alive the momentum of trilateral cooperation. The 6th Network of Trilateral Cooperation Think-Tanks (NTCT) National Focal Points Meeting and the 2021 NTCT Conference were convened in December, in which universities and research institutes discussed ideas on trilateral economic cooperation in the post COVID-19 Era and trilateral security cooperation in the long run.

In the area of economic cooperation, trilateral Cooperation gained substantial outcomes. In November 2021, the government bodies in charge of intellectual property held the 21st TRIPO Head Meeting, reporting respectively on the current status of their national IP systems, and reviewed the latest TRIPO cooperation activities in the areas of trademark and design, trial and appeal, human resources, and IP societies. The next month, the 9th Consultative Meeting on Consumer Policy among China, Japan and Korea was held online, where participants exchanged information on each country's consumer policy trends and issues in the era of COVID-19 such as e-commerce, misleading representations and SDGs, as well as cross-border enforcement cooperation and consumer dispute resolution. The three countries also kept deepening cooperation in the field of sustainable development. The 22nd Tripartite Environment Ministers' Meeting was held online in December 2021.

In the area of socio-cultural cooperation, the Culture City of East Asia (CCEA) program continues to thrive, a program in which every year one city in each is selected from among the cities in the three countries that are aiming to develop their ties through culture and the arts; that city hosts a variety of cultural and artistic events to introduce modern arts and culture, traditional culture, and various lifestyles. In October 2021, the 14th China-Japan-ROK Cultural Content Industry Forum was held. Later in December, the 14th Tripartite Health Ministers' Meeting was convened online.

Hwang The three countries declared their vision for the future in Chengdu in 2019, but still, I assume that there must have been inevitably limited cooperation over the past few years due to COVID-19. What outcomes and results have you achieved since your appointment?

Ou The TCS has devoted itself to keeping the steady momentum of the Trilateral Cooperation against the backdrops of the unprecedented difficulties and challenges. In the 14 months since the 6th Consultative Board's appointment, the TCS witnessed the giant vessel of Trilateral Cooperation keeping its pace by continuing the mechanisms and dialogues mainly through online channels. As previously mentioned, a series of ministerial-level meetings have taken place since the inauguration of this Consultative Board, in which the TCS played a supporting role. Trilateral Cooperation mechanical projects at various levels across all spectrums, were convened and carried out successfully, giving strong impetus to the post-pandemic recovery of the economy and socio-cultural exchanges of the three countries against the headwinds of the changing situation in this region. The TCS contributed its due part by faithfully fulfilling its functions as mandated.

Beyond the inter-governmental mechanisms, the TCS has carried out many of its own initiatives as well. In November 2021, the TCS, alongside United Nations organizations, hosted a high-level forum on the carbon neutrality goals of the three nations, in which officials and leading experts from national and international organizations deliberated on the implications of the COP26 outcome on national climate actions, and identified potential areas and modalities for cooperation between the three countries and with other developing countries. In February 2022, we carried out two youth exchange programs, the Young Ambassador Program and the Trilateral Youth Speech Contest, bringing together young people from different countries utilizing creative online methods. Likewise, March 2022 saw the introduction of the inaugural Virtual Marathon, where runners made full use of mobile applications and a dedicated website to run together, despite the physical limitations caused by the pandemic.

Apart from the above, the TCS also launched online the Trilateral Statistics Hub, a one-stop location for various indicators related to the trilateral cooperation. The TCS also released numerous publications, such as the An Evolving Trilateral Cooperation: Reality and Outlook, the Trilateral

Economic Report, and the Research Report on CJK Local City Exchange 2022, which all broaden public awareness of trilateral cooperation and TCS while reaching out to the public.

Hwang How would you evaluate the history of TCS over the past 11 years? I am curious about the achievements and challenges that TCS has had in its history.

Ou The past decade since the establishment of TCS is no doubt a crucial phase in the course of trilateral cooperation. Having gone through a global economic crisis, the Trilateral Cooperation became more vigorous; not only its scope of cooperation expanded to nearly 30 pragmatic areas, but also the cooperation itself morphed into a genuinely institutionalized framework, with the Trilateral Summit Meeting as the heart, the 21 Ministerial Meetings as the brain, over 70 working-level consultations and dialogues as the body, and more than 100 projects as its outcomes. Successful projects such as the CAMPUS Asia student exchange program and Culture City of East Asia local government exchange program, launched in the first half of the last decade, have continuously reshaped our perceptions towards the true meaning of trilateral cooperation. Regardless of disparities, there is endless potential to unleash it if it serves the well-being of the people in the three countries.

The establishment of the TCS as a permanent secretariat, further ensures a steady development of the Trilateral Cooperation in the context of dynamic changes in regional and international landscapes as well as ups-and-downs in bilateral relations. The development of TCS can roughly be divided into two chapters. The first half of the decade from 2011 to 2015 was the period of organization building and quantitative growth. Beginning to communicate with various ministries and departments, TCS focused on broadening its reach in existing governmental cooperation platforms from the working to ministerial level. It was this solid foundation that paved the way for the second chapter of TCS, which can be characterized by qualitative growth through pragmatic contributions in both governmental and non-governmental sectors. Since 2016, TCS began to propose and implement more cooperative projects on topics such as economy, education, environment, culture and disaster management. The International Forum for Trilateral Cooperation, the Trilateral Journalist Exchange Program, the Trilateral Entrepreneurs' Forum, and the Trilateral Common Vocabulary Dictionary are some of TCS' flagship projects.

Hwang What is the particular reason for Korea, China, and Japan to cooperate? Why do we actually need it?

Ou As important members of the international community, China, Japan and Korea are the engines of global economic development. According to the Statistics Hub of TCS, the GDP of the three countries rank second, third and tenth in the world in 2021, and the total economic volume accounts for 25.5% of the world's total; the trade volume of the three countries accounts for 21.9% of the world's total, and patent applications account for 50.7% of the world's total; Container port throughput accounts for 36.9% of the world's total. These figures clearly show that China, Japan and Korea are economically active, innovative and powerful. Such cooperation between the three countries has a pivotal position and influence in the world. The cooperation among the three countries is on a win-win basis which has been bringing concrete outcomes to the people of the region and even beyond. A cooperative, prosperous and stable Northeast Asia is no doubt the common interest and shared value of the region. So that the trilateral cooperation is not optional but rather imperative.

Hwang Could you assess the environment for promoting trilateral cooperation these days?

Ou The world we live in today is turbulent, and its changes have not been profound like this in a century. The COVID-19 pandemic continues to rage, the geopolitical environment is getting worse, the international security situation is turbulent, and traditional and non-traditional security threats are on the rise. The world economic growth continues to slow down, major economies face the risk of economic recession, the problem of unbalanced development among countries is exacerbated, the global industrial chain and supply chain are readjusted, and the prices of energy, food and bulk commodities continue to rise, which intensifies inflation in various countries. The surge of dollar appreciation intensifies the inflation output of the United States, and made the currencies of many countries, including China, Japan and Korea, face extremely severe depreciation pressure.

Hwang Can you explain both the pros and cons of this issue?

Ou At the same time, the trilateral cooperation also faces complex internal challenges. Due to historical, territorial and other reasons, the three countries continue to experience difficulties in bilateral relations and weak political mutual trust. The mature and stable industrial chain and supply chain between the three countries are also facing challenges due to interference from external factors. Due to the reduction of face-to-face communication opportunities and the amplification effect of the online world, it is difficult to effectively identify the "massive" information on the internet, especially negative and even deepfaked information. There is a downward trend in mutual favorability.

But the shared culture of China, Japan and Korea tells us such a fact: the more difficult times are, the more we must strengthen our confidence. Looking back at the history of trilateral cooperation, we can clearly know that the more crises and challenges we face, the more important the strategic significance of the trilateral cooperation is. Because of the Asian financial crisis in 1997 that China, Japan, Korea and ASEAN countries joined hands to deal with it, that the prosperity and stability of the region could be maintained. After more than 20 years of development, the trilateral cooperation has become a stabilizer and driving force for peace and prosperity in Northeast Asia. Trilateral cooperation was born in response to common crises and has been strengthened in the process of jointly responding to larger crises.

Hwang How can the three governments promote trilateral cooperation?

Ou In the face of complex internal and external challenges, we must clearly realize that trilateral cooperation is the key to maintaining peace and security, economic prosperity and people's happiness in Northeast Asia. The cooperation among the three countries should be strengthened in the following areas:

First, to accumulate political mutual trust. The governments of the three countries should strive to maintain close communication and avoid the suspension of the trilateral cooperation mechanism due to difficulties in bilateral relations. The trilateral cooperation and bilateral relations should complement each other to form a virtuous circle. The more difficulties the bilateral relationship encounters, the less it should harm the trilateral cooperation.

Second, to consolidate the ties of economic and trade interests. The three countries should continue to implement the RCEP agreement, continue to promote trade and investment liberalization and facilitation and strive to promote innovation cooperation between the three countries in various fields such as digital economy, green economy, supply chain, industrial chain, smart agriculture and advanced manufacturing. Especially when the global supply chain is restructured and more emphasis is placed on regionality and security, it is more important to strengthen trilateral cooperation to maintain the resilience of the industrial chain and supply chain.

Third, to strengthen policy communication and coordination for a stable financial situation. The three countries should maintain communication on financial and monetary policies, work with ASEAN countries to maintain financial stability in East Asia, ensure long-term fiscal sustainability, and jointly deal with downside risks of the regional economy and the negative spillover effects, so as to ensure that the East Asian economy can withstand the downside risks of the global economy.

Hwang The expression 'people's happiness' is quite impressive.

Ou Besides the improvements in economic security circumstances, it is to restore and expand people-to-people and cultural exchanges in the region. By holding more and richer face-to-face cultural exchange activities, people from all fields of the three countries, especially young people, can deepen mutual understanding and friendship, enhance mutual recognition and goodwill, and build a strong public opinion foundation for mutual trust and cooperation among the three countries.

Hwang Would you introduce any cases if there are any key projects that you would like to pursue during your remaining period?

Ou First, we plan to hold the annual Trilateral Entrepreneurs' Forum. We will also carry out our annual Trilateral Journalist Exchange Program as a tour for journalists as well as SNS influencers of the three countries, promoting Culture Cities of East Asia across China, Japan, and Korea.

The Trilateral Visionary Group is also another concept we have under preparation, in which we will invite high-level politicians/governmental officials or renowned academics specializing in strategic planning of the three countries to attend closed strategic dialogues and share visionary insights on the progress, challenges, and opportunities of the trilateral cooperation in political, economic, and socio-cultural areas.

We will also be implementing projects that engage all sectors of the three countries. This includes our annual flagship program, the International Forum for Trilateral Cooperation, which brings together eminent scholars/ policy makers to share and offer new insights into the political climate, economic cooperation, and social-cultural ties among the three countries. Next year, we plan to return to our rotational hosting pattern with our first forum outside of Korea, to be held in Qingdao, China. We also plan to hold the Young Scholars' Forum back-to-back with the previous forum, in which rising scholars of the three countries present their research on the various facets of Northeast Asian relations, and network with other like-minded scholars, broadening existing regional cooperation by involving young leaders with new perspectives, and opening a dialogue to address timely issues.

Speaking of youth, which is the key area of the TCS' efforts, we will also be giving special attention to them in February next year when we hold our inaugural Youth Month, when we unveil the Trilateral Youth Exchange Network, which will integrate our existing youth programs to promote interaction between participants and alumni, and to provide a platform for the exchange of experiences and mutual learning for young people from the three countries.

Roles and cooperation of East Asia for the transition of civilization

Oct 27, 2022

Park Jinsu

Director, Asian Cultural Studies Research Institute at Gachon University

Lee Wookyon

Professor, Department of Chinese Culture at Sogang University

The 20th century was a terrifying era of war not only in the West, but also in East Asia. The East-West conflict during the Cold War that dominated decades of the late 20th century after World War I and II maintained a balance of power under the cloak of ideological confrontation, but there was a blatant armed conflict on one side of the Earth at the same time. East Asia, where Korea and Vietnam are located, is in fact the region where the Cold War was the 'hottest.' Even if the Cold War ended as the Berlin Wall fell in 1989 and the Soviet Union collapsed in 1991, North Korea's nuclear issue and China's cross-Strait problems still exist. In the meantime, China's economy rose rapidly for the past 30 years. The US-China trade friction today is gradually turning into a diplomatic and military confrontation, and a full-fledged hegemony competition has begun. Now, a number of population around the world are feeling anxious about East Asia possibly becoming the front line of the "new Cold War" again. Where is East Asia standing now? Where is East Asia going? What direction should East Asia head toward, as it is at a historical and civilizational crossroads? This week's discussion invites two experts from Chinese Studies and Japanese

Studies, respectively, to figure out the answers to these questions. Professor Lee Wookyon of the Department of Chinese Culture at Sogang University and Director Park Jinsu of the Asian Cultural Studies Research Institute at Gachon University have contributed their viewpoints today.

Hwang Although the momentum has been slightly dampened, it seems human history entered a new phase in many ways as the world was combating against COVID-19 since 2020. Moreover, after Russia's invasion of Ukraine in February, the world is concerned about the instability of nuclear war. How do you view the world today?

Park To begin with, my research area is Japanese literature and comparative literature. Basically, comparative literature is an academic field established in France about 120 years ago. From the late 19th to early 20th century, there was a dark foreboding of World War I sinking heavily throughout all of Europe. France's defeat in the Franco-Prussian War in 1871 led the French to realize they needed more knowledge and a deeper understanding of Germany, which suddenly emerged as a modern industrial country. Although France was a border-facing neighbor, it began to reflect that it was too indifferent to Germany, and that it knew too little about Germany as a result. Entering the 20th century, this necessity grew rapidly. In a way, comparative literature is a study born of people's desperate desire to somehow avoid the crisis of war just around the corner by knowing and understanding their neighbors better. Today, conflicts between the world's leading giants are taking place, although it is not quite the same with the two previous World Wars and the Cold War era in the 20th century. The desperate need to know our neighbors can be exactly applied to East Asia, where we are living today. How safe is East Asia from war? And how much deeper do we understand people in neighboring countries than the Europeans did 120 years ago? I sometimes feel the need for us to think about these things.

Hwang The world is now facing an era of historically intensifying turmoil. This era even makes us feel like we are standing at a turning point in civilization. What meaning does this East Asia where we are living have?

Lee East Asia abandoned its own unique institutions, values and views as the principal actors during the modern transition period and transplanted them with modern Western institutions, values and new views. However, it is now necessary to reflect on the meaning of the institutions, values, and views of East Asian traditions along with a reflection on modern times, as we are in a transitional period of civilization's history. This process of self-reflection is to think of modernity as a kind of historical process away from blindness to modernity, and to re-examine the values of tradition and modernity in terms of building a new civilization in the future. This is a third reason and practice that opens up a new civilization through reflection and re-examination of modern times and traditions while looking at modern light and darkness in a balanced manner.

Park There hasn't been a single day without confusion since human history began to be written. However, the distinction from the past is that the great sphere of regions that can be grouped into the "wide" cultures of East Asia, Europe and the Middle East have been able to exchange stronger and more direct influences with each other since modern times. This phenomenon may have accelerated to today so that the world, in a good or bad sense, has become more complex and more variable, facing new problems that we have not experienced before, which we may feel and accept as "confusion." Modern East Asian societies have changed more than those of any other region in the world, and have developed internal strength through extreme historical experiences. Again, compared to any other region in the world, East Asia is a representative region that is currently struggling to find solutions to the sharp problems humanity is facing.

Hwang Since when did this concept of "East Asia" begin to be actively used?

Park The view of East Asia puts Korea, China, and Japan in one region and considers three of them in an equal sense. It actually has not been so long since we started using this term a lot. I remember often encountering researchers using the expression "East Asia" when I was a graduate student in the 1990s. Perhaps it is closely related to the situation in which interest in East Asian culture and history increased significantly in Korean society and academia since the 1990s. These trends must have been caused by political and economic changes back then, such as the collapse of the socialist sphere, the global expansion of capitalism, the progress of bloc formation -- symbolized by the launch of the European Union in 1993 -- and the establishment of diplomatic relations between Korea and China in 1992. As all these factors were combined, there emerged a need to view East Asia -- including Korea, China and Japan -- as a region from a historical, cultural and economic perspective. Therefore, an academic approach was required. It gradually spread to the general public, and from 2012, "East Asian History" was adopted as a Korean high school history subject in addition to "Korean History" and "World History." In the end, the term "East Asia" has been frequently used only in the last 20 or 30 years at the longest.

Hwang Then do you mean we did not have the idea of bringing the region into one in the past?

Park Yes, no one who lived in the Chinese continent, the Korean Peninsula, and the Japanese archipelago had the idea of bringing the region together until the 1980s. Instead, concepts such as "Orient," "Asia," and "(Greater) East Asia" was used as a countermeasure to the West or by positioning ourselves at the corresponding point to the West by internalizing its Orientalism. Since modern times, East Asia's cultural interest was all toward the West and the US. This trend did not change much until the World War II or the Cold War. Therefore, there were not many cases where people in this area were interested in each other's language or culture, and exchanges were not activated in accordance with this disinterest.

Hwang There is also a great confusion going on in the international order, and East Asia is no exception.

Lee As mankind is facing a new turning point in world history after going through COVID-19, another crisis and turning point is occurring at the same time. In other words, a turning point in a new world history -- the new crisis of the US-China competition -- is coming ahead. In this era of a new crisis and turning point, East Asia is a key site. China and the US are clashing on the Korean Peninsula and the Taiwan Strait. East Asia is the front line of the US-China confrontation. As East Asia, as well as China, is a direct party in the US-China competition, it is facing an urgent task to respond to a new shift in world history of the US-China competition while facing a crisis in humanity in terms of the history of civilization. In short, East Asia is standing in front of a double crisis and a double transitional period.

Hwang Meanwhile, China has been trying to transcend modernity in a socialist way since we have entered modern times.

Lee Yes, those transcendences sometimes resulted in another Chinese version of modernism in the name of socialism or in the name of a socialist market economy. On the other hand, however, China has always sought to pursue its own character that is distinct from the American-style modernity, and this intention is even more so in the Chinese Dream era. Not only the Chinese Communist Party, but the Chinese people are the same as well. Whether we call it China's pursuit of "Chineseness" or the realization of "Socialism with Chinese characteristics," China now envisions its own paths, values, institutions, cultures, and views on humanity as alternatives to American modernity. The more China builds such plans, the more the US is wary of China. The confrontation between the US and China is going beyond competition over economic and technological hegemony and toward the clash of civilizations. Following the US' Trump administration, the Biden administration gave up hope that China would converge on US-style values and systems in the future. Therefore, the US has started to contain China and pressure the Chinese Communist Party because of the complex nature of the US-China confrontation.

Hwang How do you see US-China relations? Is it difficult to view it optimistically?

Lee Now the US is overreacting to China's flows, and China is also overreacting to the US' flows. Both are building higher and thicker barriers to their respective institutions, values and culture. Just like how autoimmune diseases occur in people with strong immune systems who try to protect themselves too much, if the US and China respond by building thick and strong defenses to protect themselves from the outside, it will cause overreactions which will cause problems to their immune systems and eventually destroy them.

Hwang Is there any possible way to cure those autoimmune diseases?

Lee Yes, there are two ways. One is to seal oneself in a vacuum so that nothing from outside can enter into one's boundary, and the other is to lower one's immune barrier, and adapt oneself to what is coming from the outside without overreacting. The former is actually impossible in reality unless one is in a closed hospital room. What is feasible in reality is the latter one. The latter way is to neutralize oneself with the outside factors, change one's body and to create a new self. Through this process, the third self, a brand new self is born, which is basically not the one of the past or another's self. In the era of diseases, where COVID-19 is prevalent, we must gain the wisdom of life given by the phenomenon of disease. Based on these wisdoms, we hope the US-China competition can turn into an opportunity to renew each other and open a third era, not a polarized world in confrontation. In the face of the COVID-19 crisis, it is a global task to redesign a new third civilization while examining the light and darkness of modernity in a balanced way, beyond being blind to modernity, and to find a solution in the US-China era.

Hwang However, it seems this task must be more desperate for East Asia.

Lee Yes, it is because East Asia is the region that is most exposed to the double crisis that the world is facing, or maybe the double turning point. And above all, it is because East Asia is directly exposed to the risk at the same time. Therefore, in this double crisis and double turning point, how to transit this reality into a new opportunity for mankind and how to set it as a starting point for imagining a new civilization is a more severe issue for East Asia than in any other part of the world. East Asia has richer modern experience than any other region. It has a history of joining the line of advanced Western countries through catching up with Western modernity through compressed growth. It has also pursued socialist modernity in a different direction from Western modernity. On the other hand, it also has abundant resources from its traditional civilization that can critically reflect on modern times. In East Asia today, the world crisis and the world's contradictions are all concentrated in one region.

Hwang When we look at it from this perspective, East Asia must be heavily responsible, as it has become a key site of world history at a turning point of civilization and a historical era.

Lee Again, East Asia is more directly exposed to crisis than any other region in the world. It has abundant traditional and civilizational assets and various modern and contemporary historical experiences that can help it creatively break through the era. This is why cooperation within East Asia is critical in the face of a double crisis or a double turning point. East Asia should have new civilized grounds altogether. East Asia should jointly gather and contemplate together for new civilized grounds. East Asia's wise response to the civilizational crisis through mutual cooperation will be an alarm of beginning of a new civilization and a new history that departs from East Asia to the world. In the midst of re-grounding and re-examining the wisdom of East Asian traditional civilization and the light of modern civilization, East Asia's joint efforts and cooperation in designing and practicing a new civilization are desperately needed -- not only for East Asia, but also for humanity.

Hwang What can East Asia do in this crisis and transitional period?

Park Korea, China and Japan have miraculously overcome several challenges in East Asia that began in the 19th century by sometimes colliding, cooperating, influencing and referring to each other. If we successfully achieve the goal of peaceful coexistence and co-prosperity in East Asia today in the 21st century, we will be able to contribute to peace and prosperity not only within East Asia, but also for mankind as a whole. The most serious problem to overcome at this point is that all three countries -- Korea, China and Japan -- are obsessed with their own country-centered historical and cultural views. We need to break away from these narrow-minded one-nation attitudes as soon as possible. Another problem is one that has existed since before modern times. Although the general aspects have changed, it is still necessary to completely discard the great power-centrism. Even in the 21st century, there is no true sense of East Asia in East Asia, regardless of Korea, China and Japan. There is only "conceptual (fictional) East Asia" centered on each country. Now is a time in which we must think together about how to coexist peacefully with one another in the "East Asia" unit, not just for our own interests.

Lee Above all, we need a civilizational reason that grounds why we are seeking a new civilization. In other words, we have to link the civilizational reason for how the COVID-19 era has attempted to redesign and rebuild a new civilization to mankind, with East Asia's crisis solution in the era of US-China competition. The United States' institutions, values, and views on humanity symbolize modern times. These were the lights that symbolized modern times, and many countries around the world including East Asia, walked toward the light and went on the path of modernization and Americanization. Nevertheless, now the darkness embedded in the path is getting darker. The crisis of the US is another name for the crisis in modern times.

Hwang What are the specific ways for countries to peacefully coexist in the "East Asia" unit?

Park Firstly, it is essential to create a real opportunity for mutual understanding based on mutual consideration. In particular, history education matters. Until now, in many cases, the three countries have often described ancient and modern history based on their own country-centered views that lacks objectivity. It sure must be difficult to describe a complete common history, but at least the position of the other country should also be narrated together to enable a more transparent and objective understanding of history for the next generation. It is not easy, but it has to be done for the future of East Asia. Next, more people should be able to speak the language of the other country than now and understand each other's traditions and cultures more deeply. I sometimes imagine a scene in which teenagers from Korea, China and Japan read each other's literature, listen to each other's music (not only popular music, but folk songs and children's songs), watch each other's movies, and communicate with each other in polite and appropriate language. The "national sentiment" of the older generation was always an obstacle to trilateral relations and was not so helpful for common development.

We still need new multilateral cooperation in this region

Oct 19, 2022

Paik Wooyeal

Professor, Department of Political Science and International Studies at Yonsei University

Jeong Hanbum

Professor, Department of International Studies at Korea National Defense University

There are not many cases when Northeast Asia was under stable security. As China's path toward a military power and Japan's normalization are recognized as the regional arms race, mutual checks and confrontations are intensifying among countries in the region. Recently, North Korea launched multiple missiles and the regional security is fluctuating again at a time we cannot rule out the possibility of another nuclear test. At least, we could somewhat reduce the threat posed by North Korea in the past, as there were six-party talks as a mechanism to deal with North Korea's nuclear program. However, such efforts have gone to nothing due to North Korea's resistance and differences between the participants in the six-party talks. Meanwhile, neither China nor Japan has newly established or promoted multilateral cooperation in the region. Unlike the neighbors, Korea's respective governments have continued to propose its own multilateral cooperation ideas. The proposals did not end as successful maybe because the practical environment was yet created or due to the problems of the driving force within the government itself. Nevertheless, it is necessary for

Korea to reorganize its multilateral cooperation strategy by expanding its perspective to all regions outside Northeast Asia, namely Southeast Asia, Oceania, South Asia, and Northwest Europe, away from the fixed concepts and framework of Korea-China-Japan. Indeed, considering the US, which is the basis of Korea's national security, we can still think of building bold strategic changes by comprehensively considering, organizing, and trying new combinations of other countries or approaches in accordance with policy areas within the traditional Asia-Pacific region. And the need for such multilateral cooperation is not diminishing at all. To continue the further discussion, this week's interview invites professor Paik Wooyeal at the Department of Political Science and International Studies of Yonsei University and professor Jeong Hanbum at Department of International Studies of Korea National Defense University.

Hwang How would you assess the changes in current international affairs?

Jeong It currently seems to be the end of liberal international order. Due to the decline of the US leadership, the rise of America first, the rapid rise of China, Russia's return to the international stage, and Japan's rearmament are underway. Additionally, the friendly countries such as Germany, India, and Saudi Arabia are strengthening their independent routes, which is becoming one of the centrifugal forces. Resolving the nuclear issues of Iran and North Korea has virtually failed. The proliferation of democracy in Iraq, Syria, and Afghanistan was also a failure. As multilateralism based on the liberal trade order declines and protectionism reappears as the US and China focus on economic security, international organizations such as the WTO are becoming nominal.

Hwang What about the changes in the East Asian circumstances?

Jeong China's rapid growth is an opportunity for the prosperity of East Asia, but at the same time, it is creating security instability due to its competition for power. On the other hand, Japan has lost its confidence because of its prolonged slump, the lost 30 years. In the case of North Korea, it is continuing to threaten nuclear development while maintaining its closed society by consolidating its power over the three-generation hereditary succession. The US and China have ended up in a win-win relationship that was based on the international division of labor, and the US is starting to contain China in earnest with the Indo-Pacific Strategy.

Hwang How do you see Korea's diplomatic and security environment?

Jeong Korea is buried under the structure of the "US-ROK alliance on North Korea" and "the US global strategy or the US-China hegemony competition." There is no discourse and strategy on the collapse of the liberal order, the hegemonic competition, the return of Russia, and Japan's attempt to be the military power. We need to build a strategic thinking to lead this country in the future international community. There is a need for multilateral diplomacy and a way to overcome the dilemma in an environment where it is difficult to implement multilateral diplomacy. Therefore, the need for multilateral diplomacy is rather increasing due to the emergence of US-China strategic competition and protectionism.

Hwang How is the discussion on multilateral cooperation in the region going on?

Jeong Actually, various mini-multilateral cooperation has been proposed in the following of the US Indo-Pacific Strategy. For now, multiple responses are all mixed up on whether to participate, because of multilateral cooperation's openness. There is fierce sensing going on between countries in the region over a lack of trust, sincerity and leadership. Due to economic relations with China, many countries in the region are facing a dilemma in participating in the US-led multilateral cooperation.

Hwang Then how is Korea's multilateral cooperation policy?

Paik In general, several policies were established during the Kim Daejung government, including the 1997 ASEAN+3 Forum. It includes India, Australia and New Zealand along with 13 other countries and functions as the basic structure for East Asian multilateral cooperation with the East Asia Summit, where the US and Russia participated in earnest since 2010.

Hwang When was a time Korea took the initiative in promoting multilateral cooperation in East Asia?

Paik We can find the origin of Korea's initiative in multilateral cooperation from the Kim Daejung and Park Geunhye governments. The Park government's "Northeast Asian Peace and Cooperation Initiative" could be more clarified, as it went through several East Asian diplomatic strategies in the Lee Myungbak and Roh Moohyun governments. Then most of this initiative was inherited into the "Northeast Asian Platform for Peace and Cooperation" by the Moon Jaein government, which basically maintained the continuity of multilateral cooperation in Northeast Asia. This means that regardless of conservative and liberal governments, this diplomatic strategy was supported as "bipartisan." In detail, eight Korea-China-Japan summits (the last in 2019), five Korea-China-Japan foreign minister talks (the last in 2015), and dozens of working-level talks were continuously held at Track 1 and 1.5.

Hwang However, both the Northeast Asian Peace and Cooperation Initiative and Northeast Asian Platform for Peace and Cooperation are barely maintaining its reputation without achieving their goals in general.

Paik Yes, this happens in accordance with the proliferation of exclusive mini-multilateral cooperation organizations based on blockages among like-minded countries due to the intensifying US-China competition, excessive politicization and securitization across the economy, science and technology, and human exchanges where the high quality of transition took place from the separation of politics and economy to the amalgamation of politics and economy, and low expectations or a perception at the level of disregard toward (North) East Asian multilateral cooperation within Korea and other countries (especially

China and Japan). In addition, the deterioration of the three bilateral relations between the three countries (Korea-Japan, Korea-China, and Japan-China), especially the deterioration of the bilateral relationship between Korea and Japan, has a significant impact on the level of mini-multilateral cooperation in Northeast Asia.

Hwang Nevertheless, what is the reason that such a multilateral cooperation attempt is necessary?

Paik Above all, it is because Korea in 2022 does not perfectly fit into the others' current "state capacity" and status or positions within and outside of the region, as the countries went through absolute and relative changes for a period and their respective situations are different. It is an undeniable fact, therefore, it is necessary to seek a practical form of East Asian multilateral cooperation strategy that is optimized for the environment-conditions of a completely new global, (North) East Asian region.

Jeong We must consider an appropriate harmony of security interests that share strategic interests with the US and economic interests that share practical interests with China. As an ally, the US approaches the economy from a security perspective. Recent collaborations such as the Indo-Pacific Economic Framework and Chip 4 can be the typical example. This emphasis on economic security has been strengthened since the Ukraine war, while China is complaining that such cooperation is intended to exclude and contain China. The counterstrategy accordingly requires an approach that goes case by case and field by field based on national interest, rather than an all-or-nothing approach that follows one side either the US or China. In general, it is desirable to set military security in the direction of strengthening bilateral alliance with the US, and deal with economic security by setting joint responses with related countries.

Hwang Please give us more specifics on what direction we should head toward multilateral cooperation.

Jeong First of all, in order to solve the problem of sluggish cooperation due to the US-China strategic competition and intensifying conflict, we should actively take advantage of using the existing regional cooperation. In other words, in order to offset the negative effects that come from strategic competition between great powers, regional cooperatives such as the East Asia Summit and the ASEAN Regional Forum or other neutral actors such as ASEAN should be actively utilized. Complementarily, it is important to practice the "Trilateral Cooperation Vision for the Next Decade" agreed at the Eighth Korea-China-Japan Summit in Chengdu, China, in December 2019. If we decide to participate in the US-led economic and security consultative group due to the inevitable US-China strategic competition, we must put efforts to resolve the conflict with China. Korea, China and Japan are not only facing geographical proximity, but also will lose if the conflict escalates because of the economic interdependence. In order to eliminate unnecessary misunderstandings between the three countries and promote cooperation, it is necessary to regularize cooperation, including the regularization of the trilateral summit. In order to accelerate negotiations on the Regional Comprehensive Economic Partnership and the Korea-China-Japan Free Trade Agreement, and to promote cooperation and friendship among future generations of Korea-China-Japan, it is essential to promote youth exchanges as well.

Hwang There still are conflicting factors in the trilateral relationship between Korea, China and Japan, and three bilateral relationships between Korea-Japan, Korea-China, and Japan-China.

Paik Among the three countries, Korea is the most active one in trilateral mini-multilateral cooperation. It is because Korea is relatively the weakest country in the region from the past-present-future, and has to deal with China and Japan, which are global strong powers, as well as the US, the stakeholder which essentially is involved in these relations, and North Korea. In this sense, by nature, an expanded multilateral cooperation structure including three parties or a trilateral mini-multilateral cooperation is the most useful choice for Korea rather than a bilateral one. However, most of the multilateral cooperation efforts led by Korea in (North) East Asia have gone nowhere and failed to elicit meaningful responses and policy changes from the other two countries. It is expected to be more difficult after 2022.

Hwang Beyond the existing inertia, what can be the most realistic, viable and interdependent way for multilateral cooperation in the mid-to-long-term?

Paik The most important breakthrough of inertia is Korea breaking out of the existing form of Korea-China-Japan trilateral cooperation. Of course, this does not mean that Korea should abolish some of the achievements established so far, namely, the Korea-China-Japan Summit or the Trilateral Cooperation Secretariat. I am saying that the trilateral cooperation mechanism which was similarly established can be revived in accordance with appropriate global and regional environmental changes. However, although Korea is the one that desires for Korea-Japan-China trilateral cooperation the most, we must remind that China and Japan do not count Korea's utilization high in the system, and even Korea is facing intensified bilateral conflicts with Japan and China.

Hwang Do you see the relationship between Korea and Japan as the biggest problem facing the Korea-China-Japan cooperation.

Paik First of all, maybe we should refrain from proposing diverse forms of (mini) multilateral cooperation to Japan. Japan builds its diplomatic strategy centered on the US' mini-multilateral cooperative groups amid the US-China structural change and based on Korea's "bypass" stance. Additionally, the way Japan is recognizing Korea as the weakest link in its deterrence strategy against China would not be any help because Japan wants to exclude Korea from its relationship with China. However, Korea-Japan-led mini-multilateral cooperation is highly desirable in several strategic aspects, it is undoable. Once again, the most important prerequisite for revitalizing the Korea-Japan-led mini-multilateral cooperation system is the normalization of bilateral relations.

Hwang Do you have any other words to add?

Paik Basically (mini) multilateral cooperation led by China, Japan, the US, and maybe others can expand the scope and depth of Korean multilateral diplomacy and can anticipate the so-called the "boomerang effect" that goes beyond the existing Northeast Asian-centered thinking. However, it cannot be overemphasized that Japan and China should always be mindful in this new direction of multilateral cooperation strategy. The multilateral strategy centered on Korea, China and Japan presupposes openness that can be incorporated into the modified existing form or the new form of multilateral cooperation at any time.

Jeong The possibility of global multilateral cooperation is decreasing and the possibility of regional mini-multilateral cooperation is increasing. In principle, it is necessary to be wary of getting caught up in strategic competition between great powers. In situations where choices are inevitably forced, policies must be decided from the standpoint of national interest, and policy decisions that aim not to fall behind in the US-led international order must come first. In the direction of strengthening bilateral alliances with the US, participation in US-led supply chains and value chains related to economic security is desirable, if possible. However, participation in regional military and security consultative groups that target China should be cautious. The problem with China must be solved through another separate kind of effort. There can be active cooperation with Japan on the economy, but we should tread carefully on security issues. Also, we need to actively use the existing regional consultative groups in preparation for more intensified strategic competition in the region in the future. To complement that, the Korea-Japan-China regional cooperation agreed upon at the Korea-China-Japan summit should be promoted. Apart from the Korea-US-Japan cooperation, it is also important to run Korea-China-Japan cooperation in parallel.

KOREA, CHINA and the WORLD

Author	Hwang Jaeho
First Printed	2023.03.17
First Published	2023.03.23
Director	Yunsung Koh
Executive Contents Creator	Sunho Shin
Contents Creator	Haejung Jang Jaeeun Roh Daeun Byun
Designer	Sunah Choi Daewook Kim
Published by	HANKUK UNIVERSITY OF FOREIGN STUDIES KNOWLEDGE CONTENTS & PRESS 107, Imun-ro, Dongdaemun-gu, Seoul 02450, Korea Tel.) 82-2-2173-2497 Fax.) 82-2-2173-3363 E-mail) press@hufs.ac.kr Online) http://press.hufs.ac.kr
Printed by	Twinbell Tel.) 82-2-2088-1810
ISBN	979-11-5901-737-7 [03340]
Price	28,000 Won